THE NEW GROVE®
MASTERS OF ITALIAN OPERA

The New Grove® Series

The Composer Biography Series

French Baroque Masters
Italian Baroque Masters
Bach Family
Handel
Haydn
Mozart
Beethoven
Schubert
Early Romantic Masters, Volume 2
Russian Masters, Volume 1
Wagner
Masters of Italian Opera
Twentieth-Century English Masters
Twentieth-Century American Masters
Second Viennese School
Gospel, Blues and Jazz
Modern Masters

The Musical Instrument Series

The Organ
The Piano
Early Keyboard Instruments

THE NEW GROVE®

Masters of Italian Opera

ROSSINI   DONIZETTI
BELLINI
VERDI   PUCCINI

Philip Gossett
William Ashbrook
Julian Budden
Friedrich Lippmann
Andrew Porter
Mosco Carner

W. W. NORTON & COMPANY
NEW YORK   LONDON

First published in
The New Grove Dictionary of Music and Musicians,®
edited by Stanley Sadie, 1980

First American Edition in book form with additions 1983

ISBN 0-393-30361-6

Printed in the United States of America

W. W. Norton & Company, Inc.
500 Fifth Avenue, NY, NY 10110
W. W. Norton & Company Ltd.
10 Coptic Street, London WC1A 1PU

1 2 3 4 5 6 7 8 9 0

Contents

List of illustrations

Illustration acknowledgments

We are grateful to the following for permission to reproduce illustrative material: Edward T. Cone, Princeton, New Jersey (fig.1); Accademia Filarmonica, Bologna (fig.2); Museo Teatrale alla Scala, Milan (cover, figs.3, 8, 12, 29); Richard Macnutt, Tunbridge Wells (figs.4, 5, 25); Mansell Collection, London (cover, fig.6); British Library, London (fig.7); Mary Evans Picture Library, London (fig.9); Museo Donizettiano (fig.10); Bibliothèque Nationale, Paris (figs.11, 18); Biblioteca Comunale, Palermo (cover, fig.13); Archivio Storico Ricordi, Milan (figs.14, 21, 22, 24, 26, 27, 31); Pierpont Morgan Library (Mary Flagler Cary Music Collection), New York (figs.15, 19, 23); International Museum of Photography at George Eastman House, Rochester, New York (fig.16); Civici Musei Veneziani d'Arte e di Storia, Venice (fig.17); SPADEM, Archives Photographiques, Paris (cover, fig.20); Metropolitan Opera Archives, New York (fig.28).

General abbreviations

A	alto, contralto	Mez	mezzo-soprano
acc.	accompaniment, accompanied by	movt	movement
appx	appendix	n.d.	no date of publication
B	bass	ob	oboe
b	bass [instrument]	obbl	obbligato
b	born	off	offertory
Bar	baritone	orch	orchestra, orchestral
bc	basso continuo	org	organ
bn	bassoon	ov.	overture
c	circa	perf.	performance, performed (by)
cl	clarinet	pr.	printed
collab.	in collaboration with	prol	prologue
conc.	concerto	pubd	published
d	died	qnt	quintet
db	double bass	qt	quartet
edn.	edition	*R*	photographic reprint
eng hn	english horn	recit	recitative
		repr.	reprinted
facs.	facsimile	rev.	revision, revised (by/for)
fl	flute	RISM	Répertoire International des
frag.	fragment		Sources Musicales
Gl	Gloria	S	San, Santa, Santo [Saint];
grad	gradual		soprano
gui	guitar	str	string(s)
		sum.	summer
hn	horn	sym.	symphony, symphonic
inc.	incomplete	T	tenor
inst	instrument, instrumental		
		U.	University
Jg.	Jahrgang [year of publication/volume]	v, vv	voice, voices
		va	viola
Ky	Kyrie	vc	cello
		vn	violin
lib	libretto		

Symbols for the library sources of works, printed in *italic*, correspond to those used in *RISM*, Ser. A.

Preface

This volume is one of a series of short biographies derived from *The New Grove Dictionary of Music and Musicians* (London, 1980). In its original form, the text was written in the mid-1970s, and finalized at the end of that decade. For this reprint, the text has been re-read and modified by the original authors and corrections and changes have been made. In particular, an effort has been made to bring the bibliographies up to date and to incorporate the findings of recent research.

The fact that the texts of the books in this series originated as dictionary articles inevitably gives them a character somewhat different from that of books conceived as such. They are designed, first of all, to accommodate a very great deal of information in a manner that makes reference quick and easy. Their first concern is with fact rather than opinion, and this leads to a larger than usual proportion of the texts being devoted to biography than to critical discussion. The nature of a reference work gives it a particular obligation to convey received knowledge and to treat of composers' lives and works in an encyclopedic fashion, with proper acknowledgment of sources and due care to reflect different standpoints, rather than to embody imaginative or speculative writing about a composer's character or his music. It is hoped that the comprehensive work-lists and extended bibliographies, indicative of the origins of the books in a reference work, will be valuable to the reader who is eager for full and accurate reference information and who may not have ready access to *The New Grove Dictionary* or who may prefer to have it in this more compact form.

S.S.

Bibliographical abbreviations

AcM	*Acta musicologica*
AMw	*Archiv für Musikwissenschaft*
AnMc	*Analecta musicologica*
DBI	*Dizionario biografico degli italiani*
ES	*Enciclopedia dello spettacolo*
HMYB	*Hinrichsen's Musical Year Book*
IMSCR	*International Musicological Society Congress Report*
JAMS	*Journal of the American Musicological Society*
LaMusicaE	*La musica: Enciclopedia storica*
Mf	*Die Musikforschung*
ML	*Music and Letters*
MMR	*The Monthly Musical Record*
MQ	*The Musical Quarterly*
MR	*The Music Review*
MT	*The Musical Times*
MZ	*Muzikološki zbornik*
NRMI	*Nuova rivista musicale italiana*
NZM	*Neue Zeitschrift für Musik*
ÖMz	*Österreichische Musikzeitschrift*
PNM	*Perspectives of New Music*
PRMA	*Proceedings of the Royal Musical Association*
RaM	*La rassegna musicale*
RBM	*Revue belge de musicologie*
RdM	*Revue de musicologie*
RIM	*Rivista italiana di musicologia*
RMI	*Rivista musicale italiana*
SovM	*Sovetskaya muzïka*
ZfM	*Zeitschrift für Musik*
ZIMG	*Zeitschrift der Internationalen Musik-Gesellschaft*

GIOACHINO ROSSINI

Philip Gossett

CHAPTER ONE

Introduction

No composer in the first half of the 19th century enjoyed the measure of prestige, wealth, popular acclaim or artistic influence that belonged to Rossini. His contemporaries recognized him as the greatest Italian composer of his time. His achievements cast into oblivion the operatic world of Cimarosa and Paisiello, creating new standards against which other composers were to be judged. That both Bellini and Donizetti carved out personal styles is undeniable; but they worked under Rossini's shadow, and their artistic personalities emerged in confrontation with his operas. Not until the advent of Verdi was Rossini replaced at the centre of Italian operatic life.

Yet the image of Rossini as man and artist remains distorted. As a man he most often appears the indolent raconteur, the gourmet, the spirit of an elegant Second Empire salon. This image results largely from the nature of extant biographical sources. Almost all surviving documentation concerning Rossini's life derives from the period after he withdrew from operatic composition in 1829. Of his active career little is known but what Stendhal related in his brilliant but unreliable *Vie de Rossini*, what Rossini recounted to visitors in Paris some 40 years later, and what can be pieced together from the bald facts of his performed works and a few surviving early letters. The fascinating insights into a composer's growth that can be gleaned from the correspondence of Bellini or Verdi, the interrelations of the composer and his librettists, the aesthetic creeds formulated in moments of artistic inspiration, all these are totally lacking.

The general view of Rossini the composer is equally mistaken. Until recently Rossini's historical position was distorted by the prominence of his great comic operas, which are among the last and finest representatives of *buffo* style. His ties with the 18th century were consequently emphasized, while his position in the 19th was misunderstood. Superb as the *buffo* operas are, Rossini is historically more important as a composer of *opera seria*. He threw off 18th-century formulae and codified new conventions that dominated Italian opera for half a century. Between 1810 and 1850 Italian opera was reformed in many ways: techniques of singing and melodic style altered drastically; the Romantic theatre routed dramatic conventions that had tyrannized both theatre and opera, thus offering a new wellspring of operatic subjects and techniques; the self-image of the composer changed, that of the craftsman giving way to that of the creative artist, while each individual work of art consequently gained new significance. But throughout, Italian opera depended upon the musical forms, the style of orchestration, the rhythmic vitality and the role of music in defining and shaping the drama first developed fully in the operas of Rossini.

CHAPTER TWO

Early years

Gioachino (Antonio) Rossini was born in Pesaro, a small city on the Adriatic in the region known as the Marches, on 29 February 1792. His immediate paternal ancestors can be traced in Lugo, while his mother's family came from Urbino. Both his parents were musicians. Giuseppe Antonio Rossini was a horn player of some ability, having preceded his son into membership in the Bologna Accademia Filarmonica in 1801. During his early career he performed in military bands and served the ceremonial function of public *trombetta*, the position he obtained in Pesaro when he took up residence there in 1790. The building into which he moved also housed the Guidarini family, whose daughter Anna he married on 26 September 1791.

Rossini's earliest years, spent in Pesaro, were not peaceful. The Napoleonic wars, bringing with them French and papal soldiers in confusing alternation, were particularly hard on Giuseppe, whose enthusiasm for the cause of liberty displeased the papal authorities and resulted in his brief imprisonment in 1800. Memories of his father's misadventures may have dampened Gioachino's enthusiasm for Italian nationalism later in his life. The child was frequently left with his maternal grandmother while his parents toured opera houses in the region, his father playing in the orchestra, his mother singing small roles.

By the time the family moved to Lugo in 1802,

Rossini's father was teaching him to play the horn, while a local canon, Giuseppe Malerbi, whose musical knowledge and fine collection of scores seem to have exercised a generally beneficent influence on the child's musical taste, instructed him in singing and composition. Many youthful compositions by Rossini have been found among the papers of Malerbi. After a throat ailment forced Anna to retire from her theatrical career, the family established permanent residence in Bologna. That Gioachino was immensely gifted as a singer must have been soon apparent, for in June 1806 he followed his father into the Accademia Filarmonica, a singular honour for so young a man. His early musical activities are poorly documented, but they certainly included singing (his performance as the boy, Adolfo, in Paer's *Camilla* at the Teatro del Corso in Bologna during the autumn season of 1805 is attested to by a libretto printed for the occasion), composition (several works can be assigned to these years, including the six *sonate a quattro* probably written in 1804, several masses and religious works, overtures, etc) and instrumental performance (he often served as *maestro al cembalo* in theatres during this period). A rich merchant from Ravenna, Agostino Triossi, was an early patron of Rossini's: many of the boy's compositions were prepared for private performance at Triossi's home.

In Bologna, Rossini studied music privately with Padre Angelo Tesei. His progress was rapid and by April 1806 he was able to enter the Liceo Musicale. There he followed courses in singing, the cello, piano and, most important, counterpoint under Padre Stanislao Mattei, the director of the Liceo and successor to Padre

Martini. Rossini, always an eminently practical man, did not react well to the more esoteric processes of counterpoint. He later reported to his friend Edmond Michotte that Mattei considered him the 'dishonour of his school'. Nonetheless, Rossini profited enormously from prolonged exposure to more 'serious' musical styles than those prevailing in Italian theatres. He devoured the music of Haydn and Mozart, later referring to Mozart as 'the admiration of my youth, the desperation of my mature years, the consolation of my old age', and was forced to submit to exercises in strict composition. Though he culled only what could be of direct use to him in a practical career, the sureness of his harmony, clarity of his part-writing (hardly marred by occasional 'forbidden' progressions) and precision of his orchestration derive ultimately from this traditional training.

During his student years Rossini wrote little: a few instrumental pieces, some sacred music and a cantata, *Il pianto d'Armonia sulla morte d'Orfeo*, which won a prize at the Liceo and was performed there for an academic convocation on 11 August 1808. It is often said that he supplied many arias for insertion into operas performed in Bologna, but this claim has never been systematically investigated. His first opera was commissioned, perhaps as early as 1807, by the tenor Domenico Mombelli, who together with his two daughters formed the nucleus of an operatic troupe. As Rossini later told Ferdinand Hiller, Mombelli asked him to set some numbers from a libretto entitled *Demetrio e Polibio*. Not even knowing the entire plot, he proceeded one number at a time until the entire score was finished. Though this was Rossini's first opera, it was not performed until 1812, after four other works had brought the young composer advance publicity. It is not clear how much of the opera is Rossini's and how much may have been supplied or tampered with by Mombelli; but with it Rossini was initiated into the realities of Italian operatic life.

CHAPTER THREE

First period, 1810–13

The first decade of the 19th century was a period of transition in Italian opera. The deposited mantles of Cimarosa and Paisiello were unfilled. The Neapolitan *buffo* tradition was in decline, and the operas of Farinelli or Fioravanti merely repeated its gestures without its substance. Though the conventional world of Metastasian *opera seria* had dissolved, the future was murky. Composers set heavily revised Metastasian texts, or imitations of them, to music in which typical 18th-century devices were precariously balanced with more progressive features. The simple tonal procedures of older *opera seria* were inadequate for longer ensembles and elaborate scenas, yet no Italian composer could or would adopt the more sophisticated tonal schemes of Mozart. As librettos turned from classical history to semi-serious subjects, medieval epic, and ultimately Romantic drama, the orchestral forces of the 18th century proved increasingly inadequate. As characters emerged from the cardboard figures of earlier days, melodic lines required more careful delineation, while the indiscriminate improvisation of vocal ornaments became less palatable. As Italian composers such as Paisiello, Cherubini and Spontini travelled to other European capitals, particularly Paris, Italian opera felt the influence of other national schools.

These challenges to a dying tradition drew little response from even the best composers of the decade,

Johannes Simon Mayr or Ferdinand Paer. Though they brought new orchestral richness to Italian opera and began to construct larger scenic complexes than were found in the post-Metastasian period, they seemed incapable of fusing a new style from the disparate elements demanding their attention. Stendhal, in his forthright manner, found these composers essentially wanting. Mayr was learned, able, 'the most correct composer', but only with Rossini did a composer of genius appear. Indeed, for Stendhal, Rossini's very earliest works are his best, with *Tancredi* an apotheosis of the freshness that illuminates them. One need not follow Stendhal in denigrating Rossini's mature operas in order to recognize the charm of his first operas. Amid the resplendent glories of *Guillaume Tell* one can still yearn with Stendhal for 'the freshness of the morning of life', the spontaneity and sheer melodic beauty of a piece such as the duet 'Questo cor ti giura amore' from *Demetrio e Polibio*.

Rossini's operatic career began in earnest in 1810, with a commission from the Teatro S Moisè of Venice to compose the music for Gaetano Rossi's one-act *farsa*, *La cambiale di matrimonio*. According to a student of Giovanni Morandi, cited by Radiciotti, a German composer scheduled to write the opera reneged on his contract. Through the good offices of Morandi and his wife, the singer Rosa Morandi, friends of the Rossinis, the inexperienced Gioachino was approached instead. It was a fortunate opportunity, as he later recalled:

That theatre also made possible a simple début for young composers, as it was for Mayr, Generali, Pavesi, Farinelli, Coccia, etc, and for me too in 1810. . . . The expenses of the impresario were minimal since, except for a good company of singers (without chorus), they were limited to the expenses for a single set for each *farsa*, a modest staging, and a few days of rehearsals. From this it is evident that everything tended to facilitate the début of a novice composer, who could, better than in a four- or five-act opera, sufficiently expose his innate fantasy (if Heaven had granted it to him) and his technical skill (if he had mastered it).

Five of Rossini's first nine operas were written for the S Moisè.

It was a full year before Rossini's next opera, *L'equivoco stravagante*, was performed in Bologna on 26 October 1811. The libretto, in which the heroine's poor lover convinces the rich imbecile preferred by her father that the girl is really a eunuch disguised as a woman, was considered in such bad taste that the Bolognese authorities closed the show after three performances. But Rossini had no time to be upset by this fiasco, since the Teatro S Moisè was already awaiting his next *farsa*. *L'inganno felice*, which had its Venetian première in January 1812, was Rossini's first truly successful work, remaining popular throughout Italy during the next decade.

Commissions from other theatres followed rapidly. Despite statements from writers north of the Alps about the decadence of Italian music in this period, operatic life was in one sense remarkably healthy. Many important centres existed, and theatres and impresarios sought to outdo one another in obtaining new works, exploring new talent, training new musicians. That there was much bad music composed and performed is undeniable, but a flourishing, lively culture could give a composer the opportunity to come to maturity, and Rossini did not lack for opportunity. His sacred opera *Ciro in Babilonia* was presented in Ferrara during Lent, followed by yet another work for S Moisè, *La scala di seta*. The pinnacle of Rossini's first period, though, was the première of his two-act *La pietra del paragone*, at the Teatro alla Scala, Milan, on 26 September 1812. Just as Verdi, 30 years later, was assisted by Giuseppina Strepponi in obtaining his entrée to La Scala, so Rossini benefited from the recommendations of two singers who had taken part in his earlier operas, Maria Marcolini and Filippo Galli, both of whom were to sing in the cast of *La pietra del paragone*. The work was an unquestionable triumph. Rossini told Hiller that it earned him exemption from military service. He hurried back to Venice, where he composed two more *farse* for the

1. Gioachino Rossini: drawing by Thomas Lawrence (1769–30)

Teatro S Moisè, *L'occasione fa il ladro* and *Il Signor
Bruschino*. It is distressing that, 50 years after
Radiciotti destroyed the myth of the latter opera's being
a jest at the impresario's expense, the story continues to
circulate. *Il Signor Bruschino* is perhaps the best of
Rossini's early *farse*, comic, witty and sentimental by
turns. The famous sinfonia, in which the violins occasionally beat out rhythms with their bows against the
metal shades of their candle holders or, in modern times,
against their music stands, is delightful both for its
absurdity and for the totally natural and logical way in
which the effect is woven into the composition.

In the 16 months from *L'equivoco stravagante* to
Il Signor Bruschino, Rossini composed seven operas.
With the sheer press of commitments on him, he often
used individual pieces in more than one opera. Though
famous examples of self-borrowing are found later in his
life, no compositions ever saw such service as two from
Demetrio e Polibio, the duet 'Questo cor ti giura amore'
mentioned above (which reappeared in five later operas)
and the quartet 'Donami omai Siveno' (about which
Stendhal wrote, 'had Rossini written this quartet alone,
Mozart and Cimarosa would have recognized him as
their equal'). One can understand, if not wholly respect,
the insouciance with which Rossini simplified his task of
grinding out so many operas. What is remarkable is how
much fine music they contain.

Rossini's *farse* and *La pietra del paragone* are superior to his early *opere serie*. Despite some beautiful
moments, *Demetrio e Polibio* remains colourless, while
Ciro in Babilonia, if not the fiasco that Rossini later
labelled it, is scarcely distinguishable from the host of
pseudo-religious operas prepared yearly for Lent. In the

farse and comic operas, however, Rossini's musical personality began to take shape. Formal and melodic characteristics of his mature operas appear only occasionally, but many elements emerge that remain throughout his career. A love of sheer sound, of sharp and effective rhythms, is one of them. Pacuvio's aria 'Ombretta sdegnosa' in *La pietra del paragone*, with its babbling 'Misipípí, pípí, pípí' that rapidly acquired the status of a folksong, or the younger Bruschino's funereal 'son pentito, tito, tito', proclaim a love for words and their sounds that blossomed in the first finale of *L'italiana in Algeri*. Orchestral melodies give the singer scope for *buffo* declamation. Built almost exclusively in this way is 'Chi è colei che s'avvicina?', the aria of the parodied journalist, Macrobio, in *La pietra del paragone*. But sometimes, especially in these earlier works, the orchestral bustle seems rather faceless. Thus much of the introduction in *La cambiale di matrimonio* revolves around an orchestral figure (ex.1), over which

Ex.1

the pompous Mill attempts unsuccessfully to calculate from a world map the distance from Canada to Europe and then engages in a spirited dialogue with his servants. The same figure recurs in *L'inganno felice*, during the aria 'Una voce m'ha colpito', in which Batone realizes that the woman he thought to have murdered is alive. Rather than being particularly jarring in these diverse situations, the orchestral motif is simply appropriate to neither: its very limitations make it extremely adaptable.

Alongside the comic elements is the sentimental vein that pervades much of Rossini's *opera buffa*. Florville's opening solo in the introduction of *Il Signor Bruschino*, 'Deh! tu m'assisti, amore!', Isabella's 'Perchè del tuo seno' in *L'inganno felice*, or the cavatina of Berenice in *L'occasione fa il ladro*, 'Vicino è il momento che sposa sarò' (ex.2) are all lovely examples. Rossini's vocal lines

Ex.2

Vi - ci-no è il mo-men-to che spo-sa sa - rò, Ep -

– pu-re con-ten to il co-re non ho.

here are less florid than in his later operas. Although some ornamentation would have been applied by singers, particularly in repeated passages, the style imposes limitations. Isabella in *L'inganno felice* could hardly sing in the vein of the heroines of *Semiramide* or *Elisabetta, regina d'Inghilterra*. The simplicity and balance of these melodic periods, which avoid the deformations that give Rossini's later melodies such variety, help explain their freshness and appeal. When a singer does break into coloratura, as Berenice in her expansive aria 'Voi la sposa pretendete', it normally forms a quasi-independent section before the final cadences, a procedure Rossini abandoned after his earliest operas.

Whereas Rossini grew in stature as a dramatist during his career, he was from the outset a consummate composer of overtures. Though early specimens do not exhibit all the typical characteristics of the more mature works, their appeal is immediate and genuine. Formally they are sonata movements without development sections, usually preceded by a slow introduction with a cantabile melody for oboe, english horn or french horn. The first group is played by the strings; the second group features the wind. The crescendo is part of the second group, though in these early works it is not fully standardized. Within this schema, clear melodies, exuberant rhythms, simple harmonic structure and a superb feeling for sound and balance, together with such splendid details as the wind writing in *La scala di seta* or the beating bows in *Il Signor Bruschino*, give the overtures their unique character. The qualities that make them unique as a group, though, are also the qualities which make them generic among themselves. Almost all these overtures served for more than one opera. Some of the transferences, as from *La pietra del paragone* to *Tancredi*, seem no less incongruous than the infamous vicissitudes of the overture to *Il barbiere di Siviglia*.

In a famous letter to Tito Ricordi, written in 1868, Rossini chided Boito for attempting innovations too rapidly. 'Don't think I am declaring war on innovators', he continued; 'I am opposed only to doing in one day what can only be achieved in several years . . . look, with *compassion*, at *Demetrio e Polibio*, my first work, and then at *Guglielmo Tell*: you will see that I was no snail!!!'. Still, Rossini's early works have their own charms, and to anyone who has a touch of Stendhal in his blood they remain delightful.

CHAPTER FOUR

From 'Tancredi' to 'La gazza ladra'

With no effective copyright legislation in an Italy of separate states, Rossini's earnings from an opera were limited to performances in which he participated, and payments to a composer did not match those to a prima donna. Obliged to support both himself and, increasingly, his parents, Rossini plunged into one opera after another. The period from *Tancredi* to *La gazza ladra*, which intersects with his Neapolitan years, was one of constant travelling and frenetic compositional activity. Entire operas were prepared in a month, and Rossini's masterpiece, *Il barbiere di Siviglia*, occupied him for about three weeks. During this period he produced his great comic operas, works ranging from pure *buffo* to sentimental comedy, his more 'classical' serious operas, and his finest opera in the *semiseria* genre.

Unfortunately almost nothing is known of Rossini's life during these years. Anecdotes pertaining to his amorous pursuits and filial devotion abound, but documents do not. Nor can reports from later in the century be trusted, even those originating with close friends such as Hiller, Alexis Azevedo or Edmond Michotte: so many of the statements they attribute to Rossini are palpably false that one must suspect that either they embroidered his remarks or that he saw his early life and attitudes through the tinted glasses of his old age. One can be certain only that Rossini now became the leading Italian composer. His music was played and enthusiastically received almost everywhere.

Rossini's first two operas to win international acclaim were written consecutively for Venetian theatres: *Tancredi*, the idyllic *opera seria*, given at the Teatro La Fenice on 6 February 1813, and the zaniest of all *buffo* operas, *L'italiana in Algeri*, produced at the Teatro S Benedetto on 22 May 1813. For later generations the fame of *Tancredi* appeared to rest on the cavatina 'Tu che accendi', with its cabaletta 'Di tanti palpiti'. One need not invoke the old images of gondoliers singing and juries humming the tune to gauge its appeal. Thanking Tito Ricordi for a New Year's *panettone* in 1865, Rossini assured him it was worthy of 'the greatest Publisher (donor) and the author of the too famous cavatina "Di tanti palpiti" (receiver)'. Wagner's parody, the Tailors' Song in Act 3 of *Die Meistersinger*, is

Ex.3

further evidence of its longevity. Rossini's melody seems to capture the melodic beauty and innocence characteristic of Italian opera, while escaping naivety by its enchanting cadential phrase, which instead of resting on the tonic F jumps to the major chord on the flattened third degree A♭ (ex.3). Rossini delighted in such harmonic games, even within the simplest phrase, and their piquancy gives his melodies their special charm.

But *Tancredi* is more than 'Di tanti palpiti'. It is Rossini's first great *opera seria*, and it exhibits the freshness of first maturity, of first formulated principles. There is little in *Semiramide* whose roots cannot be traced here. Formal procedures in particular, uncertain and tentative in earlier operas, assume the characteristics that were now to dominate Italian opera. It is impossible to prove that Rossini was an innovator here, since so little is known of the music of his contemporaries, but the force of his example was felt strongly by the legions of opera composers after him.

Rossini's formal procedures were compelling because they fused in a simple yet satisfactory manner the urge for lyrical expression and the needs of the drama. Although in *Tancredi* secco recitative still separates formal musical numbers, many important dramatic events occur within these numbers. There are occasional isolated lyrical moments, such as Amenaide's exquisite 'No, che il morir non è' of Act 2, but these play a decreasing role in Rossini's operas as he matured. Instead they are incorporated into larger musical units in alternation with dramatic events that motivate lyrical expression. The formal structure of standard arias, duets and first-act finales demonstrates this in various ways.

The problem of the aria is to permit lyrical expression to predominate without freezing the action. Often, especially in his cavatinas (entrance arias), Rossini com-

17

posed two successive, separate lyrical sections, an opening cantabile and concluding cabaletta, thus giving the impression of dramatic change even when actual change is slight or non-existent. More normal is the approach taken in Amenaide's 'Giusto Dio che umile adoro' of Act 2 of *Tancredi*. Amenaide is alone on the stage; after a short scena her aria begins with a lyrical solo, a prayer for the victory of her champion. In a section of contrasting tempo and tonality, the chorus enters and describes his victory. Emphatically not lyrical, the music depends instead on orchestral figures, declamatory non-periodic solos and choral interjections. The cabaletta now concludes the aria in its original key. Amenaide contemplates her joy in a lyrical period, first expressively, then in exuberant coloratura. 'The chorus and other characters immediately applaud', in the words of Pietro Lichtenthal, a contemporary detractor, 'and She [Queen Cabaletta], all kindness, returns to content her faithful audience by repeating with the same instrumental plucking the celestial melody.' Rossini's multi-sectional aria with cabaletta may not be the ideal solution to the problem of the aria, but it permits lyrical sections to co-exist with dramatic action and gives the singer, during the repetition of the cabaletta theme, the flattering option of ornamenting the melody. That the cabaletta was both useful and aesthetically satisfying was perceived by Verdi as late as *Aida*, when he wrote to Opprandino Arrivabene in reaction to criticism about his use there of a quasi-cabaletta: 'it has become fashionable to rail against and to refuse to hear cabalettas. This is an error equal to that of the time when only cabalettas were wanted. They scream so against convention, and then abandon one to embrace another! Like flocks of sheep!!'.

The duet poses a different problem. 18th-century *opera seria* tended to minimize ensembles. Under the influence of *opera buffa*, ensembles gradually infiltrated the grand Metastasian design, until by 1800 ensembles within the act and lengthy finales were the norm. As Rossini matured, the number of his solo arias (with or without assisting chorus) decreased until, in an opera such as *Maometto II*, they play a small role. There are of course purely lyrical duets, like the already-cited 'Questo cor ti giura amore' from *Demetrio e Polibio*. But Rossini's problem was to perfect a duet form that offered the characters opportunity for lyrical expression while centring on their dramatic confrontation. The duet 'Lasciami, non t'ascolto!' for Tancredi and Amenaide exemplifies his solution. Essentially in four parts, the duet begins with a confrontation that dramatically motivates the whole composition, Tancredi's belief in Amenaide's guilt and her protestations of innocence. The initial clash is presented in parallel poetic stanzas, normally set to the same or similar music. Here the settings differ only in details of ornamentation and in tonality: Tancredi's is in the tonic, Amenaide's modulates to and remains in the dominant. Once positions have been stated, the characters often continue in dialogue, though in this example an orchestral modulation (typically to the mediant major) leads directly to the second section. The latter is a lyrical contemplation of the dramatic situation. Though the characters basically have quite different views, they express them in 'pseudocanon' to the same or parallel texts, one character sing-

19

ing a lyrical phrase alone, the other repeating it while the first supplies brief counterpoints. Overlapping lyrical phrases and cadences, often in 3rds and 6ths, bring the section to a close. The third section can recall the first, but is freer in design. Action is taken, new positions defined, a motivating force established, while the music follows the events, preparing the final section, a cabaletta *a due*. Using the form outlined above, the characters reflect on their new positions, shout out new challenges, and so on. (In the *Tancredi* duet, printed editions do not show the repetition of the cabaletta theme, but it is in the autograph.)

The first-act finale is quite similar to the duet, with the standard addition of a short opening ensemble or chorus. Since more action is to be incorporated into the music, the kinetic sections are longer and more flexible. Action is advanced through passages of arioso and simple declamation over orchestral periods, often identical in both kinetic sections. The latter are followed, respectively, by a slow ensemble, called a 'Largo', and a concluding cabaletta, referred to in the finale as a 'stretta' but indistinguishable in shape and function from the normal cabaletta. The *Tancredi* finale is a pure example, but with the addition of extra internal movements the model holds for most contemporary *opera seria*. Indeed, except for a less rigid stretta, the act 'Il contratto nuziale' from Donizetti's *Lucia di Lammermoor* concludes with a textbook example of the Rossini finale, the famous sextet forming the Largo. The same holds for the first-act finale of Verdi's *Nabucco*. Once again, Rossini's underlying plan balances various forces, musical, dramatic and vocal.

The difficulty with these formal conventions is that

form too easily degenerates into formula. But the procedures do permit diverse handling and effective modifications. *Tancredi* manifests them in their pristine state. The lines are clear, the melodies crystalline, the rhythms vital without being exaggerated, the harmonies simple but with enough chromatic inflections to keep the attention. Orchestral writing is kept in perfect control, with the wind offering numerous colouristic solos. Heroic and idyllic moods dominate, and Rossini captured well the pseudo-Arcadian spirit. Though the world of *Semiramide* is implicit here, its realization seems far off.

L'italiana in Algeri, to a libretto by Angelo Anelli first set by Luigi Mosca (1808), fully shared the success of *Tancredi*. It is an *opera buffa* that moves easily among the sentimental (Lindoro's 'Languir per una bella'), the grossly farcical (the 'Pappataci' trio), the patriotic (Isabella's 'Pensa alla patria'), and the sheer lunatic (the 'cra cra, bum bum, din din, tac tac' of the first finale). Too often, critics stress the extent to which Rossini's *opera seria* is enriched through elements of the *opera buffa* without looking at the reverse: how *opera buffa* adopted elements from the *seria*. The aria 'Pensa alla patria' would have no place in a classical *opera buffa*, and this tendency develops further in *La Cenerentola*. Similarities between the genres are as important as their divergences. Of course there are no buffo arias *per se* in Rossini's serious operas, and devices such as mechanical repetition, rapid declamation to the limits of the possible, the use of large intervals in a grotesque manner ('Pappataci Mustafà') or exaggerated contrasts of tempo are part of *buffo* technique. Similarly, elaborate, orchestrally introduced scenas, often preceding major arias in Rossini's serious operas, rarely appear in the *buffo* world. The heroic *coro e cavatina* is reserved for the *opera seria*, though Rossini satirized the procedure in Dandini's mock-heroic entrance in *La Cenerentola*, 'Come un'ape ne' giorni d'aprile', or even in Isabella's 'Cruda sorte! amor tiranno!' from *L'italiana*.

But so many elements are similar. All the formal designs of the *opera seria* recur in the *opera buffa*, though treated with the greater internal freedom characteristic of the *buffo* heritage. The rhythmic verve of *opera buffa*, which depends on rapid orchestral melodies as a background for quasi-declamatory vocal lines, easily passes to the serious style and helps expand enormously the amount of action incorporated into musical numbers. Though the stretta of an *opera seria* finale would never adopt the 'bum bum' fracas of *L'italiana*, there is really scant difference in character between the close of the first-act finale in the serious *Aureliano in Palmira* and the comic *Il turco in Italia*. Nor does the orchestration differ greatly between the genres. The ease with which a single overture could introduce a serious or a comic opera is well known. This confounding of types, particularly the rhythmic vitality injected from the *opera buffa* into the *seria* and the introduction of more noble sentiments into stock *buffo* figures, is central to an understanding of Rossini's music and its effect on his contemporaries. Though the traditional *buffa* prevails gloriously in *L'italiana*, *La Cenerentola* is only four years away.

After *Tancredi* and *L'italiana*, Rossini's fame was assured. From the end of 1813 until the summer of 1814 he was largely in Milan, mounting and revising for the Teatro Re his two Venetian successes, and composing for La Scala two new operas, *Aureliano in Palmira* (26 December 1813) and *Il turco in Italia* (14 August 1814). The role of Arsace in the former was sung by the last great castrato, Giambattista Velluti. Although the castrato hero had been superseded by the contralto (Rossini's Tancredi, Malcolm in *La donna del lago*, Calbo in *Maometto II*, and Arsace in *Semiramide* are all breeches roles) and by the tenor (Othello, Rinaldo in *Armida*, Osiride in *Mosè in Egitto* and Ilo in *Zelmira*), Velluti remained a powerful figure. Rossini again wrote a part for him in his 1822 cantata *Il vero omaggio*, prepared for the Congress of Verona, but Velluti's greatest triumph was as Armando in Meyerbeer's last Italian opera, *Il crociato in Egitto* of 1824, one of the last significant castrato roles.

Velluti's importance for Rossini centres on an anecdote too widely accepted, according to which Velluti so ornamented Rossini's music that it was unrecognizable. Enraged, the composer vowed thenceforth to write out all ornamentation in full. It is an amusing story; but Rodolfo Celletti has conclusively demonstrated its fatuousness. While Rossini's melodies do tend more and more towards the decorative and florid, it is a gradual process. Rather than a matter of disciplining singers, Rossini's florid style is a mode of musical thought whose development can be traced from *Demetrio e Polibio* to *Semiramide*. At least one piece from *Aureliano* was published with Velluti's ornaments, the duet 'Mille sospiri e lagrime'. It is not certain that these are the variants he sang in Milan, but they are no more objectionable than ornamented versions of Rossini arias by other singers published in Paris in the 1820s. There is no hard evidence that Velluti had any effect on

Rossini's vocal style, and there is no quantum jump between *Aureliano* and *Elisabetta, regina d'Inghilterra*, Rossini's first Neapolitan opera and, according to legend, the first opera for which he wrote out the entire vocal part.

Aureliano was only moderately successful with the Milanese; *Il turco in Italia*, to a libretto by Felice Romani, fell flat. The fault did not lie with the opera, which is as masterful as *L'italiana* and, particularly in its Pirandellian Poet, even more sophisticated. The Milanese believed *Il turco* to be a mere inversion of *L'italiana* and claimed to hear extensive self-borrowing. But *Il turco* is actually one of Rossini's most carefully constructed comic operas, and except for a few short motifs (e.g. the opening motif of the duet 'Io danari vi darò' from *Il Signor Bruschino* is the basis for the first section of the magnificent Geronio–Fiorilla duet 'Per piacere alla signora'), the opera is newly composed. In the ensembles Rossini shines, and the quintet 'Oh guardate che accidente!' is one of the funniest he ever wrote. The trio 'Un marito scimunito!' presents the Poet projecting a plot around the misfortunes of his friends, until in fury they turn on him singing:

> Atto primo, scena prima
> Il poeta per l'intrico
> Del marito e dall'amico
> Bastonate prenderà.

Rossini's setting is unique among his ensembles. The entire piece grows from a figure in semibreves, played alone and then accompanying the orchestral motif round which the *buffo* declamation revolves (ex.4).

By the end of the year Rossini was again in Venice,

Ex.4

writing *Sigismondo* for the Carnival season at La Fenice. Although its failure was deserved, some of the numbers that critics praise in *Elisabetta, regina d'Inghilterra* were originally written for *Sigismondo*. Azevedo quoted Rossini concerning the publication of his complete works by Ricordi in the 1850s:

> I remain furious . . . about the publication, which will bring all my operas together before the eyes of the public. The same pieces will be found several times, for I thought I had the right to remove from my fiascos those pieces which seemed best, to rescue them from shipwreck by placing them in new works. A fiasco seemed to be good and dead, and now look they've resuscitated them all!

The extent and character of Rossini's self-borrowing remains to be investigated.

Rossini's next opera, *Elisabetta, regina d'Inghilterra* (4 October 1815), opens his Neapolitan period and almost exclusive involvement with *opera seria*. During the first years (1815–17) of his association with Naples, however, Rossini produced several major works for other cities, including two comic operas, *Il barbiere di Siviglia* and *La Cenerentola*, and two in the *semiseria* genre, *Torvaldo e Dorliska* and *La gazza ladra*. These works, so different as a group from his Neapolitan operas, may be examined first.

Soon after the première of *Elisabetta* Rossini went to Rome, where he wrote two operas during the Carnival season. The first, *Torvaldo e Dorliska*, opened the season at the Teatro Valle (26 December 1815). There are attractive elements in this 'rescue opera', but its reception was mediocre. 11 days before the première, Rossini signed a contract with the rival Teatro Argentina to compose an opera, to a libretto chosen by the management, for the close of carnival. After a subject offered by Jacopo Ferretti had been rejected, Cesare Sterbini, author of *Torvaldo*, was summoned. The resulting opera was *Almaviva, ossia L'inutile precauzione*, a title adopted to distinguish it from Paisiello's well-known *Il barbiere di Siviglia*, although the more common title appeared when the work was revived in Bologna during the summer of 1816. The dreadful failure of *Almaviva* on opening night is hardly surprising, if one considers the speed with which it was mounted. But stories, even by the original Rosina, Geltrude Righetti-Giorgi, which claim that Rossini extensively altered the opera are constructed on air. There is no hard evidence that a different overture was used at the première, and the standard one was unquestionably performed during the season. Since Rossini often prepared overtures last, he more probably turned to the overture of *Aureliano in Palmira* for lack of time or lack of will to compose another. (He turned to *Aureliano* and not to *Elisabetta*: the latter overture, though largely the same, differs in detail and has a heavier orchestration.) Manuel Garcia, the original Lindoro, cannot be shown ever to have inserted a serenade of his own, though Rossini may have permitted him to improvise an accompaniment to 'Se il mio nome saper voi bramate'.

The autograph contains the melody in Rossini's hand and guitar chords in another, except for an important modulation that Rossini obviously feared might be misinterpreted by his singer-guitarist. The libretto printed for the première gives essentially the same text as modern editions; the opera played on 20 February 1816 was the opera known today.

Il barbiere di Siviglia is perhaps the greatest of all comic operas. Beethoven thought well of it; Verdi wrote to Camillo Bellaigue in 1898: 'I cannot help thinking that *Il barbiere di Siviglia*, for the abundance of true musical ideas, for its comic verve and the accuracy of its declamation, is the most beautiful *opera buffa* there is'. Faced with one of the best librettos he ever set, one in which the characters are keenly sketched and the dramatic situations are planned for a maximum of effective interaction among them, one which is itself based on an excellent play by Beaumarchais, featuring the incomparable Figaro, Rossini took fire. The opera soon gained an enormous success that has never diminished. From Lindoro's miniature canzona 'Se il mio nome saper' to Rosina's delicious cavatina 'Una voce poco fa', which so perfectly captures the wily heroine, to the uproarious first-act finale, the compositions achieve in turn melodic elegance, rhythmic exhilaration, superb ensemble writing, original and delightful orchestration – particularly when heard in Alberto Zedda's critical edition (Milan, 1969), stripped of the extraneous accretions of 'tradition'. The formal models of earlier operas are adapted to specific dramatic situations with such cleverness and irony that they seem eternally fresh. Basilio's 'La calunnia' is an apotheosis of the Rossini crescendo. The orchestral phrase that is to serve for the crescendo first

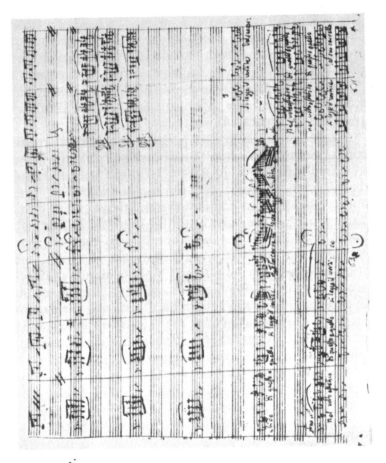

2. Autograph MS from 'La Cenerentola', first performed in Rome, 25 January 1817

appears in the strings alone, *sul ponticello* and *pianissimo*, as an orchestral background for Basilio's narration. Then a gradual increase in orchestral forces, with a movement upwards in register, a change to the regular position in the strings, and the introduction of staccato articulation, all produce the enormous crescendo as rumour spreads from mouth to mouth. Bartolo's 'A un dottor della mia sorte', on the other hand, is one of the most rapid patter songs ever written. Its concluding section is amusingly worked out, contrary to Rossini's normal procedures in vocal compositions, in strict sonata form, a wonderfully ironic comment on the pedantic character of the tutor. There is the delightful incongruity of form and content in the trio 'Ah! qual dolce inaspettato!', where the Count and Rosina go through 'obligatory' formal conventions, including a strict cabaletta repeat of 'Zitti zitti, piano piano', while their escape ladder disappears and Figaro hopelessly mimics and prods them along, only to be forced to wait out the exigencies of form. Every piece is filled with such riches. *Il barbiere di Siviglia* is an opera that can be appreciated on many levels, and what it may lack in the humanity of Mozart's *Le nozze di Figaro* it retrieves in glorious musical spirit and wit.

After two more Neapolitan operas, *La gazzetta* and *Otello*, Rossini returned to Rome, where on 25 January 1817 he produced *La Cenerentola*, with the contralto Righetti-Giorgi in the title role. *La Cenerentola* markedly turns away from the delirious style of *L'italiana* and *Il turco*. There are, of course, the normal *buffo* roles. Don Magnifico is rather conventional, but Dandini, the servant dressed as the prince and trying to sound like him, is more subtle and more amusing. The duet 'Un segreto d'importanza', in which Dandini reveals his true identity to Magnifico, is brilliantly witty, and Rossini's setting is superb. Once the secret is out, the tentative opening phrase (ex.5*a*) is transformed into the

Ex.5
(a)

Un se-gre-to   d'im-portan-za,   Un ar-ca-no   inte-res-san-te,   Io vi de-vo,   Io vi de-vo pa-le-sar

(b)

Di quest'in - giu - ria, Di quest'af - fron - to, Di quest'in - giu - ria, Di quest'af - fron- to, Il ve-ro prin - ci-pe

Mi da-rà con-to,   Mi da-rà con-to.

spirited tune of the final Allegro (ex.5*b*). In the fashion of *L'italiana* the confused Magnifico babbles:

> Tengo nel cerebro un contrabbasso
> Che basso basso frullando va,

with the requisite leaps and quick patter. What sets *La Cenerentola* apart, though, is the nature of the Cenerentola–Don Ramiro story, the sentimental tale, the transformation of the scullery maid who sings 'Una volta c'era un re' in the introduction of Act 1 into the royal maiden who, with full coloratura regalia, ends the opera with 'Nacqui all'affanno e al pianto'. The shy mouse of the duet 'Un soave non so che', with her charmingly incoherent 'Quel ch'è padre non è padre', grows into the mature woman who, in the sextet 'Siete voi? Voi Prence siete?', can, to the beautiful melody 'Ah signor, s'è ver che in petto', forgive those who have wronged her. Far removed from the tone of an Isabella or Rosina, Cenerentola is a character who anticipates the heroines of sentimental dramas, such as Bellini's *La sonnambula*.

La gazza ladra, produced in Milan on 31 May 1817, takes the process further. The rustic setting, as later in *La sonnambula*, heralds a tragi-comedy, the *opera semiseria* genre so popular in this period. Not until Verdi's *Luisa Miller* was a rustic scene permitted to serve as background to real tragedy. Some critics have deplored a lack of profundity in Rossini's characterization of the evil forces in the opera, particularly the Podestà, but this objection loses sight of the genre. The Podestà must function as a semi-*buffo* figure to sustain disbelief in the reality of the forces that appear to be bent on Ninetta's inevitable destruction. Indeed Rossini develops the characters quite carefully, avoiding both the exaggerations of *buffo* style and the postures of *opera seria*. Ninetta's simplicity, even when overwhelmed by events, differentiates her entirely from his earlier, more sophisticated heroines. In both the sweetness of the opening of her duet with Pippo, 'Ebben, per mia memoria', and the almost monotone declamation at 'A mio nome deh consegna questo anello', set over a theme used earlier in the sinfonia, Ninetta is the image of persecuted innocence. Her prayer at the start of the second-act finale, framed by a funeral march, is extremely touching, the more so for Rossini's restraint in the use of ornament. Fernando, her father, is one of the composer's finest bass roles, and his agony is vividly expressed musically. The pedlar, Isacco, is sketched with just a few touches but they are witty and telling, especially in his street song, 'Stringhe e ferri'. Though Giannetto makes a bland lover, his parents are well characterized. To begin the opera, Rossini wrote one of his finest overtures, filled with novel and striking ideas from the opening antiphonal snare drum rolls and military march, to the first group in the minor (later employed in Ninetta's prison scene), and the superb crescendo.

Rossini began his maturity close to 18th-century models, but gradually established his own approaches to musical form, melodic writing, and dramatic characterization. Since this period of his first maturity includes his better-known music, one tends to characterize his total operatic output by it and to see him as essentially Classical rather than Romantic. But if the Romantic tradition in Italian opera is defined through the works of Bellini and Donizetti, this tradition is unthinkable without the developments that Rossini's style underwent both in his first maturity and in the years immediately following, years in which the composer's base of operations was established in Naples.

CHAPTER FIVE

Naples and the opera seria, 1815–23

By 1815 Rossini's operas were played almost everywhere, but were ignored in Naples. That the
Neapolitans, with their long, flourishing native traditions, were loath to welcome a brash northerner into the
temple of Cimarosa and the still-living Paisiello is
understandable. Indeed, the advent of Rossini marked
the end of Neapolitan dominance in Italian opera. But
the powerful and shrewd impresario of the Neapolitan
theatres, Domenico Barbaia, seeking to revitalize
operatic life in Naples, invited Rossini both to compose
for his theatres and to serve as their musical and artistic
director. From 1815 until 1822 Rossini was to reign over
this domain, and the initial resistance he encountered
from the fiercely nationalistic Neapolitans gradually
dissolved as he became their adopted favourite son.

Although Rossini was granted the right to travel and
compose for other theatres, after *La gazza ladra* the
fruits of these travels paled in comparison with the
Neapolitan operas. Indeed Rossini's Neapolitan period
was important precisely because he wrote for a specific
theatre, the Teatro S Carlo, with a fine orchestra and
superb singers. He could write more deliberately and be
assured of adequate rehearsals. He could come to know
the strengths of his company and they could develop
together. The growth of Rossini's style from *Elisabetta,
regina d'Inghilterra* to *Zelmira* and, ultimately,
Semiramide, is a direct consequence of this continuity.

Not only did Rossini compose some of his finest operas for Naples, but these operas profoundly affected oper-
·atic composition in Italy and made possible the developments that were to lead to Verdi.

It is usually asserted that Rossini's first Neapolitan opera, *Elisabetta*, opened a new stylistic era, but in fact the chronologically significant point is not equally important musically. *Elisabetta* belongs to the world of *Aureliano in Palmira* and *Sigismondo*, not to the world of *Mosè in Egitto* or *La donna del lago*. To call it the first opera in which Rossini wrote out the coloratura is a great exaggeration (see above). Although it is the first of his operas in which all recitative is accompanied by strings, Mayr had done this two years earlier in *Medea in Corinto*, written for the same Neapolitans who, largely under French influence, were demanding the rejection of secco recitative in *opera seria*. Much of the music of *Elisabetta* is salvaged from earlier operas, and the new pieces offer little novelty. As Rossini's first opera for Isabella Colbran, whose highly ornamental style of singing was to affect Rossini's musical thought, *Elisabetta* is important, but it marks no significant reform or progress in the character of the *opera seria*.

The same cannot be said of *Otello*, composed a year later. After the première of *Elisabetta*, Rossini returned to Rome for *Torvaldo e Dorliska* and *Il barbiere di Siviglia*. During his absence fire destroyed the old Teatro S Carlo. While Barbaia rapidly rebuilt it, Rossini composed two operas for other Neapolitan theatres, *La gazzetta* and *Otello*. The former was given at the Teatro dei Fiorentini on 26 September 1816. This theatre was the home of traditional Neapolitan *opera buffa*, and Rossini used Neapolitan dialect for the main *buffo* role,

Don Pomponio, sung by Carlo Casaccia, who made a speciality of such parts. Indeed, when *La Cenerentola* was revived for the Teatro del Fondo in the spring of 1818, Casaccia played Don Magnifico in dialect, perhaps with Rossini's approval. *La gazzetta* was even more derivative than *Elisabetta*. It is as if Rossini were gauging his new audience by drawing together successful numbers from lesser-known operas before attempting an original work. Several numbers are lifted whole from *Il turco in Italia*, including the entire masked scene in Act 2, with the chorus 'Amor la danza mova' and the quintet, 'Oh! vedete che accidente'; a trio is taken without change from *La pietra del paragone*; and several pieces are largely derived from *Torvaldo e Dorliska*. These operas were unknown in Naples, Rossini had no desire to revive them (unlike *L'italiana in Algeri*, which he offered in 1815 contemporaneously with the production of *Elisabetta*), and thus they could be freely pillaged. After *La gazzetta* he rarely resorted to borrowing for his Neapolitan operas.

Otello, given at the Teatro del Fondo on 4 December 1816, stands out from the world of Rossini's earlier *opere serie* most strikingly in its masterful third act. The act is conceived as a musical entity, and although one can identify the Gondolier's canzona, the Willow Song and prayer, the duet, and the final catastrophe, none is truly independent. Desdemona's Willow Song is ostensibly strophic, but Rossini's handling of vocal ornamentation gives it a more sophisticated structure. The first strophe is simple, a beautiful harp-accompanied melody. The second is more ornamented, and the third is quite florid. But the storm brews without and within, and when, after a short section of arioso

3. Stage design by Alessandro Sanquirico for the 1824 Milan performance of 'Semiramide'

from the frightened Desdemona, she begins the final strophe, it is utterly barren of ornament. Finally, unable to finish, she trails off into arioso. Although the first section of the Othello–Desdemona 'duet' is traditional, its ending, which builds in intensity until Othello kills Desdemona, is not. There is no room for a cabaletta, and Rossini offers none, though the text had been fashioned to suggest the typical cabaletta structure. Throughout this act, the drama is the controlling element, and the music, while never abdicating its own rights, reinforces it. In Act 3 of *Otello* Rossini came of age as a musical dramatist.

After trips to Rome and Milan for *La Cenerentola* and *La gazza ladra*, Rossini returned to Naples, where from 1817 until 1822 most of his significant operas were written. These include *Armida* (11 November 1817), *Mosè in Egitto* (5 March 1818), *Ricciardo e Zoraide* (3 December 1818), *Ermione* (27 March 1819), *La donna del lago* (24 September 1819), *Maometto II* (3 December 1820), and *Zelmira* (16 February 1822). Though written for Venice, *Semiramide* (3 February 1823) is a fitting climax to this period and brings to a close Rossini's Italian career. The works written for other cities do not generally reach the level of the Neapolitan ones. *Adelaide di Borgogna* (Rome, 27 December 1817), *Adina* (a one-act *farsa* written in 1818, though not performed until 22 June 1826 in Lisbon and containing much borrowed music) and *Eduardo e Cristina* (Venice, 24 April 1819, but a pasticcio) are clearly inferior in quality. Though not an innovatory opera, *Bianca e Falliero* (Milan, 26 December 1819) has some very beautiful passages. The most unusual of these works is *Matilde di Shabran* (Rome, 24 February 1821), a rather serious *opera semiseria*, and the only one of these operas that Rossini produced in Naples (in an extensively revised version at the end of 1821).

Criticism of Rossini's Neapolitan operas, beginning with Stendhal, has concentrated too heavily on the singers Isabella Colbran, Andrea Nozzari, Giovanni David and Rosmunda Pesaroni, whose vocal talents left an indelible and not wholly positive mark on Rossini's style. They all specialized in florid singing that could be dazzling in its splendour but monotonous in its ubiquity. In his Neapolitan works Rossini rarely failed to exploit the characteristic strengths of these voices. Attention given to this aspect of Rossini's art was intensified by his personal relations with Isabella Colbran. When Rossini arrived in Naples, she appears to have been Barbaia's mistress. Her unusual vocal abilities, as a dramatic soprano capable of elaborate fioritura, and her Spanish beauty combined to entrance the composer. Sometime between 1815 and 1822 he replaced Barbaia as Colbran's favourite, and in 1822, in Bologna, married her. The marriage was never very fortunate, but a false image of Rossini led by the whims of his prima donna has persisted. Though she clearly exerted some influence on his musical style, the exaggeration of its importance is based on a misreading of the Neapolitan operas.

Solo singing is of course important in these works. Malcolm's cavatina 'Elena! oh tu che chiamo' from *La donna del lago*, Orestes' cavatina 'Che sorda al mesto pianto' from *Ermione*, and Arsace's cavatina 'Ah! quel giorno ognor rammento' from *Semiramide*, each a standard entrance aria with an introductory scena, a slow and florid *primo tempo* and a rousing cabaletta, are all

beautiful pieces, but they define their characters so gen-
erically that they were used almost interchangeably during the 19th century. Rossini himself put 'Che sorda al
mesto pianto' into *La donna del lago* (Naples, 1819)
and its *primo tempo* (together with a cabaletta from
Otello) into *Matilde di Shabran* (Paris, 1829). Since he
had neglected to compose a cavatina for Desdemona in
Otello, the great singer Giuditta Pasta supplied her own,
adopting 'Elena! oh tu che chiamo' for the purpose. This
same interchangeability affects the final rondos Rossini
composed for many operas. Elena's 'Tanti affetti in tal
momento', which brings down the curtain in *La donna
del lago*, found a home in many Rossini operas, at least
twice through the composer's actions (in *Bianca e
Falliero* and in the 1823 Venetian revision of *Maometto
II*). These arias, all virtuoso pieces, offer enormous
technical difficulties, but also contain simpler vocal periods and delicate orchestral shading to raise them above
the level of pure technique. What they may lack in
delineation of character they recover in the glorious
sound that wells inexhaustibly from Rossini.

Focussing undue attention on the soloists can mask
the far-reaching advances in musical thought in these
Neapolitan operas. Though *Guillaume Tell* is Rossini's
most ambitious opera, its basis is laid in Naples. And
Rossini was not first exposed to French opera in Paris:
he directed the revival of Spontini's *Fernand Cortez* at
the Teatro S Carlo in 1820, shortly before he composed
Maometto II. The importance Rossini attached to the
latter is apparent. After its indifferent reception in
Naples, he revised it for Venice in 1823, immediately
before the *Semiramide* première, and in 1826 used it to
initiate his Parisian career, as *Le siège de Corinthe*.

Similarly, the finest numbers in *Moïse*, Rossini's second Parisian opera, are already found in its Italian model, *Mosè in Egitto*.

The Neapolitan operas show an enormous expansion in musical means, particularly an increase in the number and length of ensembles, with a corresponding decrease in the prominence of solo arias, and a profound shift in the role of the chorus, which now acts not as a passive observer but as an active participant. For the musical and dramatic requirements these changes imply, Rossini created a more dramatic accompanied recitative (Ermione's soliloquy before the final duet of that opera exemplifies this), and generally made his orchestra more prominent (earning himself the criticism of being Germanic). He attacked the tyranny of the 'number' from within, and it is arguable that the Neapolitan version of *Maometto II* is more audacious in this respect than its French revision.

Most operatic reformers are credited with expanding musical means, achieving a more continuous dramatic structure, and turning from a style dependent on the solo aria. A traditional way of achieving this is seen in the second act of *Armida*. This act reveals a continuous, additive musical and dramatic structure (short choruses alternating with recitative, duets, dances, even a *tema con variazioni* for soprano), deriving from earlier French tradition and characteristic of the Gluckian reform. Such a musically shapeless but dramatically responsive series of elements is scarcely original with Rossini. Paer and Mayr both featured this technique prominently, and it occurs in Rossini's earliest operas. The finale of Act 2 of *Semiramide* is a later example of such scenic construction.

Central to Rossini's reform, though, is the internal expansion of the musical unit. The simpler forms of *Tancredi* are pressed far beyond their original confines to incorporate extended dramatic action and diverse musical elements. The introductions of *Tancredi* and *Semiramide* are recognizably in the same tradition, but the latter is enormously expanded, presenting most of the characters, establishing the main lines of the plot, and comprising an introductory solo scena, a chorus, a trio for Idreno, Oroe, and Assur, another chorus followed by a quartet in pseudo-canon, a dramatic scena for soloists and chorus, and a final cabaletta led by Semiramis but incorporating all four soloists and chorus. The music is largely continuous, themes recur from one section to another, and the entire composition forms a dramatic, musical, and tonal entity. Perhaps the most remarkable number in these operas is the first-act 'terzettone' (as Rossini called it) in *Maometto II*, 'Ohimè! qual fulmine'. Practically the longest unit in the opera, this number shows in the extreme how Rossini expanded internally standard forms. The ensemble begins as if it were to be a simple trio, with a static section followed by a kinetic one. Though normally this would address a concluding cabaletta, here a cannon shot announces Maometto's impending siege, and Anna, Erisso and Calbo leave the stage. As the scene changes, the 'trio' is left incomplete, but the music continues into a chorus and solo prayer for Anna. Erisso and Calbo return, and with the members of the initial trio reassembled, they launch a typical four-part design that concludes with a cabaletta to bring the entire scene to completion. The whole composition is tonally closed, with the initial 'Ohimè! qual fulmine' and concluding cabaletta 'Dicesti assai! t'intendo' both in E major. Tonal closure is essential to Rossini's technique, and helps unify his expanded ensembles. Though this terzettone, which fills more than a third of Act 1, incorporates many different dramatic events and musical sections, it clearly represented a unit for Rossini and must be heard as such to make formal sense. To break it up into a 'Scena e Terzetto', 'Scena', 'Coro', 'Preghiera', and 'Scena e Terzetto', as in standard vocal scores of the opera, is to substitute chaos for an effective and coherent plan. This is an extreme but characteristic example of Rossini's efforts to incorporate more musical material and dramatic action into the individual number. Though the number remains sectional, these sections define a larger design, as the composer expands, almost to the limits of intelligibility, the possibilities of those formal patterns he had established earlier as basic elements in Italian operatic structure.

Equally important is the new emphasis Rossini placed on the chorus. From an inert mass in *Tancredi*, the chorus becomes in *Mosè in Egitto* or *La donna del lago* a central character in the drama, a role further developed in Rossini's French operas. Whereas in earlier operas the chorus merely comments on the actions of the principal characters, in the first-act finale of *La donna del lago*, with its famous 'Coro dei Bardi', the chorus dominates as the various melodic strands of the finale are brought together into a powerful ensemble. The opening chorus from *Mosè in Egitto*, 'Ah! che ne aita!', draws its source from the tradition of the Bach prelude rather than from simple song forms, with the melody of ex.6 winding its way through the orchestra as the chorus intones its pleas for mercy, interspersed with cries from the soloists. The simplicity and strength of these choruses, the most famous of which is the prayer for soloists and chorus from *Mosè*, 'Dal tuo stellato soglio', further balance the florid solo writing.

Ex.6

Even Rossini's approach to the overture changed drastically in Naples. After *Elisabetta* and *Otello*, both of whose overtures were composed for other operas, the former for *Aureliano in Palmira*, the latter for *Sigismondo*, Rossini firmly avoided prefacing his Neapolitan operas with standard overtures. Indeed *Mosè*, *Ricciardo e Zoraide*, *La donna del lago*, *Maometto II* (original version), and *Zelmira* have none at all, but at most introductory orchestral material melodically related to the ensuing introductions. *Armida* has an overture, but it is not in Rossini's traditional mould. The overture to *Ermione* is the most fascinating, for although its structure largely parallels the norm, at several points during this overture the chorus is heard, from behind the curtain, lamenting the fate of Troy; in the introduction, these choral interjections are developed into a full chorus. In his operas for other cities, however, Rossini continued to supply overtures, though many are derivative and only the overture to *Semiramide* is worthy of the composer. Impresarios

43

elsewhere were presumably in a position to demand overtures, whether the composer wanted to write one or not, but in Naples Rossini could exercise his will. The absence of traditional overtures there evidently reflects an artistic decision, and it seems likely that Rossini sought to involve his audience with the drama from the opening chord. A formal overture was extraneous, and hence was sacrificed. The significance of this approach for later Italian composers needs hardly be stressed. Indeed it is to Rossini's Neapolitan operas that a generation of composers, including Bellini and Donizetti, looked for inspiration and guidance.

Rossini also composed in these years a number of cantatas for state occasions and royal visits, as well as a *Messa di gloria*. The mass is a remarkable work; it draws on both Rossini's operatic style and techniques characteristic of sacred music generally absent from the operas, such as the extensive participation of obbligato orchestral instruments in complete ritornello arias and the employment of more contrapuntal textures. Far from being pieced together from fragments of his operas, as earlier writers ignorant of the score claimed, the *Messa di gloria* is an entirely original and excellent work, as worthy of modern performance as the great sacred works of Rossini's post-operatic career.

CHAPTER SIX

Europe and Paris, 1822–9

By 1822 Rossini's operas had already gained international acclaim. Both France and England were bidding for his services, but it was Barbaia who provided the impetus for Rossini's first foreign voyages just as he had initiated the composer's stay in Naples. The men were tied professionally, personally (through Colbran) and financially. Indeed, Rossini's wealth grew from his association with Barbaia in a company running the profitable gambling tables in the foyer of the Teatro S Carlo. Assuming directorship of the Kärntnertor-Theater in Vienna at the end of 1821, Barbaia imported his Neapolitan company, together with its composer, for a Rossini festival. It began on 13 April 1822 with *Zelmira*, which had had its Neapolitan première in February, and lasted until July. Six operas were given with extraordinary success. The city of Beethoven and Schubert welcomed Rossini as a hero. He may have been introduced to Beethoven, who according to Michotte told him to write only comic operas, faintly malicious advice to a composer who had written little but *opera seria* since 1817.

After his Viennese stay, Rossini parted company with Barbaia and Naples. He returned to Italy during the summer of 1822 and remained until the autumn of 1823. At the invitation of Prince Metternich, he composed two cantatas for the Congress of Verona at the end of 1822 (both patched together from earlier works).

45

The Carnival season of 1823 found him at the Teatro La Fenice in Venice, revising *Maometto II* to open the season and composing his last opera for Italy, *Semiramide*. It is one of the few Rossini operas whose genesis can be partly followed. Gaetano Rossi, the librettist, was a guest of the Rossinis in Bologna during the autumn of 1822, and his letters to Meyerbeer frequently refer to the opera being composed.

The Rossinis spent the summer of 1823 in Bologna. On 20 October they departed for Paris and England. That they were to abandon Italian theatres for ever probably occurred to neither of them. Rossini left Italy as the most important and popular composer of his time. He had written 34 operas, the best of which formed a large proportion of the repertory in opera houses throughout the peninsula. He was 31 years old.

They stopped briefly in Paris, where many of Rossini's operas were known, even if productions at the Théâtre-Italien were often so radically altered in content that Stendhal accused its directors of attempting to sabotage Rossini's reputation in France. Royally fêted, he began negotiations concerning future activities in Paris. The Rossinis then continued to London, arriving late in 1823. A Rossini season was organized at the King's Theatre, but many of the operas were unsuccessful. *Zelmira* made a particularly poor impression because of the inadequacy of Colbran in the title role. Her voice was gone, her career effectively over. Rossini was supposed to write a new opera, *Ugo, re d'Italia.* Although he may have composed at least part of it, nothing survives. In the autograph score of *Ermione*, however, several pieces are underlaid with alternative texts, in which the character Ugo appears. Rossini, who

SIGNOR ROSSINI'S FIRST CONCERT,
ALMACK'S.
FRIDAY, MAY the 14th.

Her Excellency COUNTESS LIEVEN,	LADY GRANTHAM,
MARCHIONESS OF LANSDOWNE,	COUNTESS COWPER,
COUNTESS OF JERSEY,	LADY GWYDYR,
MARCHIONESS OF WATERFORD,	COUNTESS OF SEFTON,
MARCHIONESS OF CHOLMONDELEY,	COUNTESS OF MORLEY.
COUNTESS BATHURST.	and
MARCHIONESS OF CONYNGHAM,	The Hon. MRS. HOPE.

The Second Concert will be on *Friday* the 11th of June.

Subscriptions to both, *Two Guineas.*

Part the First.

SINFONIA—(Gazza Ladra) . . . . *Rossini.*
DUETTO—" Della casa,"—M. and Madame Ronzi De Begnis *Generali.*
QUARTETTO — "Vedi come esulta," — Madame C. Rossini,
Madame Caradori, Signor Garcia, and Signor Curioni . . *Rossini.*
SESTETTO — " E palese," — Madame Caradori, Madame C.
Rossini, Signor Curioni, Signor Placci, Signor Remorini,
and Signor Benetti . . . . *Rossini.*
CAVATINA—" Quell' istante,"—Madame Catalani . . . *Rossini.*
DUETTO—" Un se puoi,"—Madame Pasta and Signor Curioni *Rossini.*
CAVATINA—" Di piacer,"—Madame Caradori . . . . . *Cimarosa.*
DUETTO—" Se fiate in corpo avete,"—Madame Catalani and
Signor Rossini . . . . *Cimarosa.*

Part the Second.

SINFONIA—(Tancredi) . . . . *Rossini.*
TERZETTO — " Cruda sorte," — Madame Catalani, Madame
Vestris, and Signor Garcia . . . . *Rossini.*
ARIA—Madame Pasta . . . . *Zingarelli.*
TERZETTO—" In questo estremo,"—Madame C. Rossini, Ma-
dame Pasta, and Signor Garcia . . . . *Rossini.*
ARIA—" Pensa a la patria," — Madame Catalani, with chorus *Rossini.*
DUETTO—" Ebben per mia memoria," — Madame Caradori
and Madame Vestris . . . . *Rossini.*
CAVATINO—(Figaro)—Signor Rossini. . . . . *Rossini.*
TERZETTO— " Giuro alla terra," — Signor Garcia, Signor
Remorini, and Signor Benetti . . . . *Guglielmi.*
FINALE—God save the King.

*** To begin at *Nine* o'Clock.

Vouchers issued by the Ladies Patronesses, to be exchanged for Tickets,
at the *Opera Office*, 105, Quadrant.

☞ Signor Rossini respectfully begs leave to state, that having unex-
pectedly been deprived of the assistance of M. and Madame Ronzi De
Begnis, for the latter part of the Concert, Madame Caradori, although un-
well, and Signor Benetti, both at a very short notice, most obligingly
granted their services on the occasion.

had kept the *Ermione* autograph as he had those for all his Neapolitan operas, apparently intended to use at least part of this score, performed only in Naples, as the basis for his English opera. Again Rossini's first reaction to a new artistic environment was to adapt an older work rather than to compose a new one. Most of his time, though, was spent growing wealthy on the foibles of English aristocrats, who were willing to spend outrageous sums to have the composer and his wife participate in household musical gatherings or to give lessons to their spoilt daughters.

By 1 August 1824 Rossini was in Paris, where he agreed to become director of the Théâtre-Italien. He also contracted to produce his older operas there, introduce other Italian operas and compose new operas for both the Théâtre-Italien and the Opéra. By the end of 1824, after a Bolognese vacation, the Rossinis established residence in Paris, where they were to live together for almost five years. Rossini first concentrated on the Théâtre-Italien. For the coronation of Charles X he composed *Il viaggio a Reims*, performed on 19 June 1825. Much of the music of this occasional opera was re-used in *Le Comte Ory*. As director of the theatre, Rossini introduced to Paris the finest Italian singers in first-rate performances of his most advanced Neapolitan operas, including *La donna del lago*, *Zelmira* and *Semiramide*, supervising the productions and often making significant revisions. The operas he produced by other composers included *Il crociato in Egitto*, which launched Meyerbeer's phenomenal Parisian career. The two men remained close throughout their lives. With Rossini at its helm, the Théâtre-Italien enjoyed its moment of greatest glory, and until his seemingly definitive departure from Paris in 1836, Rossini continued to assist in running the theatre.

His goal, however, was to compose operas in French for the Académie Royale de Musique. By October 1826 he signed a new contract, relieving him of most formal duties at the Théâtre-Italien and permitting him to devote his energy to composition for the Opéra. An honorary post was created for him as *premier compositeur du roi* and *inspecteur général du chant en France*. Having to learn French and master the intricacies of its declamation, Rossini approached his new task gingerly. He reserved two Neapolitan works for adaptation to the French stage, withholding them from production at the Théâtre-Italien during his tenure. Thus *Maometto II* became *Le siège de Corinthe* on 9 October 1826 and *Mosè in Egitto*, on 26 March 1827, became *Moïse*.

The differences between the Neapolitan originals and Parisian revisions result from a dialectical process internal to the Neapolitan works. In the latter, extremely florid solo vocal lines, emphasizing the virtuoso and generic, co-exist with far-reaching experiments in musical structure, which seek to give musical expression to particular dramatic situations. In the Paris revisions both extremes are planed down, resulting in a more consistent, if less audacious, dramatic continuum, and a reduced gulf between declamatory lines and florid passages. Ex.7 shows the purification of a melody from the introduction of *Maometto II* (7a) in its French revision (7b). Similarly modifying his structural experiments, Rossini eliminated many internal sections from the terzettone analysed above, leaving a truncated and more conventional residue in *Le siège de Corinthe*. Arias

Ex.7
(a)

Nell' ar - duo ci - men – – – to   E

co - vran mie fos – – – se   De'

bar - ba - ri ac-cen – – ti

(b)

Bra - vant ___ le tré-pas   Il vo - le aux com-

- bats   Et s'il suc - com – be à

further decline in importance. Instead Rossini tended to compose larger units in which solo voices and chorus combine more dramatically. The scene in which Hiéros blesses the soon-to-be-martyred Greek warriors and prophesies future greatness for Greece is impressive and anticipates the patriotic scenes of Auber's *La muette de Portici* and, of course, Rossini's own *Guillaume Tell.* Three of the four original arias in *Mosè in Egitto* were omitted for Paris. The one added aria, Anaï's 'Quelle horrible destinée', is in its force of utterance and starkness of melodic line far removed from the Neapolitan florid aria.

These two revisions prepared for Rossini's great French operas, the *opéra comique Le Comte Ory* (20

August 1828) and *Guillaume Tell* (3 August 1829).
Both works effectively unite elements of Italian and
French operatic style; by fusing Italian lyricism with
French declamation and spectacle, they add another link
to the chain that will lead to grand opera. *Le Comte Ory*
is a problematical work, episodic in structure, but given
its sources, it is surprising the opera hangs together at
all. The librettists, Eugène Scribe and Charles Gaspard
Delestre-Poirson, derived the second act from their own
earlier vaudeville, adding to it a first act incorporating
music from Rossini's *Il viaggio a Reims* of 1825. The
plot has its origins in a medieval ballad that recounts
deeds of the notorious Count Ory, and Rossini used the
ballad's tune both in the orchestral prelude and the
second-act drinking chorus. Only the Countess's aria,
'En proie à la tristesse', borrowed from *Il viaggio a
Reims*, features virtuoso solo writing. More characteristic of the opera are its ensembles: the trio 'A la faveur de
cette nuit obscure' reveals a wealth of musical detail that
belies common views of Rossini's style. By this time he
could encompass and yet unify a wide variety of musical
techniques, ranging from the delicacy of this trio to a
boisterous drinking-chorus, 'Buvons, buvons soudain',
with its parody of an unaccompanied prayer, 'Toi que je
révère', and from the Italianate aria of the Countess to
Raimbaud's humorous tale of pillaging the wine cellars.
In his orchestra Rossini could create the most miraculous turns with a few instruments, but when necessary he could pound on the bass drum too. His genius
held these contrasting forces in equilibrium, and despite
some illogical turns in the plot, *Le Comte Ory* is a fine
opera.

Rossini's last opera, *Guillaume Tell*, based on
Schiller's play, is more honoured than understood. Its

occasional revivals have suffered from excessive editing, as if the music and drama would be completely indifferent to mutilation, as if music whose grandeur is built architecturally could sustain itself when the repeat of a phrase almost inevitably attracts the ignorant conductor's scissors, as if depleting the work of its personal approach to music drama would somehow render it more 'dramatic' in a Verdian or Wagnerian sense. The bitter anecdote in which the head of the Opéra met Rossini on the street and proudly reported: 'Tonight we are performing the second act of your *Tell*', only to have the composer respond: 'Indeed! All of it?', rings true; the opera must be heard as the towering entity it is to be properly appreciated. Carefully written, harmonically daring, melodically purged of excessive ornamentation (though the extremely high range of the tenor part poses problems for modern singers), orchestrally opulent, *Guillaume Tell* represents a final purification of Rossini's style.

Rossini wove into this historical panorama elements of the pastoral (with actual quotations from Swiss 'ranz des vaches'), patriotic deeds (very much in vogue on the eve of the 1830 revolutions) and superbly drawn characters. The whole is a rich tapestry of his most inspired music. Ensembles dominate and the interests of the drama are well served. Tell's declamatory solo within the finale of Act 3, 'Sois immobile', won the approval even of the mature Wagner. The great overture is unabashedly programmatic. The extensive spectacular elements, ballets and processions derive from French operatic tradition, but are effectively integrated into the opera. The chorus is central both musically and dramatically, and much of the opera revolves about magnificent choral ensembles such as 'Vierge que les

5. *Title-page of the first edition of the vocal score of
'Guillaume Tell' (Paris: Troupenas, 1829)*

chrétiens adorent' in the first-act finale, or the final
ensemble, 'Tout change et grandit en ces lieux'. Act 2, in
particular, is music-theatre at its finest; its finale, in
which the three Swiss cantons, each characterized
musically, are called together to plan the revolt, is perhaps the greatest single scene Rossini ever wrote.

CHAPTER SEVEN

Retirement

After *Guillaume Tell* ... silence. For almost 40 years Rossini lived on, lauded by many, execrated by some, begged to compose; but no more operas issued from his pen. There are no simple reasons for such a personal decision, if indeed it was consciously made. That Rossini was tired in body and mind, indeed was a semi-invalid for much of the rest of his life, was partly responsible. His rate of composition of operas diminished significantly during his active career, from an average of three new operas a year from 1811 to 1819 to only one a year from 1820 to 1823, and even fewer in Paris. *Tell* absorbed more of his energy than any other work, and letters and contemporary reports show that while Rossini composed it he considered terminating his operatic career. The financial security he had now gained may also have been a contributory cause.

Political and artistic events of the next years probably solidified his resolve to abandon his career at its height. Before the première of *Tell* he had negotiated a contract with the government of Charles X, in which he was assured a lifetime annuity, independent of his activities, although he did declare his readiness to write at least four new operas, one every other year, for the Opéra. During negotiations he had threatened to withdraw *Guillaume Tell* before its performance if the annuity was not guaranteed. With the agreements signed and *Tell* launched, Rossini and his wife returned to Bologna for a vacation, his next Parisian opera scheduled for 1831. He contemplated composing a *Faust* based on Goethe, but never received a completed libretto. Instead, his vacation was abruptly shattered by news of the 1830 Revolution, in which Charles X was dethroned and contracts under the old regime were suspended. In early September 1830, Rossini left for Paris alone, relations with his wife having grown strained. He hoped quickly to regulate his financial affairs, but the courts did not decide the future of his annuity until six years later. The administration of the Opéra had changed hands. Rossini had been so closely associated with the old regime that his influence there was gone, but he maintained ties with the Théâtre-Italien, actively supporting the production of works by his younger contemporaries, particularly Donizetti and Bellini. Mostly he was kept in Paris by a protracted legal battle to maintain his right to the annuity provided by Charles X. He composed little; two works, the *Stabat mater* and the *Soirées musicales*, were important. During a trip to Spain in 1831 with his banker friend Alexandre Aguado, Rossini was commissioned by Fernandez Varela, a state counsellor, to set the *Stabat mater*. He wrote only half the score (nos.1 and 5–9) before asking his friend Giovanni Tadolini to complete six additional movements. It was almost ten years before Rossini replaced Tadolini's handiwork, and then only under pressure from his Parisian publisher, Eugène Troupenas. Rossini's conduct was not motivated by pure laziness: by 1832 he was not well, and, whether psychological or not, his ills augured a period of morbid sickness that lasted for 25 years. In this sickness he was nursed and comforted by Olympe Pélissier. Their long affair, which began in Paris early in the 1830s, culminated in marriage in 1846, after the death of Isabella Colbran.

In Paris Rossini did complete the set of eight chamber arias and four duets known as the *Soirées musicales*, pieces which prove that Rossini's departure from the operatic stage had nothing to do with any decline in his inspiration. They embrace a wide range of moods: the dramatic *Li marinari*, the Tyrolean *La pastorella dell'Alpi*, the Neapolitan abandon of the ever-popular *La danza*. Melodically attractive, they are filled with beautiful details manifesting Rossini's skill; note, for example, the unanticipated G and D harmonies near the end of the B♭ major *La serenata*. These pieces were probably composed individually for various society figures during the early 1830s and then collected into a volume for publication by Troupenas in 1835.

All these factors – illness, changes in the artistic and political climate, financial security, general exhaustion – together with the enormous success of Meyerbeer's first French operas, *Robert le diable* (1831) and *Les Huguenots* (1836), which took to an extreme many techniques of *Tell* while abandoning the 'classical' tendencies of that opera, created a physical and artistic climate in which the composition of new operas had little savour for Rossini. But the reports of rivalry between Rossini and Meyerbeer seem fundamentally false. Whatever he thought about Meyerbeer's 'grand operas', Rossini remained on good personal terms with Meyerbeer from 1825, when he introduced him to the Parisian public, until his death in 1864, for which Rossini composed a *Chant funèbre*.

With the pension affair settled in his favour, Rossini took a short trip to Germany with another banker,

6. Gioachino Rossini: photograph by Carjat

Lionel de Rothschild, meeting both Mendelssohn and Hiller. Mendelssohn, despite himself, came away enormously impressed, writing to his mother and sister: 'intelligence, vivacity and polish at all times and in every word; and whoever doesn't think him a genius must hear him hold forth only once, and he'll change his mind immediately'. Hiller became a friend for life. By the end of the summer of 1836 Rossini returned to Paris to tidy up his affairs, departing again on 24 October for Italy. He did not take Olympe, but soon afterwards, in February 1837, she followed him to Bologna.

An account of the events of Rossini's life between the time he left Paris and his return in 1855 makes depressing reading. He was continually ill, did almost nothing, seemed indeed to be living on the brink of spiritual, if not physical, death. He and Olympe established a salon in Milan during the winter of 1837–8 and gave a number of musical soirées similar in style to the more famous Parisian ones of the 1860s. But the death of his father in 1839 further weakened Rossini (his mother had died in 1827 during rehearsals for *Moïse*). His only activity was as honorary consultant to the Bologna Liceo Musicale. There, starting in 1840, he attempted to regenerate the conservatory and improve its curriculum. It is known that he played at least a small role in the performance of his works there, since in the library of the conservatory is a set of orchestral parts for the quartet from *Bianca e Falliero*, 'Cielo, il mio labbro inspira', in which the part for second horn is in Rossini's hand. A note on the manuscript reads: 'Original writing of Rossini. May 1844'. But his health was poor, urethral disorders in particular requiring prolonged and painful treatment, and so Rossini could do little for the conservatory.

When, after the death of Varela, the original version of the *Stabat mater* fell into the hands of the Parisian publisher Aulagnier, who printed it and arranged a performance, Rossini, partly at the prompting of Troupenas and partly because the work published by Aulagnier was a composite, disowned this version and decided to complete the work himself. The revised *Stabat mater* was ready by the end of 1841. The first performance, arranged by the brothers Léon and Marie Escudier, was in Paris at the Théâtre Italien on 7 January 1842. It was received with enormous enthusiasm. The first Italian performance, at Bologna, followed in March under the direction of Donizetti. Among the soloists were Clara Novello and Nikolay Ivanov, who became a close friend of Rossini and for whom, at Rossini's request, Verdi expressly composed some substitute arias. Donizetti, reporting the reception of the *Stabat mater* in Bologna, wrote:

The enthusiasm is impossible to describe. Even at the final rehearsal, which Rossini attended, in the middle of the day, he was accompanied to his home to the shouting of more then 500 persons. The same thing the first night, under his window, since he did not appear in the hall . . .

The *Stabat mater* is often said to be operatic. If by this is meant that the work is lyrical rather than symphonic in conception, it seems a harmless statement. But it is important to recognize that the statement is really a disguised attack on its style, affirming by implication that the piece is neither specifically religious in quality nor deeply felt. Leaving aside the thorny problem of what is theoretically appropriate for religious music, Rossini's setting of the *Stabat mater* contains almost no music that would normally enter into his operas, whether for reasons of structure, orchestration, melody,

7. Autograph MS from the second layer of Rossini's compositions for the 'Stabat mater', composed 1841

use of chorus or a host of other considerations. No doubt the tenor aria 'Cujus animam' is melodically rich, but no similar Andantino maestoso movement exists in any Rossini opera, especially with the wealth of orchestral detail present here. One need not point to the specifically 'sacred' conceptions, the magnificent unaccompanied quartet, 'Quando corpus morietur', with its sinking chromatic lines, the final choral fugue on 'In sempiterna saecula amen', or the dramatic interaction between soprano and chorus in 'Inflammatus', in order to recognize that Rossini was striving to apply his artistic talents to the service of sacred music. From beginning to end there is a spirit quite unlike that of the operatic world that Rossini had abandoned a decade before completing his hymn to the Virgin. The opening movement, beginning with the dark sonority of cellos doubled by bassoons leading to the tutti at 'juxta crucem lacrimosa', is a stunning testimony to the vitality and success of his efforts.

Though it did not stir Rossini to further composition, he seems to have been genuinely moved by its triumph. He was particularly grateful to Donizetti for directing the Bolognese performance, but was unsuccessful in convincing the younger *maestro* to assume the directorship of the Bologna Conservatory. Physically Rossini remained weak, and in search of medical help he travelled with Olympe to Paris in 1843. They soon returned to Italy, where Rossini remained indolent. In 1845 Isabella Colbran died, and on 16 August 1846 Rossini married Olympe Pélissier, with whom he had now lived for almost 15 years. He composed some trifles, mostly drawn from earlier works, adapting the famous 'Coro dei Bardi' from *La donna del lago* to

unveil a monument to Tasso in 1844 and to praise Pope
Pius IX in 1846. He also prepared a short cantata,
derived in part from pieces in *Le siège de Corinthe*, in
honour of the new pope.

The revolutionary movements that swept Italy in
1848 marked a significant turning-point in Rossini's
life. He found himself out of favour with many
Bolognese townsmen for what they considered his lack
of enthusiasm towards the movement for national unity.
Prompted by demonstrations directed against them, the
Rossinis left Bologna for Florence. He always recalled
this period in extremely morbid terms, claiming that his
life and that of his wife had been in danger, and speaking
of the Bolognese as assassins. The incident, together
with his physical ills, further demoralized him. He
stayed with Olympe in Florence or took cures at
Montecatini or Lucca. Contemporary reports about him
(from Emilia Branca Romani, Giuseppina Strepponi,
and many others) give uniformly depressing and pes-
simistic accounts. In a letter of 1854 Rossini wrote of
'the deplorable state of health in which I find myself for
five long months, a most obstinate nervous malady that
robs me of my sleep and I might say almost renders my
life useless'. In the hope that French doctors might be
able to help him where the Italians failed, the Rossinis
decided to return to Paris in the spring of 1855.

CHAPTER EIGHT

A new life

The last years of Rossini's life must be understood
against the background of physical illness and mental
exhaustion that he had suffered during the previous 20
years; for it is no exaggeration to say that, in Paris,
Rossini returned to life. His health improved
dramatically; his famous sense of humour returned; he
bought a parcel of land in the suburb of Passy and built
a villa; he rented city quarters on the rue de la Chaussée
d'Antin, where before long he reigned over one of the
most interesting and elegant salons in Paris. Even more
remarkably, he began to compose again. The first new
work was the *Musique anodine*, six settings of Rossini's
favourite text for albumleaves, 'Mi lagnerò tacendo'. But
these pieces, which are dedicated (14 April 1857) to 'my
dear wife Olimpia as a simple testimony of gratitude for
the affectionate and intelligent care she offered me during my too long and terrible sickness', have far more
scope than the albumleaves he continued to dash off
during his retirement. They were to begin a surge of
composition that ultimately included over 150 piano
pieces, songs, small ensembles and the *Petite messe
solennelle*. Most of the shorter pieces were first performed at the Rossinis' 'Samedi soirs', whose par-
ticipants included most of the great artists and public
figures living in or passing through Paris.

Rossini referred to these pieces as his *Péchés de
vieillesse*, the 'Sins of Old Age', and in them he turned

his wit into musical terms, incorporating in various measure grace and charm, sharp parody, a dash of sentiment, and throughout a unique combination of sophistication and naivety. He refused to permit their publication, and although some did appear in the 19th century, they remained barely known until the Fondazione Rossini began editing them in the 1950s. Since then they have received increasingly sympathetic attention. Their historical position remains to be assessed, but it seems likely that their effect, direct or indirect, on composers like Camille Saint-Saëns and Erik Satie was significant.

Many of the piano pieces are parodies, but parodies so appealing and plausible that they could sometimes be mistaken for the things they parody, were it not that blatant excesses and Rossini's superb titles reveal his intention. One of the best is the *Petit caprice* (*style Offenbach*), allegedly a *quid pro quo* after Offenbach's outrageous 'Trio patriotique' in *La belle Hélène*, 'Lorsque la Grèce est un champ de carnage' (with its wonderful line 'Tu t' fich' pas mal de ton pays!'), brought Rossini's *Guillaume Tell* trio, 'Quand l'Helvétie est un champ de supplices' to the stage of the Théâtre des Variétés. The tempo indication 'Allegretto grotesco' leads the way, as does the bizarre fingering (intended to

Ex.8

protect against the 'malocchio' of Offenbach, which in Italian superstition brought ill luck), but once the music begins one feels surrounded by a slightly tipsy Offenbach cancan. The chromatic inflection of the main theme (ex.8) is suggestive. Then, within an apparently innocent F major context, Rossini first deploys a curious melodic D♭, and finally rings out a truly bizarre F♯; the piece continues as if nothing has happened, and modulates naively back to the tonic and the main theme.

Although Rossini referred to himself as a 'pianist of the fourth class', these pieces are often technically challenging, but they are also constantly delightful. The *Prélude prétentieux* is just that, with a fugal subject and development that parody one contrapuntal cliché after another. *Mon prélude hygiénique du matin*, with its opening C major and A minor arpeggios, is sure to bring a wistful smile to those whose piano practice has started each day with appropriate exercises. The absurd dance rhythms of the *Fausse couche de polka-mazurka* and the asthmatic theme of the *Valse torturée*, in which the tonic is defined by the chord progression D major – D augmented – D diminished – D major, take salon music as their target. Bach and Chopin are never far from the surface, but they are viewed through a level of ironic respect that renders Rossini's homages a pleasure.

The songs and choruses are less inventive but no less enjoyable. *La chanson du bébé*, with its refrain, 'Pipi . . . maman . . . papa . . . caca', is a charming spoof on the nursery. *L'amour à Pékin*, Rossini's nod at the whole-tone scale, is preceded by several piano vignettes, harmonizations first of the chromatic scale, then of the whole-tone scale, but the song itself is a disappointment.

It is a straightforward *romance*, with the whole-tone scale appearing only briefly in a cadential context (using the harmonization worked out previously in the piano vignette). The descriptive *Choeur de chasseurs démocrates*, written by Rossini at the request of the Baroness de Rothschild for the visit of Napoleon III in December 1862 to the Château de Ferrières, is a fine hunting chorus. The D major tonality of the main section is nicely balanced in the centre by Rossini's use of chromatic sequences, a frequent device in these late works. Among the songs there are more traditional, sentimental, even maudlin compositions, such as *L'orphéline du Tyrol*, or the *Chanson de Zora*. But even without a layer of ironic distance these pieces have more appeal than one might expect, for Rossini at his most conventional remains a remarkable composer.

The finest work of Rossini's late years, and indeed one of his greatest achievements, is the *Petite messe solennelle* for 12 voices, two pianos and harmonium, written for the Countess Louise Pillet-Will and first performed at the consecration of her private chapel in March 1864. Rossini later orchestrated the work, for fear that someone else would do it if he did not, but the mass is most effective in its original form. In an introductory note to 'le bon Dieu', Rossini referred to the mass as 'the last mortal Sin of my Old Age', and in an envoi at the end of the autograph score he addressed God as follows: 'Dear God. Here it is, finished, this poor little Mass. Have I written sacred music [*musique sacrée*] or damned music [*sacrée musique*]? I was born for *opera buffa*, you know it well! Little science, some heart, that's all. Be blessed, then, and grant me a place in

Paradise'. There is something enormously appealing about this ironic naivety. Whatever Rossini's public defences that caused him to gain a reputation for coldness and aloofness, in his greatest music they fall and here he sang the praises of God *con amore*. From 1857 until his death, Rossini was among subscribers to the critical edition of the works of Bach. Many of his piano compositions reveal his knowledge of Bach, and this is true also of the *Petite messe*. There is no mere imitation, but an attempt to return to historical traditions while holding fast to a modern compositional vocabulary. And through all the contrapuntal writing, elaborate chromaticism and harmonic audacity, beautiful melodies abound. Some pieces, such as the tenor aria 'Domine Deus rex coelestis,' reminiscent of 'Cujus animam' from the *Stabat mater*, are frankly operatic in the prominence they give to good tunes. But even knowing the contrapuntal movements of his earlier sacred works, one is unprepared for the richness of the double fugues on 'Cum Sancto Spiritu' and 'Et vitam venturi saeculi Amen'. The entire Credo (with its tempo indication 'Allegro cristiano') is a masterpiece of economy. A few musical ideas are basic to the entire composition, with the text and music 'Credo' acting as a refrain. The 'Crucifixus' is set apart from its surroundings, a soprano aria with the simplest possible accompaniment, the melody studded with chromatic alterations, the middle section modulating rapidly through the octave by minor 3rds. Here, as elsewhere in the mass, Rossini tended to be somewhat literal about his chromatic techniques, but within the context they seem entirely appropriate. The *Petite messe solennelle* has continued to impress later generations as a deep revelation of the man whose outward character often seemed a mere witticism.

In his last years Rossini lived in honoured retirement, a composer whose fame rested on work done 40 years before, and yet a composer who after a long silence had recovered his voice. Neither an anachronism, then, nor part of current musical trends, he was content to write for himself and his circle, while expounding to those who would listen his attitudes towards art and stories of his youth. Accounts of these years were published by many, including Hiller, Saint-Saëns and Hanslick. The most significant (even if perhaps in part invented) is the alleged transcription made by Edmond Michotte of the meeting between Rossini and Wagner in 1860. Rossini's last letters too are filled with aesthetic judgments and precepts to Italian composers. He wrote in 1868 to Lauro Rossi, head of the Milan Conservatory: 'Let us not forget, *Italians*, that Musical Art is all ideal and expressive . . . that Delight must be the basis and aim of this Art: Simple Melody – clear Rhythm'. And in an aside, referring to modern tendencies in Italian music, he added: 'these new gross philosophers . . . are simply supporters and advocates of those poor musical composers who lack *ideas*, *inspiration*!!!'. He expressed similar thoughts later that year in a letter to the Milanese critic Filippo Filippi, a champion of Wagnerian ideals in Italy. Here Rossini also entered into other favourite themes, the decline in vocal art and the need to seek 'expressive' rather than 'imitative' music. Though aware of his own compositional growth in 20 years of writing opera, he objected to instant progress, the search for extreme novelty that he observed in composers who fell under Wagner's influence. He railed against those who spiced their writings with 'certain dirty words, such as Progress, or Decadence, Future, Past, Present, Convention, etc', adding:

Do not think, my dear doctor Filippi, that I favour an anti-dramatic system, no indeed; and though I was a virtuoso of Italian bel canto before becoming a composer, I share the philosophic maxim of the great poet who said:

All genres are good,
Except the boring one.

It might be said that Rossini's ideals never changed. When he abandoned composition in 1829 the world was changing, but when he took up his pen again he foreshadowed a movement of neo-classicism one of whose earliest proponents was his young admirer Saint-Saëns, and whose effects can be felt still in the music of Stravinsky. Just as his operas had defined the nature of opera for the first half of the 19th century, the *Péchés de vieillesse*, the music that cultivated Paris flocked to hear at the 'Samedi soirs', cast their spell on a younger generation of French composers.

Rossini fell seriously ill in the autumn of 1868. Soon afterwards, on 13 November, he died in his villa in Passy. His funeral was attended by thousands, and memorial services were held throughout France and Italy. He was buried in Père Lachaise cemetery in Paris. Olympe, who had hoped to be buried with him, was persuaded to permit Rossini's remains to be transported to Italy after her death. This occurred in 1887, and at a solemn ceremony on 2 May 1887 Rossini found his final resting-place at Santa Croce in Florence.

In his will, Rossini left a large endowment to found a

conservatory in his birthplace, Pesaro. He also left to Pesaro his remaining autographs, including those of the *Péchés de vieillesse*. The Fondazione Rossini, through its *Bollettino* and its *Quaderni rossiniani*, has been instrumental in the revival of interest in Rossini since the early 1950s, and has issued editions of many of Rossini's unpublished compositions. Work began during the 1970s on a critical edition of Rossini's music and the early volumes appeared at the beginning of the 1980s.

WORKS

Editions: Quaderni rossiniani, a cura della Fondazione Rossini (Pesaro, 1954–) [QR]
Edizione critica delle opere Gioachino Rossini, ed. Fondazione Rossini (Pesaro, 1979–) [vols. in square brackets are in preparation] [EC]

BC — Teatro del Corso, Bologna	NFi — Teatro dei Fiorentini, Naples	RAr — Teatro Argentina, Rome
FC — Teatro Comunale, Ferrara	NFo — Teatro del Fondo, Naples	RV — Teatro Valle, Rome
LC — Teatro de S Carlos, Lisbon	PI — Théâtre-Italien, Paris	VB — Teatro S Benedetto, Venice
MS — Teatro alla Scala, Milan	PO — Opéra, Paris	VF — Teatro La Fenice, Venice
NC — Teatro S Carlo, Naples	RAp — Teatro Apollo, Rome	VM — Teatro S Moisè, Venice

* – autograph   † – authenticated MS copy

Numbers in the right-hand column denote references in the text.

OPERAS
(composed shortly before first performance unless otherwise stated)

Title and genre	Libretto	First performance	MS, publication	
Demetrio e Polibio (dramma serio, 2)	V. Viganò-Mombelli	RV, 18 May 1812, composed before 1809	Milan, 1825–6	5, 8, 11, 14, 19, 23
La cambiale di matrimonio (farsa comica, 1)	G. Rossi, after Camillo Federici's play (1790)	VM, 3 Nov 1810	Milan, 1847	8, 12
L'equivoco stravagante (dramma giocoso, 2)	G. Gasparri	BC, 26 Oct 1811	Milan, 1851	9, 11
L'inganno felice (farsa, 1)	G. Foppa, after G Palomba's lib for Paisiello (1798)	VM, 8 Jan 1812	Leipzig, 1819; full score, Rome, 1827	9, 12, 13
Ciro in Babilonia, ossia La caduta di Baldassare (dramma con cori, 2)	F. Aventi	FC, ?14 March 1812	Milan, 1852	9, 11
La scala di seta (farsa comica, 1)	Foppa, after Planard: L'échelle de soie, lib for P. Gaveaux (1808)	VM, 9 May 1812	Milan, 1852	9, 14
La pietra del paragone (melodramma giocoso, 2)	L. Romanelli	MS, 26 Sept 1812	*I-Mr; Milan, 1846	10, 11, 12, 14, 35
L'occasione fa il ladro (burletta, 1)	L. Prividali	VM, 24 Nov 1812	*F-Pc; Milan, 1853	11, 13
Il Signor Bruschino, ossia Il figlio per azzardo (farsa giocosa, 1)	Foppa, after A. de Chazet and E.-T. Maurice Ourry: Le fils par hazard (1809)	VM, Jan 1813	*Pc; Milan, 1854	11, 13, 14, 24
Tancredi (melodramma eroico, 2)	G. Rossi and L. Lechi, after Voltaire (1760)	VF, 6 Feb 1813	*Fonds Michotte, Brussels, *private collection, Brescia, *I-Ms; Mainz, ?1816–19; [EC, I/x]	8, 14, 15, 16, 17, 18, 19, 20, 21, 22, 23, 41, 42
L'italiana in Algeri (dramma giocoso, 2)	A. Anelli, orig. for L. Mosca (1808)	VB, 22 May 1813	*Mr, Ms; Mainz, 1818–20; EC, I/xi	12, 16, 21, 22, 24, 29, 30, 35

Title and genre	Libretto	First performance	*MS, publication	
Aureliano in Palmira (dramma serio, 2)	G.-F. Romanelli	MS, 26 Dec 1813	*frag. in Fonds Michotte, Brussels; Milan, 1855	22, 23, 24, 26, 34, 42
Il turco in Italia (dramma buffo, 2)	F. Romani, after Caterino Mazzdà's lib for F. Seydelmann (1788)	MS, 14 Aug 1814	*I-Mr; Leipzig, 1821; [EC, I]	22, 23, 24, 29, 35
Sigismondo (dramma, 2)	Foppa	VF, 26 Dec 1814	*Mr; Milan, 1826	25, 34, 42
Elisabetta, regina d'Inghilterra (dramma, 2)	G. Schmidt, after Carlo Federici's play (1814) based on S. Lee: The Recess (novel, 1783–5)	NC, 4 Oct 1815	*Fondazione Rossini, Pesaro; Bonn and Cologne, 1819–20	13, 24, 25, 26, 33, 34, 35, 42
Torvaldo e Dorliska (dramma semiserio, 2)	C. Sterbini, based on J.-B. de Coudry: Vie et amours du chevalier de Faubles (1790) and any of the Lodoïska libs (set by Cherubini, Kreutzer, Mayr etc) derived from it	RV, 26 Dec 1815	*F-Pc; Milan, 1855	25, 26, 34, 35
Almaviva, ossia L'inutile precauzione, later called Il barbiere di Siviglia (commedia, 2)	Sterbini, after the play by Beaumarchais (1775) and G. Petrosellini's lib for Paisiello: Il barbiere di Siviglia (1782)	RAr, 20 Feb 1816	*I-Bc; Paris, 1820–21; full score, Rome, 1827	14, 15, 25, 26, 27, 29, 34, 113, 195
La gazzetta (dramma [opera buffa], 2)	Palomba, after Goldoni: Il matrimonio per concorso (1763)	NFi, 26 Sept 1816	*Nc; Paris, 1855	29, 34, 35
Otello, ossia Il moro di Venezia (dramma, 3)	F. Berio di Salsa, after Shakespeare	NFo, 4 Dec 1816	*Fondazione Rossini; Leipzig, 1819–20	23, 29, 34, 35f, 39, 42
La Cenerentola, ossia La bontà in trionfo (dramma giocoso, 2)	G. Ferretti, after Perrault: Cendrillon (1697), C.-G. Etienne's lib for N. Isouard (1810) and F. Fiorini's lib for S. Pavesi: Agatina, o La virtù premiata (1814)	RV, 25 Jan 1817	*Baf, Fondazione Rossini; Paris, 1822–3; [EC, I]	21, 22, 25, 28, 29, 30f, 35, 37
La gazza ladra (melodramma, 2)	G. Gherardini, after d'Aubigny and Caigniez: La pie voleuse (1815)	MS, 31 May 1817	*Mr; Bonn and Cologne, 1819–20; EC, I/xxi	15, 25, 31f, 35, 37
Armida (dramma, 3)	Schmidt, after Tasso: Gerusalemme liberata	NC, 11 Nov 1817	*Fondazione Rossini; Paris, 1823–4	23, 37, 40, 43
Adelaide di Borgogna (dramma, 2)	Schmidt	RAr, 27 Dec 1817	Milan, 1858	37
Mosè in Egitto (azione tragico-sacra, 3)	A. L. Tottola, after F. Ringhieri: L'Osiride (1760)	NC, 5 March 1818	*F-Pc; Paris, 1822; full score, Rome, 1825	23, 34, 37, 40, 42f, 43, 49, 50
Adina (farsa, 1)	G. Bevilacqua-Aldobrandini	LC, 22 June 1826; composed 1818	*Fondazione Rossini; Milan, 1859	37
Ricciardo e Zoraide (dramma, 2)	Berio di Salsa, after Ricciardetto, epic poem by Niccolò Forteguerri (d 1735), cantos xiv and xv	NC, 3 Dec 1818	*I-Nc; Mainz, 1821–2; full score, Rome, 1828	37, 43

Work	Libretto	Première	Sources; publication	Page refs
Ermione (azione tragica, 2)	Tottola, after Racine: Andromaque	NC, 27 March 1819	*F-Po, excerpt in Fondazione Rossini; Milan, 1858	37, 38, 43, 46f
Eduardo e Cristina (dramma, 2)	Schmidt, rev. Bevilacqua-Aldobrandini and Tottola from original lib for Pavesi: Odoardo e Cristina (1810)	VB, 24 April 1819	Paris, 1826–7	37
La donna del lago (melodramma, 2)	Tottola, after Scot: The Lady of the Lake	NC, 24 Sep 1819	*Fondazione Rossini; Paris, 1822–3; [EC, I]	23, 34, 37, 38, 39, 42, 43, 48, 61
Bianca e Falliero, ossia Il consiglio dei tre (melodramma, 2)	Romani, after A. van Arnhault: Blanche et Montcassin (1798)	MS, 26 Dec 1819	*I-Mr; Milan, 1828	37, 39, 58
Maometto II (dramma, 2)	C. della Valle, after own play Anna Erizo (1820)	NC, 3 Dec 820	*Fondazione Rossini, *excerpt in US-NYp; Vienna, 1823	19, 23, 37, 39, 40, 41f, 43, 46, 49
Matilde (di) Shabran ossia Bellezza, e cuor di ferro (melodramma giocoso, 2)	Ferretti, after F.-B. Hoffmann's lib for Méhul: Euphrosine (1790) and J. M. Boutet de Monvel: Mathilde (play, 1799)	RAp, 24 Feb 1821	*Fonds Michotte, Brussels; Vienna, 1822; full score, Rome, 1832	37, 39
Zelmira (dramma, 2)	Tottola, after Dormont de Belloy (1762)	NC, 16 Feb 1822	*F-Pc, excerpt in Fonds Michotte, Brussels; Vienna, 1822	23, 33, 37, 43, 45, 46, 48
Semiramide (melodramma tragico, 2)	Rossi, after Voltaire (1748)	VF, 3 Feb 1823	*I-Vi; Vienna, 1823; full score. Rome. 1826	13, 17, 21, 23, 33, 36, 37, 38, 39, 40, 41, 43, 46, 48, 166, 199, 236
Il viaggio a Reims, ossia L'albergo del giglio d'oro (dramma giocoso, 1)	L. Balocchi	PI, 19 June 825	orig. material F-Pc, *excerpts in I-Rc	48, 51
Le siège de Corinthe [rev. of Maometto II] (tragédie lyrique, 3)	Balocchi and A. Soumet, after lib for Maometto II	PO, 9 Oct 1826	*excerpts in F-Pc, Po, I-FOc and elsewhere; Paris, 1826; full score, Paris, 1827	39, 49, 62, 111
Moïse et Pharaon, ou Le passage de la Mer Rouge [rev. of Mosè in Egitto] (opéra, 4)	Balocchi and E. de Jouy, after lib for Mosè in Egitto	PO, 26 March 1827	*excerpts in F-Pc, US-NYp, STu, private collection of H. Moldenhauer and elsewhere; full and vocal scores, Paris, 1827	40, 49, 58, 111, 209
Le Comte Ory [partial rev. of Il viaggio a Reims] (opéra comique, 2)	E. Scribe and C. G. Delestre-Poirson, after their own play (1817)	PO, 20 Aug 1823	*excerpts in Fonds Michotte, Brussels, and F-Po; full and vocal scores, Paris, 1828	48, 50, 51, 115
Guillaume Tell (opéra, 4)	Jouy, H.-L.-F. Bis and others, after Schiller (1804)	PO, 3 Aug 1829	*Pc; full and vocal scores, Paris, 1829	8, 14, 39, 50, 51, 53, 54, 56, 64

Note: 11 operas pubd in Early Romantic Opera, vii–xvii (New York, 1976–) [facs.: 5 autographs, 1 contemporary copy, 5 printed scores]

SACRED

Title, performing forces	Composition, first performance	MS, publication	Remarks
[student compositions, incl.]:	1802–9	*Civico Liceo Musicale Giuseppe e Luigi Malerbi; Lugo	
Kyrie a tre voci, 2 T, B, orch			
Gloria, A, T, B, male chorus, orch			
Laudamus, A, orch			
Gratias, T, male chorus, orch			
Domine Deus, 2 B, orch			
Qui tollis, T, orch			? for Messa (Ravenna)
Laudamus, Qui tollis, T, orch			
Quoniam, T, orch			
Crucifixus, S, A, orch			
Dixit, 2 T, B, orch			
De torrente, B, orch			
Gloria Patri			
Sicut erat, 2 T, B, orch			
Magnificat, 2 T, B, orch			
Messa (Bologna), 3 sections	Bologna, Chiesa della Madonna di S Luca, 2 June 1808	I-Bc (3 MSS, incl.2*)	composite mass by students at the Liceo Musicale
Christe eleison, 2 T, B, orch			
Benedicta et venerabilis, grad, 2 T, B, orch			
Qui tollis; Qui sedes, S, hn, orch			
Messa (Ravenna), solo male vv, male chorus, orch	Ravenna, 1808	full score *RAs*, *excerpts in Istituto Musicale Pareggialo G. Verdi, Ravenna, and in Civico Liceo Musicale Giuseppe e Luigi Malerbi; Lugo	only Kyrie, Gloria and Credo
Messa, solo male vv, male chorus, orch	?1802–9	*Mc [microfilm; location of autograph unknown]	only Kyrie, Gloria and Credo
Messa (Rimini), S, A, T, B, orch	Rimini Cathedral, 1809	F-Pc; Paris, 1881	lost, mentioned in Radiciotti (1927–9), iii, 253
Laudamus, ? S, orch			

Title, genre, performing forces	Composition, first performance	MS, publication		
Quoniam, B, orch	Sept 1813	full and vocal scores, Milan, 1851		44
Messa di gloria, solo vv, chorus, orch	Naples, S Ferdinando, 24 March 1820	†*Nc,* *frag in Fonds Michotte, Brussels; Paris, 1860		
Preghiera 'Deh tu pietoso cielo', S, pf	c1820	Naples, 1828		
Tantum ergo, S, T, B, orch	1824	Biblioteca Comunale, Rieti		
Stabat mater, 2 S, T, B, chorus, orch				55, 59, 60, 66, 103, 272
1st version	1832, Madrid, Cappella di S Filippo El Real, Good Friday, 1833	*GB-Lbm,* Paris, 1841	12 nos., 6 by Rossini, others by G. Tadolini	
2nd version	1841, PI, 7 Jan 1842	*Lbm,* full and vocal scores, Paris, 1841-2	10 nos., all by Rossini	
3 choeurs religieux, female vv, pf	Paris, Salle Troupenas, 20 Nov 1844	Paris, 1844		
1 La foi (P. Goubaux)				
2 L'espérance (H. Lucas)				
3 La charité (L. Colet)				
Tantum ergo, 2 T, B, orch	Bologna, Chiesa di S Francesco dei Minori, 28 Nov 1847	*I-Mr:* full and vocal scores, Milan, 1851		
O salutaris hostia, S, A, T, B	29 Nov 1857	pubd in *La maîtrise* (15 Dec 1857)	facs. in Azvedo	
Laus Deo, Mez, pf	1861	pubd in Il Trovatore Arlotto Florence, 1861)		
Petite messe solennelle				63, 66f, 132
1st version, 12 (solo) vv, 2 pf, harmonium	1863, Paris, home of Countess Louise Pillet-Will, 14 March 1864	*Fondazione Rossini Paris, 1869	for 4 solo vv, chorus of 8vv	
2nd version, 12 (solo) vv, orch acc.	1867, PI, 24 Feb 1869	*Fondazione Rossini full score, Paris, 1869		

CANTATAS, INCIDENTAL MUSIC, HYMNS AND CHORUSES

Title, genre, performing forces	Composition, first performance	MS, publication
Il pianto d'Armonia sulla morte di Orfeo (G. Ruggia), cantata, T, chorus, orch	Bologna, Liceo Musicale, 11 Aug 1808	*I-Bc

Title, genre, performing forces	Composition, first performance	MS, publication
La morte di Didone, cantata, S, chorus, orch	1811, VB, 2 May 1818	F-Pn; excerpts, Milan, 1820–21
Dalle quete e pallid'ombre, cantata (P. Venanzio), S, B, pf	Venice, 1812	*I-Ms
Egle ed Irene, cantata, S, A, pf	Milan, 1814	*Vnm; Milan, 1820
Inno dell'Indipendenza ('Sorgi, Italia, venuta è già l'ora') (G. Giusti), hymn	Bologna, Teatro Contavalli, 15 April 1815	lost
L'Aurora, cantata, A, T, B, pf	Rome, Nov 1815	USSR-Mcm; ed. in SovM (1955), no.8, p.60
Le nozze di Teti, e di Peleo (A. M. Ricci), cantata, 3 S, 2 T, chorus, orch	NF, 24 April 1816	*I-Nc
Edipo a Colono (Giusti, after Sophocles), incidental music, B, chorus, orch [orchestration completed anon.]	before 1817	*US-NYpm; 1 aria, Paris, c1850
Giunone, cantata, S, chorus, orch, for 'La venuta di S[ua] M[aestà]', Ferdinando di Borbone	?1817–21	*NYp
Omaggio umiliato (A. Niccolini), cantata, S, chorus, orch	NC, 20 Feb 1819	*I-Nc; version for pf solo, Paris, 1864
Cantata . . . 9 maggio 1819 (G. Genoino), for Francis I's visit, S, 2 T, chorus, orch	NC, 9 May 1819	microfilm in US-NYp
La riconoscenza (Genoino), cantata, S, A, T, B, chorus, orch	NC, 27 Dec 1821	*Fondazione Rossini; Milan, 1826
La Santa Alleanza (G. Rossi), cantata, 2 B, chorus, orch	Verona, Arena, 24 Nov 1822	lost
Il vero omaggio (Rossi), cantata, Sopranista, S, 2 T, B, chorus, orch	Verona, Teatro Filarmonico, 3 Dec 1822	lost, largely based on La riconoscenza 23
Omaggio pastorale, cantata, 3 female vv, orch	Treviso, ?1 April 1823 (MS dated 17 May 1823)	*I-TVco
Il pianto delle muse in morte di Lord Byron, canzone, T, chorus, orch	London, Almack's Assembly Rooms, 9 June 1824	*GB-Lbm; London, 1824
De l'Italie et de la France, hymn, ?for Charles X's coronation, S, B, chorus, orch	PI, ?19 June 1825	*Fondazione Rossini: full score, QR ix, 62
Cantata per il battesimo del figlio del banchiere Aguado, 6 solo vv, pf	Paris, home of A.-M. Aguado, 16 July 1827	* Lbm; Paris, 1827, as 3ème quartetto da camera
L'armonica cetra del nume, in honour of Marchese Sampieri, solo vv, chorus, pf	Bologna, home of Sampieri, 2 April 1830	mentioned in Radiciotti (1927–9), iii
Giovànna d'Arco, cantata, S, pf, rev. with str for recit	Paris, 1832, rev. 1852	*Fondazione Rossini; QR xi, 1
Santo Genio dell'Italia terra (G. Marchetti), for tercentenary of Tasso's birth, chorus, orch	Turin, Palazzo Carignano, 11 March 1844	* Fonds Michotte, Brussels 62

Title, genre, performing forces		MS, publication	Remarks	
Su fratelli, letizia si canti (Canonico Golfieri), for Pope Pius IX, chorus, orch		Bologna, Piazza Maggiore, 23 July 1846	I-Bc; Milan, 1847	62
Cantata in onore del Sommo Pontefice Pio Nono (Marchetti), 4 solo vv, chorus, orch		Rome, Senate (Campidoglio), 1 Jan 1847	*frags. in Fondazione Rossini	62
Segna Iddio ne'suoi confini (F. Martinelli), chorus of the Guardia Civica di Bologna, acc. arr. D. Liverani for band		Bologna, Piazza Maggiore, 21 June 1848	*Bc	
È foriera la Pace ai mortale (G. Arcangeli, after Bacchilde), hymn, Bar, male vv, pf		26 June 1850	in private collection of Baroness F. De Renzis Sorrino (Florence); QR xii, 1	
Dieu tout puissant (E. Pacini), hymn, Bar, chorus, orch, military band		Paris, Palais de l'Industrie, 1 July 1867	*Fondazione Rossini; London, 1873 as National Hymn; QR xii, 21	

MISCELLANEOUS VOCAL

Title, genre, performing forces	Composition	MS, publication	Remarks
Se il vuol la molinara, S, pf	?1801	*US-NYpm; Milan, 1821	
Dolce aurette che spirate, T, orch	1810	I-Bc	
La mia pace io già perdei, T, orch	1812	Bc	
Qual voce, quai note, S, pf	1813	MS in private collection (Brescia)	
Alla voce della gloria, B, orch	1813	*Ms; Milan, 1851	
Amore mi assisti, S, T, pf	c1814	*US-NYpm	
3 compositions for G. Nicolini: Quinto Fabio	1817		
1 Coro e cavatina 'Cara Patria, invitta Roma', S, chorus, orch		F-Pc; Rome, 1822	first pubd as 'Alme fide a questi accenti
2 Aria 'Guidò Marte i nostri passi', T, chorus, orch		I-PAc	
3 Duet 'Ah! per pietà t'arresta', 2 S, orch		MS in collection of Opera Rara (London)	possibly not by Rossini
Il trovatore ('Chi m'ascolta il canto usato'), T, pf	1818	*US-Wc; Naples, 1818	
Il Carnevale di Venezia ('Siamo ciechi, siamo nati') (Rossini, Paganini, M. d'Azeglio, Lipparini), 2 T, 2 B, pf	carn. 1821	Milan, 1847	*facs. in G. Monaldi: 'Una canzone inedita di Rossini', Noi e il mondo (1925), Aug
Beltà crudele ('Amori scendete') (N. di Santo-Magno), S, pf	1821	*F-Pc and I-FOc; Naples, 1847	3rd *facs in ... Subirà: La música en la Casa de Alba (Madrid, 1927)
La pastorella ('Odia la pastorella') (Santo-Magno), S, pf	c1821	Naples, 1847	copy of 1st ecn. not located; 2nd edn. Milan c1850
Canzonetta spagnuola 'En medio a mis colores' ('Piangea un dì pensando'), S, pf	1821	F-Pc; Naples, 1825	

Title, genre, performing forces	Composition	MS, publication	Remarks
Infelice ch'io son, S, pf	1821	*A-Wgm	2nd *facs. ed. L. Schmidt, *Emil Naumanns illustrierte Musikgeschichte* (Dresden, 9/1928)
			also known as Addio di Rossini
Addio ai viennesi ('Da voi parto, amate sponde'), T, pf	1822	I-Nc; Vienna, 1822	
Dall'Oriente l'astro del giorno, S, 2 T, B, pf	1824	*GB-Lbm; London and Paris, 1824	London 1st edn. not located
Pidiamo, cantiamo, che tutto sen va, S, 2 T, B, pf	1824	I-Nc; London, 1824	
In giorno si bello, 2 S, T, pf	1824	GB-Lbm; London, 1824	
3 quartetti da camera			
1 (unidentified)		Paris, 1827	copy of 1st edn. not located
2 In giorno si bello, 2 S, T, B, pf	1827	Paris, 1827	
3 Oh giorno sereno, S, A, T, B, pf	1827	Paris, 1827	
Les adieux à Rome ('Rome pour la dernière fois') (C. Delavigne), T, pf/harp	1827	pubd in C. Delavigne: 7 *messéniennes nouvelles* (Paris, 1827)	
Orage et beau temps ('Sur les flots inconstans') (A. Betourne), T, B, pf	c1830	*in private collection of R. Macnutt (Tunbridge Wells, Kent); Leipzig, n.d.	
La passeggiata ('Or che di fiori adorno'), S, pf	1831	pubd in *Cartas españolas* (Madrid, 11 April 1831)	also known as Anacreontica
La dichiarazione ('Ch'io mai vi possa lasciar d'amare') (Metastasio), S, pf	c1834	Milan, 1834-5	
Les soirées musicales	c1830-35	Paris, 1835; * of no.2 only, US-Wc	55, 56, 129
1 La promessa ('Ch'io mai vi possa lasciar amare') (Metastasio), S, pf			
2 Il rimprovero ('Mi lagnerò tacendo') (Metastasio), S, pf			
3 La partenza ('Ecco quel fiero istante') (Metastasio), S, pf			
4 L'orgia ('Amiamo, cantiamo') (C. Pepoli), S, pf			
5 L'invito ('Vieni o Ruggiero') (Pepoli), S, pf			
6 La pastorella dell'Alpi ('Son bella pastorella') (Pepoli), S, pf			
7 La gita in gondola ('Voli l'agile barchetta') (Pepoli), S, pf			

Work	Date	Sources	Notes
8 La danza ('Già la luna è in mezzo al mare') (Pepoli), T, pf			
9 La regata veneziana ('Voga o Tonio benedetto') (Pepoli), 2 S, pf			
10 La pesca ('Già la notte s'avvicina') (Metastasio), 2 S, pf			
11 La serenata ('Mira, la bianca luna') (Pepoli), S, T, pf			
12 Li marinari ('Marinaro in guardia stà') (Pepoli), T, B, pf			
2 nocturnes (Crével de Charlemagne), S, T, pf 1 Adieu à l'Italie ('Je te quitte, belle Italie') 2 Le départ ('Il faut partir')	c1836	Paris, 1836	
Nizza ('Nizza, je puis sans peine', 'Mi lagnerò tacendo') (E. Deschamps and Metastasio), S, pf	c1836	Paris, c1837	
L'âme délaissée ('Mon bien aimé') (Delavigne), S, pf	c1844	Paris, 1844	*Facs. in La France musicale (Paris, 1844); also pubd as L'âme du Purgatoire
Recitativo ritmato ('Farò come colui che piange e dice') (Dante), S, pf	1848	*Fondazione Rossini (2 copies); Florence, 1800	originally composed as Mi lagnerò tacendo
La separazione ('Muto rimase il labbro') (F. Uccelii), S, pf	c1858	Paris, c1858	
2 nouvelles compositions (Pacini), S, pf 1 A Grenade ('La nuit règne à Grenade') 2 La veuve andalouse ('Toi pour jamais')	c1860	*Fondazione Rossini; Paris, c1863; QR v, 90 (no.1)	
Mi lagnerò tacendo (Metastasio), numerous versions composed as albumleaves, of which the following are representative:			
L'amante discreto, S, pf	1835	*F-Pc (2 copies), Pn, I-FOc; Milan, 1839	
Mi lagnerò tacendo, S, pf	before 1847	*F-Pn, I-Baf, private collection of R. O. Lehman (New York)	
Mi lagnerò tacendo, S, pf	?1833–9	*F-Pc (3 copies); pubd in Gazette musicale (Paris, 1840)	also pubd Paris, c1840, as Beppa la napolitaine
Mi lagnerò tacendo, S, pf	1850	*GB-Lbm, I-Sc; ed., London, 1959	*Facs. in E. Winternitz: Musical Autographs from Monteverdi to Hindemith (Princeton, 1955), plate 103
Mi lagnerò tacendo, S, pf		*in private collection of M. and R. Floersheim (Switzerland)	

Title, key, performing forces	Composition	MS, publication	Remarks
6 sonate a quattro, G, A, C, B♭, D, 2 vn, vc, db	c1804	*US-Wc; Milan 1825–6, for str qt (nos.1, 2, 4–6), QR i, 1 (no.3)	source for 1st edn. not known
Sinfonia 'al conventello', D, orch	c1806	Istituto Musicale Pareggiato G. Verdi. Ravenna	
5 duets, E♭, E♭, B♭, E♭, E♭, 2 hn	c1806	ed., Hamburg, 1861	
Sinfonia, D, orch	1808	I-Bc; QR viii, 1	rev. as ov. to La cambiale di matrimonio
Sinfonia, E♭, orch	1809	Bc	
Grand'overtura obbligata a contrabasso, D, orch	c1809	Istituto Musicale Pareggiato G. Verdi, Ravenna	
Variazioni a più istrumenti obbligati, F, 2 vn, va, vc, cl, orch	1809	Bc; QR ix, 1	
Variazioni di clarinetto, C, cl, orch	1809	Bc; parts, Leipzig, 1824; QR vi, 57	
Andante e Tema con variazioni, F, fl, cl, hn, bn	1812	*F-Pc; Paris and Mainz, 1827–8; QR vi, 18	
Andante con variazioni, F, harp, va	c1820	Naples, 1820–24; QR vi, 1 lost	mentioned in Radiciotti (1927–9)
Passo doppio, military band	1822	*Pc, I-FOc	
Waltz, E♭, pf	?1823		3rd *facs. in Revue et gazette musicale (Paris, 1841)
Serenata, E♭, 2 vn, va, vc, fl, ob, eng hn	1823	US-NYp; parts, Leipzig, 1829; QR vi, 31	
Duetto, D, vc, db	1824	ed., London, 1969	*sold at Sotheby's, London (1968)
Rendez-vous de chasse, D, 4 corni da caccia, orch	1828	*F-Pc; Paris, 1828; QR ix, 45	
Fantasie, E♭, cl, pf	1829	Paris, 1829	
Mariage du Duc d'Orléans, 3 military marches, G, E♭, E♭, military band	1837	parts, Leipzig, 1837	
Scherzo, a, pf	1843, rev. 1850	*Pc, rev. version in I-MOc; ed., Milan, n.d.	
Tema originale di Rossini variato per violino da Giovacchino Giovacchini, A, vn, pf	1845	*Fonds Michotte, Brussels; I-Fc (theme only)	

March ('Pas-redoublé'), C, military band — 1852 — Milan, 1853

Thème de Rossini suivi de deux variations et coda par Moscheles Père, E, hn, pf — 1860 — Leipzig, n.d.

La corona d'Italia, E♭, military band — 1868 — *frag., Fondazione Rossini; Rome, 1878

PÉCHÉS DE VIEILLESSE (1857–68)   63, 69, 70

Complete set of autograph MSS in Fondazione Rossini; for a somewhat different ordering, see autograph catalogue of these pieces in Fonds Michotte, Brussels

Vol.i: Album italiano
1 Quartettino 'I gondolieri', S, A, T, B, pf; QR vii, 1
2 Arietta 'La lontananza' (G. Torre), T, pf (London, c1880); QR iv, 12
3 Bolero 'Tirana alla spagnola' (Rossinizzata) (Metastasio), S, pf; QR iv, 30; music identical with vol.xi, no.3
4 Elegia 'L'ultimo ricordo' (G. Redaelli), Bar, pf; QR iv, 19
5 Arietta 'La fioraja fiorentina', S, pf; QR iv, 5
6 Duetto 'Le gittane' (Torre), S, A, pf (London, c1880)
7 Ave Maria su due sole note, A, pf; QR iv, 51
8–10 La regata veneziana, 3 canzonettas, Mez, pf (Milan, 1878)
8 Anzoleta avanti la regata (Barcarolle 'Plus de vent perfide')
9 Anzoleta co passa la regata
10 Anzoleta dopo la regata
11 Arietta (Sonetto) 'Il fanciullo smarrito' (A. Castellani), T, pf, pubd in *Strenna del giornale la lega della democrazia* (Rome, 1881)
12 Quartettino 'La passeggiata', S, A, T, B, pf; QR vii, 16

Vol.ii: Album français (E. Pacini)
1 Ottettino 'Toast pour le nouvel an', 2 S, 2 A, 2 T, 2 B; QR vii, 50
2 Roméo, T, pf
3 Ariette 'Pompadour, la grande coquette', S, pf
4 Complainte à deux voix ('Un sou'), T, Bar, pf; QR v, 58
5 Chanson de Zora ('La petite bohémienne') (E. Deschamps), Mez, pf; QR v, 49   66
6 La nuit de Noël, B solo, 2 S, 2 A, 2 T, 2 Bar, pf, harmonium; QR vii, 62
7 Ariette 'Le dodo des enfants', Mez, pf; QR v, 9
8 Chansonette de cabaret ('Le lazzarone'), Bar, pf
9 Elégie ('Adieux à la vie'), sur une seule note, Mez, pf, †Fondazione Rossini; QR v, 75
10 Nocturne ('Soupirs et sourires'), S, T, pf, also with It. text as Il cipresso, e la rosa (G. Torre)   66
11 Ballade élégie ('L'orpheline du Tyrol'), Mez, pf; QR v, 31   66
12 Choeur de chasseurs démocrates, male vv, tam-tam, 2 tamburi; QR vii, 35

Vol.iii: Morceaux réservés
1 Quelques mesures de chant funèbre: à mon pauvre ami Meyerbeer (Pacini), male vv, tamburo; QR vii, 84   56
2 Arietta 'L Esule' (Torre), T, pf; QR iv, 25
3 Tirana pour deux voix ('Les amants de Séville') (Pacini), A, T, pf; QR v, 37
4 Ave Maria, chorus, org (London, 1873); QR xi, 43
5 L'amour à Pékin: petite mélodie sur la gamme chinoise (Pacini), A, pf; QR v, 81   65
6 Le chant des titans (Pacini), 4 B, pf, harmonium, arr. 4 B. orch. vocal score (London, 1873); QR viii, 66 (orch version) [originally written to text Mi lagnerò tacendo]
7 Preghiera, 4 T, 2 Ear, 2 B; QR vii, 89 [also exists with Fr. text]
8 Elégie ('Au chevet d'un mourant') (Pacini), S, pf; QR v, 17
9 Romance 'Le sylvain' (Pacini), T, pf; QR v, 1
10 Cantemus imitazione ad otto voci reali, 2 S, 2 A, 2 T, 2 B (London, 1873); QR xi, 53
11 Ariette à l'Ancienne (J.-J. Rousseau), Mez, pf (London, c1880); QR v, 69
12 Tyrolienne sentimentale ('Le départ des promis') (Pacini), 2 S, 2 A, pf

OTHER LATE WORKS

(MS in Fondazione Rossini unless otherwise stated)

Canone scherzosa a qua tro soprani democratici, 4 S, pf
Canone antisavant (Ros-ini), 3 vv
Canzonetta 'La vénitienne', C, pf; QR xviii, 33
Petite promenade de Passy à Courbevoie, C, pf
Une réjouissance, a, pf; QR xviii, 46
Encore un peu de blague, C, pf; QR xviii, 52
Tourniquet sur la gamme chromatique, ascendante et déscendante, C, pf; QR xviii, 55
Ritournelle gothique, C, pf; QR xviii, 63
Un rien (pour album): Ave Maria, S, pf; QR xi, 60
Pour album: Sogna il guerrier (Metastasio), Bar, pf
Brindisi 'Del fanciullo il primo canto', B, chorus
Solo per violoncello, a; QR vi, 5 [with added pf acc.]
Questo palpito soave, S, pf
L'ultimo pensiero ('Patria, consorti, figli') (L. F. Cerutti), Bar, (?) pf, Fonds Michotte, Brussels
Thème, E♭, pf, I-Trt, partial facs. in LaMusicaE

MISCELLANEOUS

Teodora e Riciardino, introduction to opera, sketched c1815, Fondazione Rossini
Gorgheggi e solfeggi, studies, 1v, pf, c1827 (Paris, 1827)
15 petits exercices, 1v, 1358 (Paris, c1880)
Petit gargouillement, exercice, 1v, 1867, F-Po
Giovinetta pellegrina, variations on a romance by N. Vaccai, ed. in La cronaca musicale (Pesaro, 1912)
Vocal variants, cadenzas, etc for Rossini's operas, autographs in Fonds Michotte, Brussels, F-Po, I-Mc, US-Cu, NYpm, and elsewhere

ADAPTATIONS INVOLVING ROSSINI'S PARTICIPATION

Ivanhoé (opera, E. Deschamps and G.-G. de Wailly), Paris, Théâtre de l'Odéon, 15 Sept 1823, MS excerpts in GB-Lbm, full score [Paris, 1826] [adapted by A. Pacini, from several of Rossini's operas]
Robert Bruce (opera, A. Reyer and G. Vaëz), PO, 30 Dec 1846, full score (Paris, 1847) [adapted by A.-L. Niedermeyer from several of Rossini's operas, especially La donna del lago]

WORKS NOT TRACED OR OF UNCERTAIN AUTHENTICITY

(*sacred*)

Miserere, solo vv, chorus, orch; full score (Leipzig, 1831) as Trost und Erhebung

Dixit Domino, solo vv, chorus, orch, *I-Mc*

(*other vocal*)

Aria di Filippuccio ('Il secreto se si perde'), buffo v, orch, ed. (Trieste, 1892)

La calabrese ('Colla lanterna magica'), S, A, pf, *Vc*

Cara, voi siete quella, ? T, orch, ed. (Florence, 1902);

Quando giunse qua Belfior, S, orch, ?1824–35, *FOc*, ed. A. Garbelotto, 6 arie inedite (Padua, 1968)

Il rimprovero ('Se fra le trecce d'Ebano'), S, pf, ed. (Florence, 1944)

Vieni sull'onde, S, T, pf, Fonds Michotte, Brussels

L'absence, ? pubd Paris, n.d., mentioned in Radiciotti (1927–9), iii, 250; not traced

Il baco da seta, ?1862, ? pubd Paris, 1862, mentioned in Montazio, 125; not traced

(*instrumental*)

12 valzer per due flauti, on themes from Rossini's operas (Milan, c1827)

Sinfonia di Odense, A, orch, MS parts in Odense; QR viii, 17

SPURIOUS WORKS

Duetto buffo di due gatti, 2vv, pf, Fondazione Rossini; QR iv, 1

Sinfonia di Odense, A, orch, MS parts in Odense; QR viii, 17

Bibliography

BIBLIOGRAPHY
SOURCE MATERIALS

G. Mazzatinti: *Lettere inedite di Gioacchino Rossini* (Imola, 1890, rev. 2/1892 as *Lettere inedite e rare di G. Rossini*, rev. 3/1902 as *Lettere di G. Rossini*, with F. and G. Manis)

A. Allmayer: *Undici lettere di Gioachino Rossini pubblicate per la prima volta* (Siena, 1892)

G. Biagi: 'Undici lettere inedite di G. Rossini', *Onoranze fiorentine a Gioachino Rossini* (Florence, 1902), 101

R. De Rensis: 'Rossini intimo: lettere all'amico Santocanale', *Musica d'oggi*, xiii (1931), 343

F. Schlitzer: *Rossiniana: contributo all'epistolario di G. Rossini*, Quaderni dell'Accademia chigiana, xxxv (Siena, 1956)

——: *Un piccolo carteggio inedito di Rossini con un impresario italiano a Vienna* (Florence, 1959)

F. Walker: 'Rossiniana in the Piancastelli Collection', *MMR*, xc (1960), 138, 203

V. Viviani, ed.: *I libretti di Rossini* (Milan, 1965)

P. Gossett: 'Le fonti autografe delle opere teatrali di Rossini', *NRMI*, ii (1968), 936

——, ed.: *La Cenerentola: riproduzione dell'autografo esistente presso l'Accademia filarmonica di Bologna* (Bologna, 1969)

——: *The Operas of Rossini: Problems of Textual Criticism in Nineteenth-century Opera* (diss., Princeton U., 1970)

B. Cagli, P. Gossett and A. Zedda: 'Criteri per l'edizione critica delle opere di Gioachino Rossini', *Bollettino del Centro rossiniano di studi* (1974), no.1

F. Lippmann: 'Autographe Briefe Rossinis und Donizettis in der Bibliothek Massimo, Rom', *AnMc*, no. 19 (1979), 330

J. Kallberg: 'Marketing Rossini: Sei lettere di Troupenas ad Artaria', *Bolletino del Centro rossiniano di studi* (1980), 41

MEMOIRS BY CONTEMPORARIES

Stendhal: *Rome, Naples, et Florence en 1817* (Paris, 1817; Eng. trans., 1959)

G. Righetti-Giorgi: *Cenni di una donna già cantante sopra il maestro Rossini* (Bologna, 1823; repr. in Rognoni, 2/1968)

G. Carpani: *Le rossiniane ossia Lettere musico-teatrali* (Padua, 1824)

J. Ebers: *Seven Years of the King's Theatre* (London, 1828)

L. Escudier: *Mes souvenirs* (Paris, 1863–8)

G. Pacini: *Le mie memorie artistiche* (Florence, 1865, rev. 2/1872)

F. Hiller: 'Plaudereien mit Rossini (1856)', *Aus dem Tonleben unserer Zeit*, ii (Leipzig, 1868, 2/1871), 1–84

R. Wagner: 'Eine Erinnerung an Rossini', *Allgemeine Zeitung*

(Augsburg, 17 Dec 1868; repr. in *Gesammelte Schriften und Dichtungen*, viii, Leipzig, 1883, 2/1888; Eng. trans., 1895/*R*1966)

F. Mordani: *Della vita privata di G. Rossini: memorie inedite* (Imola, 1871)

G. De Sanctis: *Gioacchino Rossini: appunti di viaggio* (Rome, 1878)

G. L. Duprez: *Souvenirs d'un chanteur* (Paris, 1880)

E. Branca: *Felice Romani ed i più riputati maestri di musica del suo tempo* (Turin, Florence and Rome, 1882)

G. Dupré: *Ricordi autobiografici* (Florence, 1895, 2/1896 as *Pensieri sull'arte e ricordi autobiografici*)

A. Cametti: *Un poeta melodrammatico romano: appunti e notizie in gran parte inedite sopra Jacopo Ferretti e i musicisti del suo tempo* (Milan, 1898)

E. Michotte: *Souvenirs personnels: la visite de R. Wagner à Rossini (Paris, 1860)* (Paris, 1906, repr. in Rognoni, 2/1968; Eng. trans., 1968, ed. H. Weinstock)

——: *Souvenirs: une soirée chez Rossini à Beau-Séjour (Passy) 1858* (Brussels, c1910; Eng. trans., 1968, ed. H. Weinstock)

C. Saint-Saëns: *Ecole buissonnière* (Paris, 1913; Eng. trans., 1919, as *Musical Memories*)

GENERAL LITERATURE

Guerre aux Rossinistes (Paris, 1821)

Stendhal: *Vie de Rossini* (Paris, 1824, rev. 2/1922 by H. Prunières; Eng. trans., 1956, 2/1970 with introduction by R. N. Coe)

A. Wendt: *Rossinis Leben und Treiben* (Leipzig, 1824)

H. Berton: *De la musique mécanique et de la musique philosophique* (Paris, 1826)

J.-L. d'Ortigue: *De la guerre des dilettanti* (Paris, 1829)

P. Brighenti: *Della musica rossiniana e del suo autore* (Bologna, 1830, 2/1833)

A. Zanolini: *Biografia di Gioachino Rossini* (Paris, 1836, rev. Bologna, 1875)

M. and L. Escudier: *Rossini: sa vie et ses oeuvres* (Paris, 1854)

Castil-Blaze: *L'Opéra-Italien de 1548 à 1856* (Paris, 1856)

E. Montazio: *Giovacchino Rossini* (Turin, 1862)

A. Aulagnier: *G. Rossini: sa vie et ses oeuvres* (Paris, 1864)

A. Azevedo: *G. Rossini: sa vie et ses oeuvres* (Paris, 1864)

H. S. Edwards: *The Life of Rossini* (London, 1869, rev. 2/1881 as *Rossini and his School*)

A. Pougin: *Rossini: notes, impressions, souvenirs, commentaires* (Paris, 1871)

L. S. Silvestri: *Della vita e delle opere di Gioachino Rossini: notizie biografico-artistico-aneddotico-critiche* (Milan, 1874)

Bibliography

E. vander Straeten: *La mélodie populaire dans l'opéra 'Guillaume Tell'
de Rossini* (Paris, 1879)

Bollettino del primo centenario rossiniano (Pesaro, 1892)

L. Dauriac: *La psychologie dans l'opéra français: Auber, Rossini,
Meyerbeer* (Paris, 1897)

——: *Rossini: biographie critique* (Paris, 1906)

A. Sandberger: 'Rossiniana', *ZIMG*, ix (1907–8), 336; repr. in
Ausgewählte Aufsätze (Munich, 1921)

E. Istel: 'Rossiniana', *Die Musik*, x/19 (1910–11), 1

A. Soubies: *Le Théâtre-Italien de 1801 à 1913* (Paris, 1913)

E. Celani: 'Musica e musicisti in Roma (1750–1850)', *RMI*, xxii
(1915), 257–300

G. Fara: *Genio e ingegno musicale: Gioachino Rossini* (Turin, 1915)

A. Cametti: 'La musica teatrale a Roma cento anni fa', *Regia Accademia
di Santa Cecilia: annuario* (Rome, 1915–30)

F. Vatielli: *Rossini a Bologna* (Bologna, 1918)

A. Casella: 'Some Reasons why a Futurist may Admire Rossini', *The
Chesterian*, ii (London, 1920), 321

H. de Curzon: *Rossini* (Paris, 1920)

V. Cavazzocca Mazzanti: 'Rossini a Verona durante il Congresso del
1822', *Atti e memorie dell'Accademia di agricoltura, scienze e lettere
di Verona*, 4th ser., xxiv (Verona, 1922), 53–112

G. Radiciotti: *Gioacchino Rossini: vita documentata, opere ed influenza
su l'arte* (Tivoli, 1927–9)

——: *Aneddoti rossiniani autentici* (Rome, 1929)

J.-G. Prod'homme: 'Rossini and his Works in France', *MQ*, xvii (1931),
119

G. H. J. Derwent: *Rossini and some Forgotten Nightingales* (London,
1934)

F. Toye: *Rossini: a Study in Tragi-comedy* (London, 1934,
2/1954/R1963)

H. Faller: *Die Gesangskoloratur in Rossinis Opern und ihre Ausführung*
(Berlin, 1935)

Rossiniana (Bologna, 1942)

A. Capri: 'Rossini e l'estetica teatrale della vocalità', *RMI*, xlvi (1942),
353

A. Della Corte: 'Fra gorgheggi e melodie di Rossini', *Musica*, i (1942),
23

U. Rolandi: 'Librettistica rossiniana', *Musica*, i (1942), 40

L. Ronga: 'Vicende del gusto rossiniano nell'ottocento', *Musica*, i
(1942), 6

——: 'Svolgimento del gusto rossiniano al novecento', *Musica*, ii (1943),
184

G. Roncaglia: *Rossini l'olimpico* (Milan, 1946, 2/1953)

F. Barberio: 'La regina d'Etruria e Rossini', *RMI*, lv (1953), 64

Rassegna musicale, xxiv/3 (1954), 209–303 [special issue]
Bollettino del Centro rossiniano di studi (1955–60, 1967–)
L. Rognoni: *Rossini* (Parma, 1956, 2/1968, rev. 3/1977)
F. Schlitzer: *Rossini e Siena*, Quaderni dell'Accademia chigiana, xxxix (Siena, 1958)
A. Toni and T. Serafin: *Stile, tradizioni e convenzioni del melodramma italiano del settecento e dell'ottocento* (Milan, 1958)
R. Bacchelli: *Rossini e Esperienze rossiniane* (Milan, 1959)
E. N. McKay: 'Rossinis Einfluss auf Schubert', *ÖMz*, xviii (1963), 17
D. W. Schwartz: 'Rossini: a Psychoanalytic Approach to the Great Renunciation', *Journal of the American Psychoanalytic Society*, xiii (1965), 551
R. Celletti: 'Vocalità rossiniana', *L'opera*, ii (Milan, 1966), 3
F. d'Amico: *L'opera teatrale di Gioacchino Rossini* (Rome, 1968)
G. Barblan: 'Rossini e il suo tempo', *Chigiana*, xxv (1968), 143–79
F. Bisogni: 'Rossini e Schubert', *NRMI*, ii (1968), 920
A. Bonaccorsi, ed.: *Gioacchino Rossini* (Florence, 1968)
R. Celletti: 'Origini e sviluppi della coloratura rossiniana', *NRMI*, ii (1968), 872–919
——: 'Il vocalismo italiano da Rossini a Donizetti: Parte I: Rossini', *AnMc*, no.5 (1968), 267
M. Fabbri: 'Ignoti momenti rossiniani', *Chigiana*, xxv (1968), 265
P. Gossett: 'Rossini and Authenticity', *MT*, cix (1968), 1006
F. Lippmann: 'Per un'esegesi dello stile rossiniano', *NRMI*, ii (1968), 813–56
H. Weinstock: *Rossini: a Biography* (New York, 1968)
F. Lippmann: 'Rossinis Gedanken über die Musik', *Mf*, xxii (1969), 285
P. Gossett: 'Gioachino Rossini and the Conventions of Composition', *AcM*, xlii (1970), 48
J. Loschelder: 'L'infanzia di Gioacchino Rossini', *Bollettino del Centro rossiniano di studi* (1972), no.1, p.45; no.2, p.33
——: 'Rossinis Bild und Zerbild in der Allgemeinen musikalischen Zeitung Leipzig', *Bollettino del Centro rossiniano di studi* (1973), no.1, p.23; no.2, p.23; (1977), no.3, p.17
A. Caswell: 'Vocal Embellishment in Rossini's Paris Operas: French Style or Italian?', *Bollettino del Centro rossiniano di studi* (1975), no.1, p.5; no.2, p.5
Chigiana, xxxiv (1977) [special issue]
P. Fabbri: 'Presenze rossiniane negli archivi ravennati: Due inediti, un autografo ed altro', *Bollettino del Centro rossiniano di studi* (1978), 5
F. Lippmann, ed: *Die stilistische Entwicklung der italienischen Musik zwischen 1770 und 1830 und ihre Beziehungen zum Norden: Rome*

Bibliography

1978 [also pubd as *AnMc*, no.21 (1982)]

P. Fabbri: 'Alla scuola dei Malerbi: altri autografi rossiniani', *Bollettino del Centro rossiniano di studi* (1980), 5

F. Lippmann: 'Rossini – und kein Ende', *Studi musicali*, x (1981), 279

STUDIES OF INDIVIDUAL WORKS

H. Berlioz: 'Guillaume Tell', *Gazette musicale*, i (1834), Oct–Nov, 326, 336, 341, 349; Eng. trans. in *Source Readings in Music History*, ed. O. Strunk (New York, 1950)

J. L. d'Ortigue: *Le 'Stabat' de Rossini* (Paris, 1841)

A. Aulagnier: *Quelques observations sur la publication du 'Stabat Mater' de Rossini* (Paris, 1842)

J. A. Delaire: *Observations d'un amateur non dilettante au sujet du 'Stabat' de M. Rossini* (Paris, 1842)

A. W. Ambros: 'Die "Messe solennelle" von Rossini', *Bunte Blätter*, i (Leipzig, 1872), 81

G. C. Hirt [pseud. of L. Torchi]: 'Di alcuni autografi di G. Rossini', *RMI*, ii (1895), 23 [on *Péchés de vieillesse*]

G. Romagnoli: 'Gioacchino Rossini, Giulio Perticari e la "Gazza ladra" ', *Vita italiana*, iii (1897), 106

A. Cametti: 'Il "Guglielmo Tell" e le sue prime rappresentazioni in Italia', *RMI*, vi (1899), 580

G. M. Gatti: *Le 'Barbier de Séville' de Rossini* (Paris, 1925)

H. Prunières: 'L' "Edipo a Colono" de Rossini', *RdM*, xiv (1933), 32

P. Ingerslev-Jensen: 'An Unknown Rossini Overture: Report of a Discovery in Odense', *MR*, xi (1950), 19 [on so-called *Sinfonia di Odense*]

P. R. Kirby: 'Rossini's Overture to "William Tell" ', *ML*, xxxiii (1952), 132

A. Melica: 'Due operine di Rossini', *Musicisti della scuola emiliana*, Chigiana, xiii (1956), 59 [on *L'inganno felice* and *L'occasione fa il ladro*]

G. Confalonieri: 'Avventure di una partitura rossiniana: l' "Adina ovvero Il califfo di Bagdad" ', *Le celebrazioni del 1963 e alcune nuove indagine sulla musica italiana del XVIII e XIX secolo*, Chigiana, xx (1963), 206

J. W. Klein: 'Verdi's "Otello" and Rossini's', *ML*, xlv (1964), 130

A. Porter: 'A Lost Opera by Rossini', *ML*, xlv (1964), 39 [on *Ugo, re d'Italia*]

A. Damerini: 'La prima ripresa moderna di un'opera giovanile di Rossini: "L'equivoco stravagante" (1811)', *Chigiana*, xxii (1965), 229

A. Zedda: 'Appunti per una lettura fiologica del "Barbiere" ', *L'opera*, ii (Milan, 1966), 13

89

P. Gossett: 'Rossini in Naples: some Major Works Recovered', *MQ*, liv (1968), 316 [on *Le nozze di Teti, e di Peleo, Messa di gloria*, etc]

M. Tartak: 'The Two "Barbieri" ', *ML*, l (1969), 453

G. Carli Ballola: 'Una *pièce à sauvetage* da Salvare', *Bollettino del Centro rossiniano di studi* (1971), 11 [on *Torvaldo e Dorliska*]

P. Petrobelli: 'Balzac, Stendhal e il *Mosè* di Rossini', *Conservatorio di musica 'G. B. Martini' di Bologna: Annuario 1965–1970* (1971), 205

B. Cagli: 'Le fonti letterarie dei libretti di Rossini', *Bollettino del Centro rossiniano di studi* (1972), no.2, p.10 [on *Maometto II*]; (1973), no.1, p.8 [on *Bianca e Falliero*]

G. Carli Ballola: 'Lettura dell'*Ermione*', *Bollettino del Centro rossiniano di studi* (1972), no.3, p.13

S. Martinotti: 'I "peccati" del giovane e del vecchio Rossini', *Quadrivium*, xiv (1973), 249–72

M. Tartak: 'Matilde and her Cousins', *Bollettino del Centro rossiniano di studi* (1973), no.3, p.13

P. Isotta: 'I diamanti della corona: grammatica del Rossini napoletano', *Mosè in Egitto*, Opera: collana di guide musicali, iv (Turin, 1974)

Chigiana, xxxiv (1977) [special issue]

P. Gallarati: 'Dramma e ludus dall'*Italiana* al *Barbiere*', *Il melodramma italiano dell'ottocento: studi e ricerche per Massimo Mila* (Turin, 1977)

P. Gossett: *The Tragic Finale of 'Tancredi'* (Pesaro, 1977)

F. Tammaro: 'Ambivalenza dell'*Otello* rossiniano', *Il melodramma italiano dell'ottocento: studi e ricerche per Massimo Mila* (Turin, 1977)

P. Gossett: 'Le sinfonie di Rossini', *Bollettino del Centro rossiniano di studi* (1979)

M. Donà: 'Un'aria di Rossini per un'opera di Nicolini nella Biblioteca Comunale di Civitanova Marche', *AnMc*, no.19 (1979), 320

C. Questa: *Il ratto del serraglio: Euripide, Plauto, Mozart, Rossini* (Bologna, 1979) [on *L'italiana in Algeri*]

M. Viale Ferrero: '*Guglielmo Tell* a Torino (1839–1840), ovvero una *Procella* scenografica', *RIM*, xiv (1979), 378

P. Gossett: 'The Overtures of Rossini', *19th Century Music*, iii (1979–80), 3

——: 'Rossini e i suoi "Péchés de vieillesse" ', *NRMI*, xiv (1980), 7

M. Conati: 'Between Past and Future: the Dramatic World of Rossini in *Mosè in Egitto* and *Moïse et Pharaon*', *19th Century Music*, iv (1980–81), 32

GAETANO DONIZETTI

William Ashbrook

Julian Budden

CHAPTER ONE
Life

I Education and early career

Gaetano Donizetti was born in Bergamo on 29 November 1797. Baptized as Domenico Gaetano Maria Donizetti, he was the fifth of the six children of Andrea and Domenica (Nava) Donizetti who were then living in extreme poverty in the Borgo Canale on the north-west slope of the old city. The house, now no.14, has been a national monument since 1926, and the dark basement apartment is open to visitors. A tradition that the Donizetti family was of Scottish origin was proved by Caversazzi's research (1924) to be without foundation. There was no tradition of music in the family, although Gaetano's eldest brother Giuseppe (1788–1856) served as a military bandsman and in 1828 moved to Constantinople to become chief of music to the Ottoman armies. Another brother, Francesco (1792–1848), played the drum in a Bergamo band.

The opportunity that allowed Gaetano to emerge from this unpromising background came from Johannes Simon Mayr, who was to be the dominant figure in his musical education. Since 1802 Mayr had been *maestro di cappella* at S Maria Maggiore, Bergamo, while pursuing a distinguished career as an opera composer throughout Italy. He persuaded a local charitable institution to open a free music school, primarily to train choirboys but also to impart a well-grounded musical education. The school opened in 1806, and

Gaetano was in the first group of scholars to be enrolled, attending until 1814. Mayr was a thorough, punctilious teacher, familiar with a wide variety of music, particularly that of the Viennese school. He and the teachers chosen by him (Salari, Gonzales and Capuzzi) exposed Donizetti to a musical regimen then scarcely available elsewhere in Italy. Indicative of Mayr's beneficent discipline is the series of string quartets that Donizetti composed (chiefly 1819–21) while awaiting the definitive start of his career.

Donizetti, for all his quickness and talent, was a high-spirited student, as appears from the school's records with their awards of prizes and reprimands. Mayr always supported Donizetti, and his belief in his student's exceptional talent was unwavering. The libretto of a pasticcio put together by Mayr for a student performance in 1811, *Il piccolo compositore di musica*, gives a vivid picture of Donizetti as an exuberant and talented 14-year-old. When Mayr believed that Donizetti's musical horizons needed broadening, he arranged and partly paid for his transfer to Bologna, where he studied counterpoint for two years with Padre Mattei. Donizetti undoubtedly profited from this training, but Mattei's taciturn manner never aroused the respect and affection that Donizetti all his life showed towards Mayr. At Bologna he made his first attempts at composing operas, but these were not performed.

In late 1817 Donizetti returned to Bergamo. With Mayr's help he was given a contract with the company headed by the impresario Zancla, then chiefly active in Venice, for which he composed four operas. None of them made any lasting impression, and they should be regarded as apprentice work. A large number of non-operatic compositions, sacred, orchestral and instrumental, also belong to this period. Donizetti turned them out in a day, often at a single sitting, thus demonstrating a capacity for intense application and rapid work that was to remain characteristic of him until his final illness.

Much nonsense has been written about Donizetti's supposed military service. The usual story identifies one or another of his early operas as having so impressed an Austrian officer that he was summarily released from the service to pursue his career. The truth is that Donizetti was never conscripted. In 1818, as his 21st birthday approached, a lady of Bergamo, Marianna Pezzoli-Grattaroli, impressed by his promise, bought his exemption. The proof of this is contained in a letter published by Zavadini, that Donizetti wrote on 26 July 1839, in which he alluded to the event.

The real start of Donizetti's career occurred in Rome, where *Zoraida di Granata* (Teatro Argentina, 28 January 1822) had an unexpected success. He owed this opportunity to Mayr, who had turned over his contract to his pupil. As a result, the famous impresario Domenico Barbaia offered him a contract for an opera at the Teatro Nuovo, Naples. Donizetti arrived in Naples in February 1822 just before Rossini's departure from what had been since 1815 his principal arena. Bellini was still a pupil at the local conservatory. In this period Donizetti established himself as both promising and productive, but he produced no smashing successes. His first Neapolitan opera, *La zingara* (Teatro Nuovo, 12 May 1822), was so successful that it enjoyed periodic revivals there over the ensuing 15 years. During the next few years he composed two to five operas a year, ranging from one-act farces to full-length serious works, chiefly for Naples, but also for Milan, where the failure of *Chiara e Serafina* (La Scala, 1822) kept him from being invited to produce another opera there until 1830, and for Rome, Palermo and Genoa, where he fared somewhat better. Besides composing 23 operas from *La zingara* to *Anna Bolena* (Milan, Carcano, 1830), after 1827 Donizetti was also regularly preparing and conducting operas by other composers in Naples. It has become a cliché to describe this period of his career as 'Rossinian', but although the influence of the most popular opera composer of the day can be detected, symptoms of Donizetti's mature style are more common. These operas enjoyed at best a transitory success, but they are noteworthy for their variety of tone and subject, as Donizetti sought to accommodate his Romantic temperament to the Neapolitan censors' marked preference for works that ended happily.

In 1828 Donizetti married Virginia Vasselli (1808–37), the daughter of a Roman lawyer. None of their three children survived infancy. Of the sincerity of Donizetti's affection for Virginia there is no doubt, and her death during the horrors of a cholera epidemic left him grief-stricken and fostered the strain of melancholy so pronounced in his later years.

II The achievement of fame (1830)

The triumph of *Anna Bolena* marks a watershed in Donizetti's career. His first work to be given in Paris and London, it opened up for him the possibilities of an international career, although it would be nearly a decade before he could reap their full advantage. He became so dissatisfied with the limitations that Naples imposed on him that in 1832 he broke his contract there, freeing himself to accept more frequent engagements in other theatres. Not all the operas that followed *Anna Bolena* were equally successful, but the number of works that proved their hardihood in several theatres, including those that have never disappeared from the active repertory, is greater than those which failed. His first opera following the break with Naples, *Ugo, conte di Parigi* (Milan, La Scala, 13 March 1832) was a fiasco, but Donizetti more than righted the balance with *L'elisir d'amore* (Milan, Canobbiana, 12 May 1832), composed in less than a month to a libretto adapted by Romani from Scribe's *Le philtre*, set by Auber (1831). In 1833 he produced in Rome two operas, *Il furioso all'isola di San Domingo* and *Torquato Tasso*, that brought him under the stimulating influence of the 23-year-old baritone Giorgio Ronconi, whose extraordinary dramatic power awakened him to the possibilities of this type of voice, until then little exploited in Italy in serious opera. *Lucrezia Borgia* (Milan, La Scala, 26 Dec 1833), based on Hugo's play, was to keep a firm hold on the stage for half a century.

In 1834 Donizetti signed a new contract with Naples to compose one serious opera a year for S Carlo. The first of these was to have been *Maria Stuarda*, but the censors objected to the tragic ending (the story that Queen Maria Cristina fainted at a rehearsal is untrue). In little more than two weeks Donizetti rearranged his score to a completely new libretto, *Buondelmonte*; not surprisingly, the result won scant applause. When *Maria Stuarda*, based on Schiller's play, was given in its original form (Milan, La Scala, 30 December 1835), the ill-health and caprices of the soprano Malibran pro-

8. Gaetano Donizetti: portrait by an unknown artist

duced a resounding failure. A large number of revivals have proved it to be an opera of considerable effectiveness, with a final scene of great beauty and power. Early in 1835 Donizetti went to Paris at Rossini's invitation to give *Marino Faliero* at the Théâtre-Italien. Produced in the wake of the extraordinary success of Bellini's *I puritani*, the opera made little effect, although a revival at Bergamo (1966) revealed some striking anticipations of Verdi. This first visit to Paris was important because it exposed Donizetti to 'grand' opera as practised by Meyerbeer and Halévy. Further, he found a standard of theatrical and musical excellence at the Opéra-Comique and Théâtre-Italien and a level of remuneration superior to those then prevailing in Italy. He returned to Naples to bring out *Lucia di Lammermoor* at the S Carlo (26 September 1835). As performed by Persiani and Duprez, *Lucia* aroused the highest enthusiasm. Cammarano's libretto, a ruthlessly skilful reduction of Scott's *The Bride of Lammermoor*, is tautly constructed and provided Donizetti with the framework to construct a score that is a foundation-stone of Italian Romanticism. In 1839 he revised and simplified the score to fit a French translation. Although the French version is inferior to the Italian, it helped insert the work into the French national consciousness. With *Lucia* Donizetti's pre-eminence among his contemporaries was clearly established.

Donizetti's next opera, *Belisario* (4 February 1836), the first of three he was to write for Venice, was moderately successful. It reflects his Paris visit in his attempt to expand the framework and to put more emphasis on spectacle, but the total effect of its well-constructed score is, as Barblan said, oddly impersonal. Back in Naples Donizetti awaited the opening of the S Carlo season by composing two delightful comic operas to his own librettos for the Teatro Nuovo: *Il campanello* and *Betly*, both in one act (the latter later expanded to two). His opera for the S Carlo's autumn season that year was *L'assedio di Calais*, one of his most interesting. He described it as written 'in the French style' – that is, with a ballet, fewer cabalettas and many important ensemble scenes. Cammarano's strong libretto deals with the incident of the Burghers of Calais. In it, for the last time, Donizetti followed the almost extinct tradition of writing a heroic male role for a female contralto. His next three operas produced a mixed bag: *Pia de' Tolomei* (Venice, 18 February 1837), a score with a few pronounced merits, *Roberto Devereux* (Naples, 29 October 1837), a fine achievement, and *Maria di Rudenz* (Venice, 30 January 1838), burdened by a preposterous libretto, but with some finely expressive music.

In 1837, at the death of Zingarelli, Donizetti had been offered, pending royal approval, the post of director of the Naples Conservatory, where he had been teaching composition for several years. The confirmation of his appointment was delayed and finally allowed to lapse because a strong party preferred Mercadante, who was more closely identified with Naples, for the post. Further, his next opera, *Poliuto*, on which he had pinned great hopes, was banned by the royal censorship because it depicted on stage the martyrdom of a saint. The banning of *Poliuto*, coupled with his disillusionment over the directorship of the conservatory and his grief for his wife, strengthened his resolve to leave for Paris.

III **Final period and last illness (1838–48)**
Within two years of his arrival in Paris in October 1838
Donizetti had had operas performed at four Paris
theatres, much to the consternation of contemporary
French composers, particularly Berlioz, who attacked
him in the *Journal des débats*. Besides reworking some
of his Italian successes for the Théâtre-Italien and making the French version of *Lucia* for the Théâtre de la
Renaissance, he brought out *La fille du régiment* at the
Opéra-Comique (11 February 1840), followed by *Les
martyrs* at the Opéra (10 April 1840). *Les martyrs* was
Poliuto expanded from three to four acts and considerably revised to a French libretto by Scribe. It failed
to win the success Donizetti had counted on, but *La
favorite* (Opéra, 2 December 1840), after a cold start,
established itself solidly in the repertory. This score was
originally in four parts, entitled *L'ange de Nisida* and
intended for the Théâtre de la Renaissance, but when
that theatre went bankrupt before *L'ange* could be
given, Donizetti expanded the score into *La favorite*.
The oft-repeated story that Donizetti wrote Act 4 of *La
favorite* in a single night is not true; almost all of that act
formed part of the score of *L'ange*, which Donizetti had
completed in December 1839. He added to the act an
aria (now usually known as 'Spirto gentil'), which he
had already composed for the never-completed *Le duc
d'Albe*. Most of the music composed new for *La favorite*
is in Acts 2 and 3.
　　Donizetti had gone to Paris with hopes of earning
enough money to enable him to retire from the agitating
world of the opera house, as Rossini had done. But as
his health started to decline, he clung to his career with

9. Scene from Act 2 of the first production of 'Don Pasquale' at the Théâtre-Italien, Paris, in 1843: engraving from the Leipzig 'Illustrierte Zeitung' (1843)

obsessive intensity, until by 1844 he had lost the ability to concentrate sufficiently to compose works of more than a limited compass. His rounds of activity as recorded in his letters began to take on a frantic restlessness. He went to Rome for *Adelia* (11 February 1841), an unsettling near-fiasco, and to Milan for *Maria Padilla* (26 December 1841), where the censors' meddling upset him. In March 1842 he went to Bologna at Rossini's invitation to conduct the Italian première of the *Stabat mater*. Rossini's composition was a great success, and he urged Donizetti to accept the important post of *maestro di cappella* at S Petronio in Bologna. Donizetti refused this offer because he was on his way to Vienna, drawn by hopes of gaining the even more important appointment of Kapellmeister to the Austrian court. There, his newest opera, *Linda di Chamounix* (19 May 1842), aroused great enthusiasm, as did his conducting of Rossini's *Stabat mater*, and he was appointed to the post, which allowed him six months' leave each year to pursue his career elsewhere.

Donizetti's last four operas are particularly notable. Although he began to compose *Caterina Cornaro* before *Linda*, that opera was the last to be given its première in his lifetime (Naples, S Carlo, 18 January 1844). Badly performed, the opera made little impression, but revivals have shown it to be a tautly concentrated work illuminated by piercing melancholy. *Don Pasquale*, tailored to the unequalled talents of Grisi, Mario, Tamburini and Lablache, became overnight one of the glories of Paris's Théâtre-Italien (3 January 1843). Generally regarded as Donizetti's comic masterpiece, it gives no sign of his worsening condition; yet the fact that it contains a surprising amount of reworked material suggests some impairment of his inventiveness. *Maria di Rohan*, brought out in Vienna the following June, is a powerful Romantic melodrama that gave the baritone Ronconi (as Chevreuse) one of his great acting roles. Donizetti's last completed opera, *Dom Sébastien, roi de Portugal* (Opéra, 13 November 1843), is weighed down by a sombre and sometimes preposterous libretto by Scribe, but it contains pages of great nobility and monumental sadness. Donizetti was deeply disappointed that the opera failed to move the public as he had hoped. Although the score had been dismissed as 'a funeral in five acts', such a judgment is altogether too glib, and the opera, in spite of some flaws, contains passages, like the great septet in Act 4, that rank among Donizetti's finest achievements.

During the trying rehearsals of *Dom Sébastien*, Donizetti's sometimes erratic behaviour began to trouble his friends; he became increasingly subject to embarrassing lapses, and ugly gossip circulated about his uncontrollable excesses. After the Vienna season of 1845 his loyal friends in Italy hoped he would return to them, and they were alarmed when he insisted on going to Paris, from where he wrote to them wildly about the vast amount of work he had to do. This deterioration continued through 1845, and his friends appealed to Giuseppe Donizetti in Constantinople, who finally sent his son Andrea to Paris.

Finding his uncle's condition worse than he had feared, Andrea arranged a consultation of doctors on 28 January 1846. Their findings (corroborated by the autopsy of 1848) were that Donizetti was suffering from cerebro-spinal degeneration of syphilitic origin, and they recommended that he be placed in an institution.

Three days later he was moved to a sanatorium at Ivry, near Paris, where he remained for almost 17 months. Finally overcoming persistent opposition, Andrea obtained permission to move his uncle, by now helplessly paralysed and able to utter only an occasional monosyllable; on 6 October 1847 they arrived in Bergamo, where Donizetti was lodged with friends who carefully tended him until his death.

First buried in the Valtesse cemetery, in what was then a suburb of Lower Bergamo, in 1875 his remains were moved to S Maria Maggiore and placed near the monument by Vela (1855); in 1951 they were moved to another part of the church. The house where Donizetti died, now the Palazzo Scotti in Upper Bergamo, is marked by a plaque. The Istituto Musicale G. Donizetti, a continuation of the school started by Mayr in 1806, contains a Museo Donizetti that houses memorabilia and an important collection of manuscripts. Other important collections of Donizetti manuscripts are in the library of the Naples Conservatory, the Ricordi archives, Milan, and the Paris Conservatoire.

Four of Donizetti's operas were first performed posthumously. *Il Pigmalione*, his first opera, written when he was still a student at Bologna, was given in 1960 at the Teatro Donizetti, Bergamo, which makes a practice of reviving a little-known Donizetti opera each season. *Gabriella di Vergy*, composed in 1826, was given in Naples in 1869 in a version drastically modified by other hands. *Rita*, an *opéra comique* composed in 1841 to a French text by Vaëz, had its première in Paris in 1860. *Le duc d'Albe* was begun in 1839 and put aside approximately half-composed. In 1880 the publisher Giovannina Lucca obtained the rights to the opera and established a commission headed by Ponchielli to supervise the completion of the score, that task being assigned to Matteo Salvi, who had been Donizetti's pupil in Vienna. The opera was first given at the Teatro Apollo, Rome, on 22 March 1882. The chief attention aroused by the work was the discovery that Scribe had later revamped the same libretto to serve for Verdi's *Les vêpres siciliennes*. In 1959 Thomas Schippers made a second version, closer to Donizetti's original intention, which was introduced at the Spoleto Festival.

IV Donizetti's character

Over a thousand of Donizetti's letters have been printed. His correspondence gives a vivid picture of his personality and the conditions under which he worked; they could form the basis of a fascinating psychological study. He was warm and humorous, capable of deep feeling and eloquence. As his physical condition altered in his later years, his letters are a moving witness to his gradual disintegration. The obsessiveness increased and the tone of melancholy grew more inconsolable; the last letters, pathetic cries for help from a disorientated brain, were written in the first days of his confinement at Ivry.

The letters to Mayr are of particular interest because they show the constant affection and respect he felt for his old teacher. He was surprisingly fair in his comments about other composers, not at all like the morbidly jealous Bellini. Except when he thought he had been the victim of malice, he was modest about his achievements. His letters reveal no interest in the political events of his time. Nor is this surprising. Donizetti's career depended on retaining the goodwill of the regimes

10. Gaetano Donizetti: self-caricature dated 1841

Mon portrait fait par moi même

controlling the theatres for which he worked. Nevertheless, some of his close associates were political activists and exiles. If Donizetti was himself involved in such activities, no clear evidence of it has yet been recovered.

Donizetti's literary aptitude appears in the three comic librettos he wrote for himself (*Le convenienze ed inconvenienze teatrali, Il campanello* and *Betly*). They are deft and well shaped and contain frequent elements of parody. Further, he frequently took an active role in the shaping, and sometimes even the working, of librettos that others wrote for him. He was well read, with a particular affection for Dante; yet he was always at heart the practical man of the theatre, deeply involved in the practice of his craft.

CHAPTER TWO

Operas

It is by his operas that Donizetti's reputation as a composer stands or falls. In the area of comedy, his position has never been seriously challenged (Mendelssohn once shocked a number of his friends by declaring that he would like to have written *La fille du régiment*). Both *Don Pasquale* and *L'elisir d'amore* have remained in the general repertory since they were composed. In the tragic genre Donizetti was both more and less than a great composer: more in that he summed up within himself a whole epoch; less in that no single one of his tragic operas makes the impact that one expects of an unqualified masterpiece. All are subject to relapses into routine craftsmanship. Yet so central was he to the vitality of the tradition he served that when he retired it began to decay. His lesser contemporaries, Mercadante and Pacini, lacking his certainty of aim, his sense of a just relation of means to ends, soon declined into mannerism and selfconsciousness. Only Verdi succeeded in putting the Donizettian heritage to a new and valid use. Donizetti's own works survive through the grace and spontaneity of their melodies, their formal poise, their effortless dramatic pace and above all the romantic vitality that underlies their veneer of artifice.

1 General survey

Along with Bellini, Donizetti epitomized the Italian Romantic spirit of the 1830s. A more fragile spirit than its German or French counterpart, it declared itself through – and often in the teeth of – an operatic tradition of fixed, generic forms and vocal virtuosity, linked to the necessity of rapid production. If Bellini expressed Italian Romanticism in its most concentrated form, Donizetti compensated by a greater versatility and resource and a stronger feeling for dramatic movement. He also had the benefit of a more thorough musical training under Mayr and Mattei, and this contributed much to his superior fluency of technique and invention.

When Donizetti began his career in 1818, Italian music was wholly dominated by Rossini, whose formal, abundantly florid style all composers were bound to imitate, since, as Pacini wrote, 'there is no other way of making a living'. Although reputedly desirous of reform, Donizetti conformed to this style without difficulty, whether in the *seria, buffa* or *semiseria* genre, and the 30 or so works produced over the next ten years, mainly for Naples and other cities in the south, all show nimble craftsmanship and melodic fertility. In the serious and 'semi-serious' operas there is as yet little trace of individuality, which, in all the principal voice parts,

Ex.1

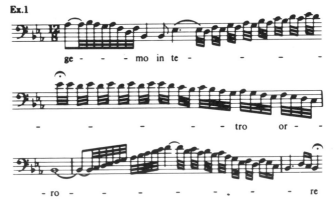

tends to sink under the weight of Rossinian *canto fiorito* and *solfeggi* (see ex.1, a passage for one of the four virtuoso basses in the heroic opera *Otto mesi in due ore, ossia Gli esiliati in Siberia*, 1827).

It is his comedies, such as *L'ajo nell'imbarazzo* (1824), *Olivo e Pasquale* (1827) and *Il Giovedì Grasso* (1828), that afford the earliest glimpse of the true Donizetti. The first, in particular, shows that blend of humour and tenderness (here enhanced by the felicity of Ferretti's verse) that is the hallmark of his comic style. Even the routine syllabic setting for the two *buffi* are floated on a characteristically fresh melody embellished with light, faintly sensuous chromatic inflections (see ex.2).

After 1828 Donizetti's own style began to take shape under the influence partly of Bellini's *Il pirata* (1827), which brought to Italian opera a new manner in which *fioritura* was both reduced and subordinated to passionate expression, and partly of Rossini's monumental French operas, such as *Le siège de Corinth* (1826) and *Moïse* (1827), which found their way to Italy in translation. Rossini's influence is noticeable in *L'esule di Roma* (1828), with its abundant choruses, and in *Il diluvio universale* (1830), an *azione tragico-sacra* whose melodic fertility amply repays its obvious debt to 'il nuovo *Mosè*'. Hints of Bellini are evident in *Alina, regina di Golconda* (1828), *Il paria* (1829) and *Elisabetta, o Il castello di Kenilworth* (1829). The next operas are marked by a tendency for *canto fiorito* to disappear from the male voices or to be relegated to the cadenzas; at the same time, the melodies shed the declamatory element inherited from Rossini to become more lyrical and periodic in Bellini's manner, or else

111

Ex.2

(Per bacco! il ma - e-stro ha perso il cer - vel-lo.) (L'a-mi-co mi

cre-de sva-nito il cer-vello.) (Oppu-re egli è un lu-po col manto d'a-

- gnello.) (O un lu-po mi sti-ma col man-to d'a-gnel-lo.)

more vivid and concise in an anticipation of Verdi's.

During this period certain works stand out as landmarks. With *Anna Bolena* (1830) Donizetti came into his own as a tragic composer. Here, for the first time, the traditional procedures were put to recognizably personal use, in the service of a drama both powerful and swift. *L'elisir d'amore* (1832) saw the perfection of sentimental comedy in a pastoral setting and remains as much a classic of its genre as does Rossini's *Barbiere* of late Classical *opera buffa*. In *Lucrezia Borgia* (1833) Donizetti explored a vein of sensational melodrama in which convention was more radically modified than ever before: the concertato and stretta that were expected to end at least one act were reduced to a few pages at the end of the prologue; not one of the duets is in the standard Rossinian three-part form that had generally served Donizetti until then. The first movement of that between Lucrezia and Alfonso ('Vi chiedo, o signore') takes the form of a dialogue; the ducttino 'Qui che fai' in the same act is conducted as a series of *parlanti* over a sinuous orchestral theme. Both served Verdi as models, in *Nabucco* and *Rigoletto* respectively.

The progress away from Rossini was gradual and not uniformly maintained. *Torquato Tasso* (1833) was a more innovatory work than *Rosmonda d'Inghilterra* (1834). Even *Lucia di Lammermoor*, generally considered the archetype of Italian Romantic opera, remained a curious blend of old and new, as may be seen by comparing the two duets 'Della tomba che rinserra' and 'Il pallor funesto orrendo'; the first was conceived lyrically throughout, the second cast in a typically Rossinian mould of complex symmetries in which the architectural element takes precedence over the dramatic. The deeply pathetic sextet with its ground-swell to climax (a legacy from Bellini that was seized on by the Italian Romantics) is framed by two movements built on the same orchestral theme – another device associated with Rossini, which artificially heightens the contrast between stasis and action. Likewise, though vocal coloratura is used effectively to depict the fragility of the heroine, some of the Mad Scene remains on a purely decorative level, even when shorn of the disfiguring cadenza for flute and voice added for or by Teresa Brambilla and still performed. The brilliant cabaletta 'Spargi d'amaro pianto' shows a curious indifference to the mood of Cammarano's text. Unlike Bellini's Elvira in similar circumstances, Lucia lacks the excuse of morbid euphoria for her roulades.

By 1836 drama has gained the upper hand in determining the structure of most duets. In *Roberto Devereux* (1837) the middle movement of that between Nottingham and Sara ('Nol sai che un nume vindice') is a dialogue over the funeral march that conducts Essex to the Tower of London, while the cabaletta allocates contrasted themes to the two soloists. Vocal virtuosity became increasingly functional. Unlike Bellini, Donizetti never wholly abandoned the declamatory flourish characteristic of the 1820s. Hence, in ex.3, the late but characteristic instance of an 'open' melody (to use Friedrich Lippmann's useful term for a melody that begins with ornamental, declamatory gestures in free time and gradually takes on a regular periodic motion as it proceeds) in the heroine's cavatina from *Pia de' Tolomei* (1836), 'O tu che desti il fulmine'.

During the years from 1839 onwards Donizetti's style was further enriched as a result of his commissions for Paris and Vienna and the need to cater to audiences more sophisticated than those of Naples or Milan. All the foreign works apart from *Dom Sébastien* have full-length overtures, mostly worked out with considerable skill, though only three (those of *La fille du régiment*, *Maria di Rohan* and *Don Pasquale*) are thematically associated with the operas to which they belong. In

Ex.3 Larghetto

O tu che de-sti il ful - mi - - ne, che al nembo il fren di-scio - - - gli, al nembo il fren discio - - - - gli, le mie dolen-ti la - gri-me in tua pieta-de ac- cer - ba.

general, the orchestration is fuller, the harmony subtler and more varied than before. Yet apart from such obvious gallicisms as the trio 'Tous les trois réunis' in *La fille du régiment* (1840) – a counterpart to the stretta 'Venez amis, retirons-nous' from Rossini's *Le Comte Ory* (1828) – and the portentous denunciation of Balthasar in *La favorite* (1840), which echoes that of Cardinal Brogni in Halévy's *La juive*, his music did not change its physiognomy in response to a French text, as Verdi's so often did. Indeed, it is a French opera, *La favorite*, that supplies one of the most evocatively Italian arias in the tenor repertory – 'Spirto gentil', originally intended for the unfinished *Le duc d'Albe* (begun in 1839). Few would maintain that it gains anything by being sung in the original French. Only *Dom Sébastien*, with its

115

preponderance of military rhythms and accompanimental 'tics', suggests a conscious attempt to imitate the grand manner of Meyerbeer.

The wider horizons offered by Parisian grand opera also benefited the last Italian operas, three of which were written for non-Italian audiences. *Linda di Chamounix* is Donizetti's ripest and most varied essay in the *semiseria* genre, including a hilarious scene for *buffo* bass and chorus, a melancholy ballad sung by a boy-minstrel, a solemn prayer for bass and chorus that serves as an act-finale, a mad scene for the heroine and a 'theme song' (here a love-duet), the singing of which by the hero recalls the distraught heroine to her right mind. In this work the current Italian idiom is sometimes invaded by harmonies of an almost Schumannesque sensibility (see ex.4).

Ex.4

tut - to scor-da a un tuo sor - ri - so. tut-to in te mi do-na a-mor

Don Pasquale (1843), Donizetti's comic masterpiece, recovered for Italy the Classical heritage of Mozart; it features a unique style of conversational recitative of freely floating lines with only an occasional string chord to underpin the modulations (until 30 years later composers were still using a continuo instrument for recitative in *opera buffa*). *Maria Padilla* (1841), *Caterina Cornaro* (composed in 1842) and *Maria di*

Rohan (1843) all hint at the way Donizetti's art would have evolved if his career had not been cut short. In the heroine's scena and cavatina in Act 1 of *Maria Padilla* the traditional Rossinian framework appears dissolved into an interplay of declamatory and lyrical elements, of vocal and orchestral melody sustaining a dramatic flow less urgent than Verdi's, yet no less continuous. *Maria di Rohan*, Donizetti's most concise tragedy, brought recitative into the heart of a formal number, thus achieving a variety of pace unusual for the time. All three works are free from the consciously grand manner that Mercadante had introduced with his *Il giuramento* (1837) and *Elena da Feltre* (1838). The most elaborate of Donizetti's concertatos is unfailingly limpid.

II Melody, form, harmony

Donizetti's melodic style was characteristic of his time and place, with little to distinguish it from that of his Italian contemporaries, who were all working in the same enclosed tradition and who, like their 18th-century forebears, availed themselves of a common stock of procedures. Donizetti had no such obvious traits as Bellini's 'heavenly length', his personal manner of articulating a melody or his continual use of simple discords on accented beats. Scholars such as Lippmann and Ashbrook, however, have drawn attention to his use of graceful, rather sensuous chromatic passing notes in the course of plain diatonic melodies, a penchant for cadences and half-cadences that descend from the fifth to the third degree of the scale, a robust, popular quality in choral and stage-band music (a trait shared with Luigi Ricci and Verdi), a fondness for lyrical melodies in triple or 6/8 time, often resulting in a characteristic

mazurka-like setting of the ubiquitous octosyllabic verse
(e.g. 'Da un tuo detto sol dipende', *Alina, regina di
Golconda*; 'Per guarir di tal pazzia', *L'elisir d'amore*;
and 'Sin la tomba è a me negata', *Belisario*). Notable
above all was Donizetti's ability to generate long,

Ex.5

Di pe - sca - to - re i - gno - bi - le

Esser figliuol cre - de - - i,   e se-co o-scu - ri in

Na - po - li   Vis - si i prim' an - ni

mie - i,   Quan-do un guer-rie-ro in - co - gni-to

Ven - ne d'in-ganno a trar - mi,

satisfying periods from plain, often predictable exten-
sions of a single rhythmic idea (e.g. 'Rayons dorés', *La
favorite*; 'O luce di quest'anima', *Linda di Chamounix*;
the prayer with chorus 'Deh, tu di un umile', *Maria
Stuarda*, and ex.5, Gennaro's solo 'Di pescator igno-
bile', *Lucrezia Borgia*).

Another characteristic melody is that which, either
due to a natural abruptness or because it reaches its
climax earlier than expected, exhausts its momentum in

varied repetitions, shortenings or expansions of the cadential phrase (see 'Mentre il cor abbandonava', *Il diluvio universale*; and 'Tu che siedi in terzo cielo', *Fausta*). This design is especially effective in cabalettas, where the repetitions not only afford a basis for virtuosity but also prepare for the desired full stop and applause (see 'Spargi d'amaro pianto', *Lucia*; and 'Mon arrêt descend du ciel', *La favorite*). In general, however, Donizetti's achievement lay less in any specific contribution to the post-Rossinian tradition than in a wideranging invention within it. His cabalettas present every possible variety from the brilliant to the expressive and sentimental. His cantabiles exploit the standard binary form in many unpredictable guises. His use of quasirecitative to diversify narrative arias is especially skilful (see 'Nella fatal di Rimini', *Lucrezia Borgia* and 'Regnava nel silenzio', *Lucia*). Particularly affecting are those sudden modulations towards the end of a period,

Ex.6

11. Autograph score
of part of the
cavatina 'Soldats, j'ai
rêvé la victoire' from
Act 1 of 'Dom
Sébastien', first
performed in Paris,
1843

increasingly common in the later operas. The most magical instance occurs in the duet 'Signorina?' in *Don Pasquale* (see ex.6).

Donizetti often combined two forms within the same number. Leicester's cavatina 'Ah rimiro il bel sembiante' (*Maria Stuarda*) is half duet, half aria with *pertichini*. Sometimes he added a strophic dimension to his cantabiles, as in 'Ah non avea più lagrime' (*Maria di Rudenz*), or the famous minor–major romanza 'Una furtiva lagrima' (*L'elisir d'amore*), the first verse of which ends in the relative minor, the second in the tonic major. There is scarcely an opera from 1830 onwards that does not contain an unobtrusive novelty of form and texture, whether it be Guido's mournful cavatina 'Questo sacro augusto stemma' (*Gemma di Vergy*), sung over a pattering recital by Rolando and the chorus of the story of Joan of Arc, the clinching of a cabaletta with a phrase taken from the cantabile, as in the duet 'Fama! Si, l'avrete' (*Anna Bolena*), or the sobbing transition from central ritornello to the second statement of the cabaletta 'Ugo è spento' (*Parisina*). As might be expected, the French works make use of the ternary form with modulating middle section (see Zaida's two *romances* in *Dom Sébastien*); all the works of this period show a more frequent use of thematic reminiscence, which, however, nowhere approaches the quasi-symphonic concept of leitmotif. In his view of opera Donizetti postulated the supremacy of the human voice and the vocally conceived period as its principle of organization; his harmony and scoring are conditioned accordingly. His tonal range is in general wider than Bellini's, his harmonies blander and yet more sophisticated (he was more sparing in the use of poignant discord). Like most of his Italian contemporaries he aimed at dramatic expression by means of vocal contour rather than harmonic nuance; hence the somewhat generalized emotion of the many cabalettas based on simple major-key harmonies in a tragic context. Nor did he fail to observe the unwritten law that any piece begun in the minor key must conclude unequivocally in the major, whether relative or tonic – a scheme that weakens many a rondò finale and in particular the remarkable stretta 'Come tigri di stragi anelanti' in Act 1 of *L'assedio di Calais*. Local colour is rare (the yodelling themes in *Betly* are an exception). There is nothing in *Il paria* to indicate that the drama is set in India. Only in the 'Danse arabe' in *Dom Sébastien* did Donizetti avail himself of the harmonic resources offered by the exotic, and, partly for this reason, his ballet music is in general trite and undistinguished.

III Orchestration and vocal writing

Donizetti followed Rossini's 'prismatic' treatment of the orchestra, tracing variegated patterns of wind colour over a neutral string background, pointing modulations with sustaining instruments, doubling melodic lines wholly or in part with solo flute, clarinet or trumpet, as the case may be. Concertante and obbligato instruments, always treated in bel canto style, frequently embellish a scena or form the basis of a prelude, with or without an accompanying harp. Instances include a glass harmonica (*Elisabetta, o Il castello di Kenilworth* and also *Lucia*, where it was later replaced by a flute), clarinet (*Torquato Tasso*), harp (*Lucia*), bass clarinet (*Maria di Rudenz*) and trumpet (*Don Pasquale*). Tuttis are usually noisy and opaque, while lyrical accompaniments keep to a plain rhythmic pattern in a more popular variant of Rossini's manner and sometimes justify Wagner's famous gibe about the big guitar. But put any score of Donizetti's beside one of Mercadante's or Pacini's and what leaps to the eye is its spareness. It seems impossible that so few notes can make the effect that they invariably do. If in his early operas Donizetti's use of wind colour may appear ornamental and hedonistic, in his later works it can be powerfully evocative. Horns play an important role in establishing the atmosphere of *Lucia di Lammermoor*.

In his treatment of the voice Donizetti followed the lead first of Rossini, then of the Bellini of *La sonnambula* and after. He was particularly responsive to the individual qualities of the singers for whom he wrote: he never attempted, as Bellini once did, to impose a plain style on a florid singer. The agility of Tacchinardi-Persiani left its mark on *Rosmonda d'Inghilterra, Lucia* and *Pia*; the more dramatic talents of Pasta and Ronzi de Begnis were given full scope in the more directly expressive final scenes of *Anna Bolena, Maria Stuarda* and *Roberto Devereux*. Confronted by a mezzo-soprano with no flexibility whatever, such as Rosine Stoltz, creator of Léonore in *La favorite*, Donizetti eschewed all decoration to achieve a noble simplicity that pervades not only the heroine's part, but the whole score, apart from the dispensable ballet. Except in *L'assedio di Calais* he followed the trend that was banishing the contralto or mezzo-soprano *en travesti* from hero to a subordinate position in the plot, such as that of the hero's or heroine's friend.

In the male parts *canto fiorito* gave way to a simpler eloquence in which syncopation usually replaces passage-work as a way of giving emphasis. Like Bellini, Donizetti treated his baritones and basses alike, but he was more successful in giving a high charge of irony to the singer's lyrical line (see 'Pour tant d'amour', *La favorite*), thereby foreshadowing Verdi. The growing incidence of important baritone roles in the later operas (in both *Maria di Rudenz* and *Maria Padilla* the baritone takes precedence over the tenor) was due to Giorgio Ronconi, who did more than any singer of his day to stimulate that forceful conception of the voice type associated with the young Verdi. For Donizetti, however, as for most of his contemporaries, the baritone remained essentially a *basso cantante* with a tessitura roughly a tone lower than that of his Verdian counterpart. On the other hand, the Donizettian tenor has a character of his own. A poet of the voice even when a villain (as in *Pia de' Tolomei*), he first took shape in his less heroic aspects in *L'elisir d'amore*, to reach his fullest incarnation as Edgardo in *Lucia*, a role that provided two famous singers of the day with their respective sobriquets: 'the tenor of the curse' (Fraschini) and 'the tenor of the beautiful death' (Moriani). Capable of great force ('Maledetto sia l'istante', *Lucia*) and even virtuosity ('Trema Bisanzio!', *Belisario*) he excelled in the portrayal of innocence betrayed. In his mature operas Donizetti's touch never failed with the tenor yet his means were of the simplest (see ex.7). Even that degree of discord is exceptional; no composer was more adept at distilling sadness from the combination of tenor voice and plain major-key harmonies, as in 'Tu che a Dio spiegasti le ali' (*Lucia*).

Donizetti's sculpting of a tenor melody can be traced in the sketches for Ernesto's aria 'Cercherò lontana terra' in *Don Pasquale*, published by Rattalino (1970).

These entirely refute the notion that the composer always wrote uncritically and at breakneck speed. Indeed, they resemble Beethoven's sketches in their painstaking adjustment of detail. But a comparison with the few known sketches by Verdi is significant. While Verdi's alterations were all directed towards a more exact representation of a particular character in a particular situation, Donizetti was here concerned purely with perfection of melodic craftsmanship in relation to the portrayal of a tenor in distress.

IV Assessment

Few of Donizetti's admirers would attempt to deny a certain generic quality in his art that recalls the outlook of a previous generation. In general, the Romantic ethos insists on the unique unrepeatable masterpiece – a description that could be more easily applied to *Norma* than to any of Donizetti's serious operas. It is sometimes said that he needed the stimulus of a romantic story in order to give of his best. In fact he was at home in almost every field from theatrical satire (*Le convenienze ed inconvenienze teatrali*) to neo-classical tragedy without a love interest (*Belisario*). For the comedies *Il campanello* and *Betly* he compiled his own

Ex.7 Larghetto

Adina credimi   te ne scon-giu - ro non puoi spo -
[sarlo]

librettos, while in *Don Pasquale* he rewrote so much of the text that the librettist refused to acknowledge paternity of it. But as with Verdi, an unusual plot elicited unusual solutions. *Lucrezia Borgia* is matched in this respect by *L'assedio di Calais*, a patriotic grand opera on the French model, with which Donizetti hoped to 'introduce a new genre to Italy'. Of its many ensembles, not one is without some surprising feature, structural and harmonic, while the fact that the juvenile lead is a mezzo-soprano allows a play of 6ths and 3rds in his duet comparable to Bellini's 'Mira o Norma'. Yet the opera failed to circulate, doubtless because of its eccentric distribution (mezzo-soprano, baritone and bass principals, the last appearing only in Act 3; two *soprani comprimari*, including the heroine, and a host of secondary roles). Donizetti never continued along this path.

Too often the idealist in Donizetti was forced to yield to the practical man of the theatre. He might welcome the freedom from Italian operatic routine afforded him by the Parisian stage; he might express a preference for the tenor ending to *Lucrezia Borgia* as against the rondò finale that he had been obliged to write for Mme Méric-Lalande in 1833. But like Rossini and generations of Italian composers before him, Donizetti believed that operas should be re-created strictly in terms of the resources available for each revival. He was always ready to adapt his scores to the demands of different singers, to expand secondary roles into principal ones, even altering the original voice type, and to provide alternative numbers for the principals themselves – a practice made all the easier by the fact that Italian opera during the 1830s was constructed from short, finite scenes. Sometimes the alternative pieces were derived

from previous scores. Thus the cabaletta from a contralto and bass duet in *Imelda de' Lambertazzi* ('Restati
pur m'udrai') was transposed for soprano and tenor,
fitted out with two preceding movements and introduced
into *Anna Bolena* as an alternative to the much shorter
duet for Anna and Percy that is printed in the definitive
score ('S'ei t'aborre'). The entire duet was modified for
Marino Faliero five years later. When Donizetti had no
time to attend to the matter himself, he would advise the
singer to use a 'pezzo di baule'. He even allowed the
stretta of *La favorite* (Act 3) to replace that of *Maria
Stuarda* (Act 2) in order to accommodate a mezzo-
soprano Maria. Some of the transferences are more
difficult to account for except on grounds of conven-
ience. Thus the Larghetto concertato in Act 2 of *Maria
di Rudenz* ('Chiuse il dì per le la ciglia') was reproduced
note for note as the Act 2 concertato of *Poliuto*, whence
it passed into Act 3 of the French version, *Les martyrs*.
A quartet finale from *Il paria* was carried over into
Torquato Tasso. The duet cabaletta 'A consolarmi af-
frettisi' that forms the 'theme song' of *Linda di
Chamounix* first appeared in *Sancia di Castiglia*, while
the overture to the same opera, all but the slow introduction, was adapted from a string quartet written in 1836.
The overture to *Les martyrs* derives mostly from one
contributed by Donizetti to a composite cantata for the
death of Malibran. Perhaps the most bizarre instance of
self-borrowing occurs in *La fille du régiment*, where
what was once Noah's solemn invocation 'Su quell'arca
nell'ira de' venti' (*Il diluvio universale*) was transformed
into the jaunty 'Chacun le sait, chacun le dit'. *La favorite* was almost entirely compiled from music written for
different contexts, yet welded together with such skill

that the listener is unaware of any incongruity. Indeed, the fact that so many of the themes are based on the ascending or descending scale gives the opera a distinctive character that is very rare in Italian opera of the time. 'Spare-part' construction, limited range of harmony, total subordination of orchestra to voice and the artificiality that attaches to the use of set forms to clothe Romantic subjects all contributed to the low esteem in which Donizetti was held in the Wagnerian age and after. *Lucia* survived as a warhorse for sopranos, with the final scene omitted. *Lucrezia Borgia* and *La favorite* were tolerated as harbingers of Verdi. Only the comedies *L'elisir d'amore* and *Don Pasquale* were thought worthy of serious attention. Since the mid-20th century, however, a change of taste, helped by the advocacy of performers such as Maria Callas, Leyla Gencer and Gianandrea Gavazzeni, has restored Donizetti to critical favour, and the revivals of his vast operatic canon continue.

CHAPTER THREE
Other works

1 Vocal chamber works

Donizetti's vocal chamber works represent a species of salon music much in vogue in Italy and elsewhere during the first half of the 19th century. They consist mostly of songs and duets with piano accompaniment to texts ranging from Metastasio (still regarded as the musician's poet *par excellence*) to Romani and professional versifiers of the time such as Guaita and Tarantini. Many of the poems are of operatic provenance and were therefore set as operatic miniatures complete with recitative; some were grouped together in publications of the type popularized by Rossini's *Soirées musicales*, with evocative titles such as *Un hiver à Paris*, *Nuits d'été à Pausilippe*, *Inspirations viennoises*, but in spite of the occasional exotic vignette (*La zingara, Il cavallo arabo*), the scene is generally Romantic Italy, even where the collective title suggests otherwise (significantly, these publications were usually issued simultaneously in Paris and Naples). Each song or duet usually has a separate dedication – to a friend, a music-loving patron or a famous singer. Songs in popular vein might have a chorus added (*La torre di Biasone*). Donizetti had a ready pen for this type of composition, and his vast production of salon music has not been fully explored. Many pieces remain in manuscript scattered in different collections throughout Europe; some were published in periodicals of the time and then forgotten.

Nor is it always easy to distinguish between a genuine 'composizione di camera' and an old operatic number jotted down in piano reduction to oblige some singer ('Fausta sempre' listed by Weinstock (1964) as a salon piece is in fact a cantabile from *Francesca di Foix*). A verbal tradition attributes the well-known Neapolitan song *Te voglio bene assaje* to him, but recent research has shown this to be doubtful (see De Mura, 1969). Like the operas, Donizetti's vocal chamber music is being revalued, but no amount of advocacy can set it beside the lieder of Schubert or Schumann, where voice and piano explore a vast range of inward feelings through an unending variety of harmony and texture. Donizetti's melodies centre on two stereotypes – the popular song and the Italian opera aria, while the piano writing rarely rises above the suggestion of a primitive orchestral accompaniment. Nonetheless, the songs are fluent, attractive and usually saved from banality by an unexpected modulation or unusual feature of design.

II Sacred works

In 1842 Donizetti submitted an *Ave Maria* to Ferdinand I of Austria, hoping to prove that 'among writers of the theatrical genre there was still a good Christian who knew a different genre, that is, the sacred one'. By that time he had certainly made good his claim. Like every Italian composer of his day he had written much liturgical music as part of his musical training. All of it suffers to some extent from that disparity of style and character that afflicted church music in Italy throughout the 19th century and which only Verdi and Rossini succeeded in overcoming – arid scholasticism in the choruses, operatic sentiment and brilliance in the solos and a general indifference to the sense of the text; yet

12. Gaetano Donizetti: portrait by Giuseppe Rillosi

there is no lack of skill or of musical resource. Mayr's teaching is particularly evident in some of the ensembles, with their echoes of Haydn and other German masters (an early *Dixit Dominus* includes a movement based on the main theme of Mozart's overture to *Die*

131

Zauberflöte). After 1824 the output diminished almost to nothing; but in 1835 Donizetti returned to religious composition, apparently in a more dedicated spirit. By then all floridity had been banished from the vocal lines, and yet of the three requiems dating from those years, that in commemoration of the death of Bellini (the only one to be published) remains a coat of many colours – a Mozartian Introit, a severely fugal Kyrie with final stretto, a Dies irae that anticipates Verdi's in theatrical force, a Judex ergo that begins in solemn, measured declamation and ends in a sentimental lilt of 6ths and 3rds, and an Offertory in the style of a Neapolitan folksong. Not until his last years as court Kapellmeister in Vienna did Donizetti find a liturgical style that was both consistent and rich in variety. This can be seen in a *Miserere* in G minor originally dedicated to Pope Gregory XVI in 1837 and rewritten in 1843. No longer is there any trace of the theatre. The movements are small but concentrated in expression. The even-numbered verses, originally to be sung to plainchant, are fully harmonized, but in a modal manner. In movements such as 'Et exultabit' and the final fugue, counterpoint is revitalized as in Rossini's *Petite messe solennelle*. The above-mentioned *Ave Maria* was justly praised by the Viennese critics for its simple dignity, one writer venturing to hope that it marked the rebirth of genuinely religious music in Italy.

III Instrumental works

The instrumental works have little importance except as evidence of a purely technical skill with which Donizetti is rarely credited. Always well written for the instruments involved, they scarcely rise above the tastes of a public for whom vocal music was paramount. The well-known Concertino in G for english horn features a melody of Schubertian freshness recalling the *Rosamunde* overture, but it soon betrays its authorship by declining into a set of purely decorative variations. Of a different order are the 19 string quartets, all but two apparently composed for musical gatherings at the house of one Bertoli in Bergamo, where Mayr often played the viola. All show a sure grasp of the possibilities of four-part string texture as well as a close thematic organization in Haydn's manner (several have monothematic finales). Donizetti also clearly aimed at giving each a different character. Nos.13–15, in A, D and F (numbering system from the collected edition of the quartets), all have finales in the minor, that of no.14 being designed as a Haydnesque fugato. No.16 in B minor recalls its opening theme in the slow movement and the finale. No.8 in F minor has a programme for each of its four movements, the last of which is a funeral march. Sometimes the material is uninteresting, as in no.12 in C, or the ideas over-ambitious, as in the slow movement of no.11, which suggests an acquaintance with Beethoven. But what ultimately prevents these quartets from entering the repertory is a basic superficiality of musical thought; they are exercises rather than genuine works of art. Most of them could be arranged for string orchestra without losing their character, and the first movement of no.19 – the most elaborate of all – did in fact furnish the basis of an opera overture.

WORKS

(*MSS are autographs unless otherwise stated*)

Numbers in the right-hand column denote references in the text.

OPERAS

vs – vocal score

Title and genre	Acts and librettist	First performance	Sources and remarks	
Il Pigmalione, scena drammatica	1	Bergamo, Donizetti, 13 Oct 1960	composed Bologna, 1816; *F-Pc*	105
L'ira d'Achille	1	not perf.	composed Bologna, 1817; *Pc* (inc.) copy *Pc*	
Enrico di Borgogna, semiseria	2, B. Merelli	Venice, S Luca, 14 Nov 1818	? also perf. as Il ritratto parlante; ov., copy *I-Bc*	
Una follia, farsa	1, Merelli	Venice, S Luca, 15 Dec 1818		
Le nozze in villa, buffa	2, Merelli	Mantua, Vecchio, carn. 1820–21	composed Bergamo, 1819; as I provinciali, ossia Le nozze in villa, Genoa, 1822; copy *F-Pc I-Mr*	
Il falegname di Livonia, o Pietro il grande, czar delle Russie, buffa	2, G. Bevilacqua-Aldovrandini, after A. Duval	Venice, S Samuele, 26 Dec 1819		
Zoraida di Granata, seria	2, Merelli; after F. Gonzales	Rome, Argentina, 28 Jan 1822	rev. (J. Ferretti), Rome, 1824; *Mr*	95
La zingara, semiseria	2, A. L. Tottola	Naples, Nuovo, 12 May 1822	copy *Nc*; vs (Paris, 1856)	95, 96
La lettera anonima, farsa	1, G. Genoino	Naples, Fondo, 29 June 1822	*Mr*; vs (Paris, 1856)	
Chiara e Serafina, o I pirati, semiseria	2, F. Romani, after R. C. G. de Pixérécourt: La cisterne	Milan, La Scala, 26 Oct 1822	*Mr*	96
Alfredo il grande, seria	2, Tottola	Naples, S Carlo, 2 July 1823	*Nc*, copy *F-Pc*	
Il fortunato inganno, buffa	2, Tottola	Naples, Nuovo, 3 Sept 1823	*I-Nc*	
L'ajo nell'imbarazzo, o Don Gregorio, buffa	2, Ferretti, after G. Giraud	Rome, Valle, 4 Feb 1824	rev. as Don Gregorio, Naples, 1826; as Il governo della casa, Dresden, 1828; *Nc* (partly autograph), excerpts (Milan, ?1827, 1837), vs (Paris, 1856; Milan, 1878)	111

Title	Libretto	First performance	Notes	Pages
Emilia di Liverpool, semiseria	2, after Scatizzi	Naples, Nuovo, 28 July 1824	rev. (G. Checcherini), Naples, 1828; also perf. as L'eremitaggio di Liverpool; Nc, copy F-Pc, vs (Paris, 1856) copy US-Bm	
Alahor in Granata, seria	2, M.A.	Palermo, Carolino, 7 Jan 1826	I-Nc	
Elvida, seria	1, G. F. Schmidt	Naples, S Carlo, 6 July 1826		
Gabriella di Vergy, seria 2nd version	3, Tottola, after Du Belloy 3, ?	Naples, S Carlo, 29 Nov 1869 Belfast, Whitla Hall, 9 Nov 1978	orig. composed 2 acts, 1826; rev. by others for 1869 perf., BGi composed c1838, GB-Lu (partly autograph)	105
Olivo e Pasquale, buffa	2, Ferretti, after A. S. Sografi	Rome, Valle, 7 Jan 1827	I-Nc; exce pts (Milan, 1830), vs (Paris, 1856)	111
Otto mesi in due ore, ossia Gli esiliati in Siberia, opera romantica	3, D. Gilardoni, after Pixérécourt: La fille de l'exilé	Naples, Nuovo, 13 May 1827	rev. (A. Alcozer), Naples, 1833; Nc, rev. by U. Fontana as Elisabeta, ou La fille du proscrit (De Leuwen and Brunswick), Paris, 1853; vs (Paris, ?1854)	111
Il borgomastro di Saardam, buffa	2, Gilardoni, after A. H. J. Mélesville, J. T. Merle and E. Cantiran de Boirie	Naples, Nuovo, 19 Aug 1827	Mr, excerpts (Milan, 1830, 1833), vs (Paris, 1856)	
Le convenienze ed inconvenienze teatrali, farsa	1, Donizetti, after Sografi	Naples, Nuovo, 21 Nov 1827	rev. (2 acts), Milan, 1831, Vienna, 1840; F-Pc (partly autograph), 2 excerpts (Milan, 1830 or 1831), vs (Paris, 1856), vs, ed. E. Riccioli (Florence, 1971)	107, 125
L'esule di Roma, ossia Il proscritto, seria	2, Gilardoni	Naples, S Carlo, 1 Jan 1828	also perf. as Settimio il proscritto; I-Mr, excerpts (Milan, 1828; Naples, 1832), with new aria, Bergamo, 1840, vs (Milan, ?1840)	111
Alina, regina di Golconda, semiseria	2, Romani, after S. J. de Boufflers	Genoa, Carlo Felice, 12 May 1828	called opera buffa on lib; rev. Rome, 1833; Nc, vs (Milan, 1842)	111, 118
Gianni di Calais, semiseria	3, Gilardoni, after C. V. d'Arlincourt	Naples, Fondo, 2 Aug 1828	Nc, excerpts (Milan, 1830 or 1831)	
Il Giovedi Grasso, o Il nuovo Pourceaugnac, farsa	1, Gilardoni	Naples, Fondo, aut. 1828	Nc, vs, without recits (Paris, 1856)	111
Il paria, seria	2, Gilardoni, after C. Delavigne	Naples, S Carlo, 12 Jan 1829	Nc, scena ed aria (Milan, 1837), vs (Paris, 1856)	111, 122, 127

Title and genre	Acts and librettist	First performance	Sources and remarks	
Elisabetta, o Il castello di Kenilworth, seria	3, Tottola, after Hugo: Amy Robsart, and Scribe: Leicester [itself after Scott]	Naples, S Carlo, 6 July 1829	Nc, vs (Paris, 1856)	111, 122
I pazzi per progetto, farsa	1, Gilardoni	Naples, Fondo, 7 Feb 1830	Nc, vs (Paris, 1856)	
Il diluvio universale, azione tragica-sacra	3, Gilardoni, after Byron: Heaven and Earth, and Ringhieri: Il diluvio	Naples, S Carlo, 28 Feb 1830	Nc, excerpts (Milan, 1834), vs (Paris, 1856)	111, 119, 127
Imelda de' Lambertazzi, seria	2, Tottola	Naples, S Carlo, 23 Aug 1830	Nc, excerpts (Milan, 1830)	127
Anna Bolena, seria	2, Romani	Milan, Carcano, 26 Dec 1830	Mr, vs (Milan, 1830 or 1831, 2/1876)	96, 97, 112, 121, 123, 127, 157
Gianni di Parigi, comica	2, Romani, after Saint-Just	Milan, La Scala, 10 Sept 1839	composed 1831; Nc, vs (Milan, 1843)	
Francesca di Foix, semiseria	1, Gilardoni, after Favart and Saint-Amans: Ninette à la cour	Naples, S Carlo, 30 May 1831	Nc	130
La romanziera e l'uomo nero, buffa	1, Gilardoni	Naples, Fondo, 18 June 1831	Nc, vs, without recits (Paris, 1856)	
Fausta, seria	2, Gilardoni and Donizetti	Naples, S Carlo, 12 Jan 1832	ov. added, Milan, 1832; rev. Venice, 1834; Nc, vs (Milan, 1832 or 1833; Paris, ?1832)	119
Ugo, conte di Parigi, seria	2, Romani	Milan, La Scala, 13 March 1832	Nc, vs (Milan, 1832)	97
L'elisir d'amore, comica	2, Romani, after Scribe: Le philtre	Milan, Canobbiana, 12 May 1832	Nc (Act 1), BGi (Act 2) (Milan, 1916), vs (Milan, 1832, 2/1869)	97, 109, 112, 118, 121, 125, 128
Sancia di Castiglia, seria	2, P. Salatino	Naples, S Carlo, 4 Nov 1832	Nc, vs (Milan, 1833)	127
Il furioso all'isola di San Domingo, semiseria	3, Ferretti, after anon. play on Don Quixote	Rome, Valle, 2 Jan 1833	rev. Milan, 1833; Mr, excerpts (Milan, 1833), vs in 2 acts (Paris, c1845)	97
Parisina, seria	3, Romani, after Byron	Florence, Pergola, 17 March 1833	BGi, vs (Milan, 1833, 2/1911); autograph facs. in Early Romantic Opera (New York, 1976-)	121
Torquato Tasso, seria [with semiseria elements]	3, Ferretti, after G. Rosini	Rome, Valle, 9 Sept 1833	Mr, vs (Milan, 1833; Naples and Rome, c1835; Paris, n.d.); also perf. as Sordello il trovatore	97, 113, 122, 127

Title and genre	Acts and librettist	First performance	Sources and remarks	
Poliuto, seria	3, Cammarano, after Corneille	Naples, S Carlo, 30 Nov 1848	composed for S Carlo, 1838, banned by censor, Nc, vs (Milan, c1850)	100, 101, 127
2nd version: Les martyrs, grand opéra	4, Scribe	Paris, Opéra, 10 April 1840	Mr (Paris, 1840), vs (Paris, ?1840/R1975; It., Milan, 1843); facs. of ?1840 edn. in Early Romantic Opera (New York, 1976–)	101, 127
La fille du régiment, opéra comique	2, J. H. V. de Saint-Georges and J. F. A. Bayard	Paris, Opéra-Comique, 11 Feb 1840	Nc (Paris, ?1840); It., Milan, 1840, vs (Milan, 1840 or 1841, 2/1879)	101, 109, 114, 115, 127
L'ange de Nisida	3, A. Royer and G. Vaëz	not perf.	composed 1839; also known as Silvia; rev. as La favorite; excerpts F-Pc	101
La favorite, grand opéra	4, Royer and Vaëz, after Baculard d'Arnaud: Le comte de Comminges	Paris, Opéra, 2 Dec 1840	Malfieri collection (Paris, 1841); facs. of 1841 edn. in Early Romantic Opera (New York, 1976–); rev. and expanded from L'ange de Nisida	101, 115, 118, 119, 123, 124, 127, 128
Adelia, o La figlia dell'arciere, seria	3, Romani and G. Marini, after anon. Fr. play	Rome, Apollo, 11 Feb 1841	I-Nc, vs (Paris, ?1843; Milan, n.d.)	103
Rita, ou Le mari battu, opéra comique	1, Vaëz	Paris, Opéra-Comique, 7 May 1860	composed 1841; Nc, vs (Paris, 1860); also perf. as Deux hommes et une femme	105
Maria Padilla, seria	3, G. Rossi, after Ancelot	Milan, La Scala, 26 Dec 1841	Mr, vs (Paris, ?1841; Milan, 1841 or 1842)	103, 116, 117, 124
Linda di Chamounix, semiseria	3, Rossi, after D'Ennery and Lemoine: La grâce de Dieu	Vienna, Kärntnerthor, 19 May 1842	rev. Paris, 1842; Mr, vs (Vienna and Milan, 1842; Paris, 1842)	103, 116, 118, 127
Caterina Cornaro, seria	prol, 2, G. Sacchero, after Saint-Georges: La reine de Chypre	Naples, S Carlo, 18 Jan 1844	composed 1842; Nc, vs (Milan, 1845/R1974; Paris, 1845)	103, 116
Don Pasquale, buffa	3, G. Ruffini and Donizetti, after A. Anelli: Ser Marc'Antonio	Paris, Italien, 3 Jan 1843	Mr (Milan, 1961), vs (Milan, 1843, 2/1871)	*102, 103, 109, 114, 116, 121, 122, 124, 126, 128*
Maria di Rohan, seria	3, Cammarano, after Lockroy [J. P. Simon]: Un duel sous le cardinal de Richelieu	Vienna, Kärntnerthor, 5 June 1843	rev. Vienna, 1844; Mr, vs (Milan, 1843, 2/1870 or 1871; Ger., Vienna, ?1843; Paris, n.d.)	104, 114, 117
Dom Sébastien, roi de Portugal, grand opéra	5, Scribe, after Barbosa Machado: Memorias ... o governo Del rey D. Sebastião	Paris, Opéra, 13 Nov 1843	F-Pc (with unpubd addns), full score (Paris, 1843–4), vs (Paris, ?1843; Milan, 1844, 2/1886); facs. of 1843–4 edn. in Early Romantic Opera (New York, 1976–)	104, 114, 115, *120*, 121, 122

Inc. and unfinished: Olimpiade (opera seria, Metastasio), composed Bologna, 1817, duet *I-BGi*; Introduzione and aria [aria adapted from Le nozze in villa] in I 101, 105*f*, 115, 264 piccioli virtuosi ambulanti (opera buffa, 1), Bergamo, sum. 1819, pasticcio perf. by students of Mayr's school; La bella prigioniera (farsa, 1), composed Naples, 1826, 2 nos., pf acc.. *BGi*; Adelaide (opera comica, begun Naples, 1834, inc. autograph *F-Pc* [partly used in L'ange de Nisida]; le duc d'Albe (grand opera, 4, Scribe and Duveyrier), begun Paris, 1839, *I-Mr* (inc), as completed by M. Salvi and others, Rome, 1882, vs (Milan, 1881 and 1882), as completed by T. Schippers, Spoleto, 1959; Ne m'oubliez pas (3, J. H. V. de Saint-Georges), composed Paris, 1842; 7 nos. *F-Pc*; La fidanzata, aria, *Pc*

CANTATAS AND OCCASIONAL WORKS

Il ritorno di primavera (G. Morando), 3 solo vv, orch, April 1818, *I-Bc*

Canto accompagnatorio, SATB, orch, for funeral eulogies of Marchese G. Terzi, Bergamo, 1819, *BGc*

Teresa e Gianfaldoni, 2 solo vv, orch, vs (Rome, 1821)

Cantata ('Questo è il suolo'), S, S, pf, Naples, for royal birth, April 1822, *BGi*

Angelica e Medoro (after Ariosto), Naples, May 1822

L'assunzione di Maria Vergine (G. B. Rusi), T, T, B, vv, orch, Rome, 1822, *BGi*

Aristea (azione pastorale, 1, G. F. Schmidt), 3 female vv, 3 male vv, orch, Naples, S Carlo, 30 May 1823, *Nc*

A Silvio amante, T, orch, ?1823, *BGi*

La fuga di Tisbe, S, pf, composed 15 Oct 1824, *F-Pc*

I voti dei sudditi (azione pastorale, 1, Schmidt), 4vv, orch, Naples, S Carlo, 6 March 1825, copy *I-Nc*

La partenza, vv, orch, Palermo, Carolino, for departure of General delle Favare, July 1825

Cantata, vv, orch, Palermo, Carolino, for king's birthday, 14 Aug 1825

Licenza, vv, orch, Palermo, Carolino, for a gala, 1825 or 1826

Saffo, solo v, vv, orch, before 1828, *BGi*, arr. v, pf (Naples, n.d.)

Il Canto XXXIII della Divina commedia (Dante), solo B, pf, Jan–Feb 1828 (Milan, 1843)

Inno reale (F. Romani), vv, orch, Genoa, for inauguration of Teatro Carlo Felice, 7 April 1828

Il genio dell'armonia (E. Visconti), solo vv, vv, ?orch, Rome, in honour of Pius VIII, 20 Dec 1829, collab. Costaguti and Capranica

Il fausto ritorno (azione allegorico-melodrammatica, D. Gilardoni), vv, orch, Naples, S Carlo, for return of king and queen from Spain, sum. 1830, *Nc*

Cantata, vv, orch, Milan, for wedding of Ferdinand of Austria, 24 Jan 1831, *BGi*

Inno, for wedding of King of Naples, Nov 1832

Il fato (J. Ferretti), Rome, for name day of Count A. Lozano, 13 June 1833

Cantata (E. and C. Carnevali), Rome, for name day of Anna Carnevali, 26 July 1833; private collection H. Steger, Vienna

La preghiera di un popolo (hymn), S, A, T, B, 4vv, orch, Naples, S Carlo, for Ferdinand II, 31 Aug 1837, *Nc*, vs (Milan, 1837)

Cantata (Donizetti), vv, orch, Naples, S Carlo, for royal birth, Aug 1838, *Nc*

Dalla Francia un saluto t'invia, T, B, B, TTBB, orch, pf, composed Paris, May 1841, perf. Bergamo, for Mayr's 78th birthday, 14 June 1841, ed. J. 3. Allitt and U. Schaffer (London and Davos, 1975)

Luge qui legis, vv, orch, Milan, funeral march for P. Marchesi, 1842, vs (Naples, n.d.)

Cristoforo Colombo, Bar, orch, Paris, Opéra, for benefit of P. Barroilhet, March 1845, scena e cavatina *Nc*

Acie Galatea, mentioned by Albinati; Gloria a Dio dei nostri padri, solo B, orch, *Nc*; Inno, for the name day of P. Pangrati, *Nc*; Niso e Violetta, v, orch, sketch *Mr*; Per il nome di Francesco I, mentioned by Albinati; Sacro è il colore, hymn, 2 vv, orch, *Nc*; Uno sguardo (F. Romani), perf Milan; La pietade col nemico or mi sembra qui delitto, solo B, orch, *BGi*

130–32

SACRED

Gloria, D, STB, small orch, 1814, *I-BGi*; Qui tollis, F, T, cl, orch, 7 Sept 1814, pts. [partly autograph] *BGi*; Kyrie, 4vv, orch, 1816, *Nc*; In gloria Dei Patris, c 4vv, 1? Sept 1816, *BGi*; Tantum ergo, TTB, orch, perf. 8 Nov 1816, *Bc*; Cum sancto, vv, orch, 16 July 1817, *F-Pc*; Kyrie, D, 4vv, orch, 1 Aug 1817, *Pc*; Kyrie, D, vv, orch, 1 Aug 1817, *I-Bc*; Gloria, C 3–4vv, orch, 28 May 1818, MS copy and partly autograph pts. *BGi*; Kyrie, c, 3vv, org, 8 Aug 1818, *F-Pc*; Credo, C, 3vv, orch, 1° April 1819, *Pc*; Magnificat, D, S, T, B, STB, orch, May 1819, *Pc*; De torrente, F, ST, orch, June 1819, *Pc*

Laudamus–Gratias, F, S/T, ob/cl, orch, 3 July 1819, *Pc*; Qui tollis–Miserere, 3vv, orch, 8 July 1819, MS property of Donizetti heirs; Gloria, 3vv, orch, 16 July 1819, *I-Nc*; Salve regina, F, solo T, orch, 5 Aug 1819, *F-Pc*; Iste confessor, D, S, T, B, STB, orch, 6 Aug 1819, *I-Nc*; Sicut erat, C, STB, orch, 9 Sept 1819, *F-Pc*; Laudate pueri, D, S, A, T, B, SATB, orch, 8 Oct 1819, *I-Nc*; Beatus vir, F, solo T, ob, cl, small orch, *F-Pc*; Cum Sancto Spiritu, D, 3–4vv, orch, 1819, *Pc*; Dixit, C, S, T, B, vv, orch, 1819, *I-Nc*; Domine ad adjuvandum, C, S, T, B, vv, orch, 1819, *F-Pc*; Domine a dextris, d, solo B, orch, 1819, *I-Nc*

Oro supplex, E, solo B, hn, orch, 1819, *BGi*; Tecum principium, S/T, ob/cl, orch, 1819, *Nc*; Miserere, 4vv, Jan 1820, copy *Nc*; Motet, solo T, cl, small orch, 29 March 1820, *F-Pc*; Miserere, 4 solo vv, vv, orch, 4 April 1820, *I-Rvat*; Tibi soli peccavi, F, solo S, basset-hn, orch, 6 April 1820, *F-Pc*; Tunc acceptabis, D, 4vv, orch, 6 April 1820, pts. *Pc*; Asperges me, Bb, SATB, orch, 8 April 1820, *Pc*; Domine Deus, Eb, solo B, cl, orch, 16 May 1820, *I-Nc*; Gloria, D, S, T, B, vv, orch, 20 May 1820, *Nc*; Kyrie–Christe–Kyrie, F, S, A, T, B, SATB, orch, 20 May 1820, copy and partly autograph pts. *BGi*; Kyrie, 4vv, orch, 20 May 1820, Eb, solo T, hn, vv, orch, 24 May 1820, MS copy and partly autograph pts. *BGi*

Gloria Patri, F, solo S, vn, orch, 28 May 1820, *F-Pc*; Qui sedes–Quoniam, c, solo T, vn, orch, 3 July 1820, *I-Nc*; Laudamus te, A, S, A, T, B, SATB, orch, 6 July 1820, *Nc*; Gratias agimus, G, solo S, fl, orch, 6 July 1820, *F-Pc*; Dominus a dextris, d, solo T, vn, orch, Aug 1820, *Pc*; Credo, C, S, T, B, vv, orch 18 Oct 1820, *I-BGi*; Libera me di sanguinibus, a, solo S, vn, orch, 30 Oct 1820, *F-Pc*; Ne procias, E, solo B, hn, orch, 29 Nov 1820, *I-Nc*; Dixit Dominus, C, S, T, B, vv, orch, 1820, MS copy and autograph pts. *BGi*; Tuba mirum, Eb, solo B, orch, 5 Jan 1821, MS copy and partly autograph pts. *BGi*; Kyrie, 4vv, orch, 26 May 1821, *F-Pc*

Kyrie, F, 4vv, orch, 26 May 1821, *I-Nc*; Miserere, c, 4vv, orch, 18 Jan 1822, *F-Pc*; Credo, D, SATB, orch, perf. 24 Nov 1824, copy by Mayr *I-BGi*; Parafrasi del Christus (S. Gatti), S, A, str orch, 1829, rev. 1844, *Nc*; Requiem, d, S, T, B, SATB, orch, for Bellini, 1835, unfinished, vs (Milan, 1870/R1974); Miserere, g, 3 male solo vv, vv, orch, org 1837, *Rvat*, rev. for solo vv, vv, orch, 1842–3, *Mr* (Milan, 1844 or 1845); Requiem, vv, orch, for Zingarelli, 1837; Requiem, vv, orch, for Abate Fazzini, 7 Nov 1837; Messa di Gloria with Credo, c, 3–4 solo vv, vv, orch, perf. 28 Nov 1837, *Nc*

Ave Maria, off, F, solo S, SATB, str orch, May 1842, *BGi*; vs (Milan, n.d.; Paris, n.d.), full score (New York, n.d.); Gloria Patri, 4vv, orch, 1843, *Nc*; Ave Maria (Dante), S, A, str orch, Jan 1844 (Milan, n.d.); Quoniam ad te, off, solo S, small orch, 1844, *Nc*; Sic transit gloria mundi, 8vv, org, 1844, *F-Pc*; Domine, Dominus noster, off, solo B, orch, Nov 1844, *I-Nc*

(undated)

Ave Maria, F, 2vv, pf, *Ms*; 3 canzoncine sacre, 2vv, pf, *Mc*: 1 Questo cor, quest'alma mia, 2 L'amor di Maria Santissima, 3 Preghiera a Maria Vergine; Christe, solo T, 2 vn, cl, db, *Rsc*; Confitebor, C, STB, bc (org), *BGi*; Credidi, D, STB, bc (org), *BGi*; 3 Credo: STB, orch, *Nc*, Eb, S, A, T, B, 4vv, orch, *Nc*, C, 4vv, orch, *BGi*; Credo breve, C, Crucifixus, F, vv, orch, orch pts. *BGi* (vocal pts. lost); 3 Cum Sancto Spiritu: C, c, 4vv, orch, both *Nc*, D, S, A, T, B, SATB, pts. *BGi*; Dies irae, c, vv, orch, inc. sketch *BGi*; Docebo, D, solo B, small orch, org, pts. (partly autograph) *BGi*

Domine ad adjuvandum, C, S, T, B, vv, wind, org, *F-Pc*; 2 Domine Deus: D, solo B, small orch, *I-Nc*, e, solo B, cl, orch, copy *BGi*; Et vitam, C, 4vv unacc., *Nc*; 3 Gloria: 4vv, orch, *Nc*, C, 4vv, orch, *Nc*, solo vv, vv, orch, *D-Dlb*; Gloria Patri–Sicut erat, C, STB, orch, MS copy and partly autograph pts. *I-BGi*; In convertendo, C, solo B, orch, *F-Pc*; Inno [to St Peter], C, solo T, small orch, *I-Nc*; Judica me Deus (S. Biava: Ps xliii), 2 children's vv, org ad lib, copy *BGi*; 5 Kyrie: c, STB, 2 ob, 2 hn, org, *BGi*, c, STB, 2 ob, 2 hn, org, *BGi*, c, S, T, B, STB, small orch, MS copy and partly autograph pts. *BGi*, d, S, A, T, B, SATB, orch, pts. (partly autograph) *BGi*, d, SATB, orch, pts. (partly autograph) *BGi*

Kyrie–Christe–Kyrie, E-G-c, T, SATB, orch, *BGi*; 2 Laudamus–Gratias: F, solo T, cl, orch, lost, A, 4vv, orch, lost; Laudate pueri, C, 3vv, orch; 2 Miserere: T, T, B, B, TTBB, 2 va, 2 vc, 2 db, org, *F-Pc*, d, 4vv, orch, pts. (some autograph) *I-BGi*; Nisi Dominus, D, solo T, orch, MS copy and partly autograph pts. *BGi*; Pange lingua, F; Preces meae, Eb, solo T, 4vv, solo insts, orch, *BGi*; Qui sedes, C, solo S, vn, small orch, *BGi*; Qui sedes–Quoniam, a, solo S, vn, orch, MS copy and partly autograph pts. *I-BGi*; 3 Qui tollis: Eb, STB, orch, MS copy and partly autograph pts. *I-BGi*; 3 Qui tollis: Eb, STB, orch, MS copy and partly autograph pts. *BGi*, Bb, solo T, small orch, pts. (partly autograph) *BGi*, E, solo T, hn, orch, pts. (partly autograph) *BGi*

Requiem, 3vv, orch, for benediction of tomb of Alfonso della Valle di
Casanova, vs (Naples, n.d.); Salve regina, F, STB, wind insts, vc, db,
F-Pc; Sicut erat, C, 4vv, orch, Pc; 3 Tantum ergo: F, solo T, orch, I-
Nc, D, solo S, org, Mc, Eb, solo T, wind insts, db, pss. BGi; Tecum
principium, F, S, T, cl, orch, partly autograph pts. BGi; Te Deum (S.
Biava), Bb, 2 children's vv, org ad lib, b, copy BGi

VOCAL CHAMBER

3 canzonette (Rome, ?1823) [A]
Collezione di canzonette, 5 songs, 3 duets, 1 qnt (Naples, n.d.) [B]
Donizetti per camera: raccolta di [9] ariette e [3] duettini (Naples, n.d.)
[C]
Nuits d'été à Pausilippe, 6 songs, 6 nocturnes (Naples, 1836; London,
1836; Milan, 1837; Paris, ?1840) [D]
Soirées d'automne à l'Infrascata, 4 songs, 1 duet (Naples, 1837; Milan
1839 [with added duet]; Vienna, 1840s, as Soirées de Paris) [E]
Un hiver à Paris 1838–1839, 5 nos. (Naples, 1839), as Rêveries
napolitaines, with added song (Paris, ?1839; Milan, 1839; Naples,
c1841; Naples, 1841 or 1842 [with 2nd added song]) [F]
Matinée musicale, 6 songs, 2 duets, 2 qts (Naples, 1841; London, 1841;
Paris, 1841; Milan, n.d.) [G]
Inspirations viennoises, 5 songs, 2 duets (Naples, 1842; London, 1842;
Milan, 1842; Paris, n.d.) [H]
Raccolta di [6] canzonette e [2] duettini (Milan, n.d.) [I]
Dernières glânes musicales, 8 songs, 2 duets (Naples, n.d.) [J]
Fiori di sepolcro: [9] melodie postume (Naples, n.d.) [K]
Donizetti: Composizioni da camera, ed. R. Mingardo (Milan, 1961) [L]
6 arie inedite, ed. C. Pestalozza (Milan, 1974) [M]

(solo v, pf)

Addio, romanza (Milan, 1844), J; Addio brunetta, son già lontano,
allegretto scherzoso, in Il sibilo (Naples, 5 Oct 1843), repr. in
Journal of the Donizetti Society, ii (1975), 155; Adieu, tu brise et
pour jamais, romance, F-Pc; Ah, non lasciarmi, no, bell'idol mio
(Metastasio), romanza, Pc; Ah, rammenta, o bella Irene (Metastasio),
cavatina (Milan, 1830 or 1831), L; Ah, si tu voulais, toi que j'aime,
canzone, I-BGi; Aimer ma rose est la sorte de ma vie, romance, I: A
mezzanotte, arietta, D, L; Amiamo, canzonetta (Milan, 1871); Amis
courons chercher la gloire, canzone, F-Pc; Ammore!, canzonetta
napoletana; Amor che a nulla amato, album leaf, 1843, I-BGi

129–30

Amor corrisposto (Bei labbri che amore formò) (Metastasio), A; Amor
marinaro (Me vojo fà na casa), canzonetta napoletana, E, L; Amore e
morte (G. L. Redaelli), arietta, E, L; Amor tiranno (Perchè due cori
insieme) (Metastasio) romanza, K; Amour jaloux, romance, F-Pc;
Anch'io provai le tenere smanie, arietta, unpubd; Antonio Foscarini
(G. B. Niccolini) (Naples, n.d.); A piè del mesto salice, canzonetta,
private collection Marchesi Medici, Rome; Au pied d'une croix,
romance, P ; Au tic-tac des castagnettes, canzonetta or aria, I

Che cangi tempora mai più non spero (Metastasio), andante, M; Che non
mi disse un dì (Metastasio), canzonetta, in Il sibilo (Naples, 2 May
1844), repr in Journal of the Donizetti Society, ii (1975), 159;
Combien la nuit est longue, romance, F-Pc; Come volgeste rapidi,
giorni de' miei primi anni, romanza, Pc; Dell'anno novello, canzonetta, I-Nlp; Del colle in sul pendio, canzonetta, B; Doux souvenirs,
vivez toujours (E. Barateau), mélodie, pubd; D'un genio che m'ac-
cende (Metastasio), B; Ella riposi alcuni istanti almeno, cavatina, M;
Elle n'existe plus, mélodie, in 2 mélodies posthumes (Milan, n.d.); È
mortal (C. Guaita), scena, H, L; E più dell'onda instabile, arietta, Nc;
Faut-il renfermer dans mon âme, mélodie, F-Pc

Fra le belle Irene è quella (Metastasio), canzonetta; Garde les moutons,
romance, pubd; Già presso il termine de' suoi martiri (Metastasio), I-
BGi; Giovanna Gray, romanza, K; Giuro d'amore (Eterno amore e
fe ti giuro), arietta, B, ; Gran Dio, mi manca il cor, F-Pc; Heureuse
qui près de toi (after Sappho), I-BGi (without acc.); I capelli (Questi
capelli bruni), romanza, C; Il barcajuolo (L. Tarantini), D, L; Il
cavallo arabo, bolero or romanza, G; Il crociato (C. Guaita), arietta
or romanza, D; Il giglio e la rosa (Non sdegnar vezzosa Irene),
canzonetta, I, J; Il m'aime encore, doux rêve de mon âme, mélodie, F-
Pc

Il mio ben m'abbandonò, melodia, I-BGi; Il mio grido getto ai venti,
romanza moresca, 1844, M; Il nome (Voi vorreste il nome amato),
arietta, C; Il pegro, canzonette, private collection Marchesa Medici,
Rome; Il pescatore (Batte il bronzo) (A. Ricciardi), K; Il pescatore
(Era l'ora) (A. de Lazières, after Schiller), F, L; Il rimprovero
(Quando da te lontano), romanza, C; Il ritorno del trovatore da
Gerusalemme, F-Pc; Il ritratto (F. Romani), impromptu, private
collection Casa Branca, Milan; Il sorriso è il primo vezzo, canzonetta, B, C

Il sospiro (C. Guaita), melodia, H, L; Il sospiro del gondoliere, barcarola, I-Nc; Il trovatore. BGi; Il trovatore in caricatura (Le troub-

adour à la belle étoile) (L. Borsini), scène bouffe or ballata, F; Io amo
la mestizia, romanza, ?1841 or 1842, private collection Marchesa
Medici, Rome; Io son pazza capricciosa, arietta; J'attends toujours
(E. de Lonlay), romance, pubd; Je vais quitter tout ce que j'aime,
romance, F-Pc; La bohémienne, ballade, Pc; La chanson de l'abeille
(H. Lucas), It. (Milan, 1844), J; La conocchia, arietta or canzone
napoletana, D, L

La corrispondenza amorosa (Cifra d'amore; Billets chéris), romanza, G,
L; La dernière nuit d'un novice (A. Nourrit), ballata, added to F, L;
La farfalla ed il poeta, canzoncina, Pc; La fiancée du timbalier (V.
Hugo), 1843, Pc; La fidanzata, romanza, K; La folle de Sainte-Hélène
(A. Nourrit), ballata, added to 1841 or 1842 Naples repr. of F; La
gondola, canzone; La gondoliera (Vieni la barca è pronta), barcarola,
G; La hart (P. Lacroix), chant diabolique; La longue douleur, pregh-
iera; La lontananza (F. Romani), arietta, E, L; L'amante spagnuolo
(L. Tarantini), arietta or bolero, E; Lamento in morte di V. Bellini
(Venne sull'ale ai zeffiri) (A. Maffei) (Milan, 1836)

Lamento di Cecco Varlungo, album leaf, Donebauer Collection, Prague;
La mère et l'enfant (A. Richomme), mélodie (Milan, 1830), J, L, acc.
arr. orch, copy I-BGi; La mia fanciulla, K; L'amor mio (L'arcano del
core) (F. Romani), K, L; La musulmane (M. Bourges), pubd; La
negra (La nouvelle Ourika), romance, G; La ninna-nonna (La mère au
berceau de son fils) (A. de Lauzières), ballata, F, L; La partenza del
crociato (Puoti), arietta or romanza, C; La passeggiata al lido (Che
bel mar) (Naples, n.d.); La prière (? P. Lacroix); La savoiarda (A.
Broffeni), romanza, K; La speranza; La sultana (L. Tarantini), ballata, F, L; La torre di Biasone (Tarantini), ballata, D

La tradita (oh ingrato, m'inganni), romanza or arietta, C; L'attente,
mélodie; La vendetta (Bedda Eurilla), canzonetta siciliana, C; La voix
d'espoir (M. Cimbal), romance; La zingara (C. Guaita), arietta, H, L;
Le crépuscule (V. Hugo), D, L; Le départ pour la chasse (P. Lacroix),
Bar/B, hn, Nc; Le dernier chant du troubadour, romance, in 2 mélodies posthumes (Milan, n.d.); Le gondolier de l'Adriatique (Crevel
de Charlemagne), nocturne; Le miroir magique (E. Plouvier), chansonette; Léonore (M. Escudier), romance (Milan, 1843), J; Le pauvre
exilé (A. de Leuven), romance

Le petit joueur de la harpe (P. Lacroix), Nc; Le petit montagnard, K; Le
pirate (S. Saint Étienne), mélodie, in Lyre française (Mainz, n.d.); Le
renégat (E. Pacini), scène, It. (Milan, 1835); Les revenants (Lacroix),
aria, F-Pc; Les yeux noirs et les yeux bleus (E. Monnier), romance;
L'étrangère, romance, private collection Marchesa Medici, Rome; Le

violon de Crémone (E. T. A. Hoffmann), romance, Pc; L'ora del
ritorno (Guaita), arietta, H; Lu trademiento (Aje, tradetore, tu m'haje
lassata), canzone napoletana, I, L; Malvina (G. Vitali), scène
dramatique (Milan, 1845), M; Malvina la bella, romanza, in Il sibillo
(Naples, 28 Dec 1843), repr. in Journal of the Donizetti Society, ii
(1975), 156; Marie enfin quitte l'ouvrage, romance, Pc

M'è Dio il tuo signore (Oh quanto in me tu puoi), G; Mentre del caro
lido, canzonetta, private collection of Marchesa Medici, Rome;
Minvela (Quando verrà sul colle), canzonetta or romanza, C; Mon
enfant, mon seul espoir, romance, Pc; Morir per te!, arietta (Naples,
n.d.); Nice, st'occhiuzzi càlali, canzonetta, private collection of
Marchesa Medici, Rome; Noé (J. de Boutellier), scène du déluge,
1839, pubd; Non amerò che te (after G. Vitali), romanza (Milan,
1842 or 1843); Non amo che te, romanza; Non giova il sospirar
(Metastasio), canzonetta veneziana, A

Non m'ami più (L'ingratitude) (Guaita), H; Non v'è più barbaro di chi
non sente (Metastasio), canzonetta, private collection of Marchesa
Medici, Rome; Non v'è nume, non v'è fato, romanza (Milan, n.d.);
N'ornerà la bruna chioma (Romani), scena e cavatina, L; O anime
affanate, venite a noi parlar (Dante: Divina commedia), Pc; Occhio
nero incendiator, canzonetta, I; O fille que l'ennui chagrine, romance,
Pc; Oh, Cloe, delizia di questo core, canzonetta, private collection of
Marchesa Medici, Rome; Oh, je rêve d'une étrangère plus douce que
l'enfant qui dors, Pc

On vous a peint l'amour (Lacroix), romance, Pc; Or che in cielo, barcar-
ola, Strenna musicale, i (1837); Or che la notte invita, canzonetta, Pc;
Oui, je sais votre indifférence, Pc; Oui, ton dieu c'est le mien (M.
Michonne), romance, Pc; Ov'è la voce magica, melodia, 1844, M;
Pace! canzonetta (Naples, n.d.); Pas d'autre amour que toi (E.
Barateau), mélodie; Perché due cori, romanza, I-Nc; Perché mai,
Nigella amata, insensibile tu sei?, romanza, F-Pc; Perché se mia tu sei
(Metastasio), romanza, Pc; Philis plus avare que tendre, romance, Pc

Più che non m'ama un angelo (L'amor funesto), romanza, also arr. with
vc/hn, 1842, L; Plus ne m'est rien, romance, Pc; Pourquoi me dire
qu'il vous aime, romance, Pc; Preghiera (Una lagrima), G, L; Quand
un soupçon mortel, romance, Pc; Quand je vis que j'étais trahie, scène
religieuse, with pf, org, Pc; Quando il mio ben io rivedrò, canzonetta,
private collection of Marchesa Medici, Rome; Quando morte coll'or-
rido artiglio, prayer, Pc; Quanto mio ben t'adoro, canzonetta, private
collection of Marchesa Medici, Rome; Quel nome se ascolto
(Metastasio), romanza

Questo mio figlio è un fiorellin d'amore, berceuse, in Album du gaulois: oeuvres inédites, i (Paris, 1869); Qui sospirò, là rise, aria, copy, with autograph annotations, J-Nc; Rendimi il core, o barbaro, canzonetta, A: Rose che ne di spiegaste, romanza, F-Pc; Se a te d'intorno scherza, romanza, in Il sibillo (Naples, 4 April 1844), repr. in Journal of the Donizetti Society, ii (1975), 158; Se lontan, ben mio, tu sei (Metastasio), canzonetta; Se talor più nol rammento, cavatina; Seul sur la terre, album leaf or romance, private collection of C. Lozzi, Bologna; Si o no, canzonetta giocosa, J; Si tanto sospiri, ti lagni d'amore, Pc; Si tu m'as fait à ton image, romance, Pc

Sorgesti alfin, aurora desiata, aria, I-Nc; Sospiri, aneliti che m'opprimete, canzonetta, private collection of Marchesa Medici, Rome; Sovra il campo della vita, larghetto, M: Sovra il remo sta curvato (L. Mira), barcarola, in Il sibillo (Naples, 22 Feb 1844), repr. in Journal of the Donizetti Society, ii (1975), 157; Spunta il dì, l'ombra spari, romanza, F-Pc; Su l'onda tremula ride la luna, B; Su questi allor, canzonetta, private collection of Marchesa Medici, Rome; Taci invan, mia cara Jole, romanza, 1835; T'aspetto ancor (Nel tuo cammin fugace), romanza (Milan, 1843), J; Te dire adieu (G. Vaëz), romanza Te voglio beneassaje, canzone napoletana, often attrib. Donizetti; Tengo no n'namurato, canzonetta napoletana, I; Troppo vezzosa è la ninfa bella, canzone, I-BGi; Trova un sol mia bella Clori (Metastasio), collection of Count G. B. Camozzi-Vertova, Bergamo; Trova un sol mia bella Clori (Metastasio), Toscanini collection, New York [different setting]; Tu me chiedi se t'adoro, arietta, 1840, F-Pc; Una prece sulla mia tomba (Non priego mai) (Redaelli), canto elegiaco or romanza, C

Una tortora innocente, romanza, I-BGi; Una vergine donzella per amore, romanza, F-Pc; Un bacio di speranza, romanza (Milan, 1845); Un coeur pour abri (A. Richomme), scène; Un detto di speranza, romanza, J; Uno sguardo (F. Romani), romanza, Casa Branca, Milan; V'era un dì che il cor beato, romanza, I-Ms; Vien ti conforta, o misera, F-Pc; Vision (E. Plouvier), mélodie; Viva il matrimonio (L. Tarantini), cavatina buffa, bass (Milan, 1843)

(duets)

Ah, non lasciarmi, no (Metastasio), I-Nc; Amor, voce del cielo, (Tarantini), notturno, D; Armida e Rinaldo (Tasso), F-Pc; Canzonetta con l'eco (Per valli, per boschi), 27 Aug 1817, I-BGi; C'est le printemps (E. Plouvier), chansonette-valse; Che cangi tempra

mai più non spero (Metastasio), unacc., BGi; Che vuoi di più? (Guaita), F: Duettino, S, S, Nc; Duet, S, S, F-Pc; Duet, 1822, collection of C. Lczzi, Bologna; Godi diletta ingrata nell'ingannarmi tu, canzonetta, P-; Ha negli occhi un tale incanto (Metastasio), B

Héloïse et Abélard (Crevel de Charlemagne), duo historique; Ho perduto il mio tesoro (Metastasio), B: I bevitori (Tarantini), notturno or brindisi, D; I due carcerati, I-Mc; I fervidi desiri (Da me che vuoi, che brami), C; Il fiore (Qui dove mercè negasti), duettino pastorale, E; Il giuramento (PalazzoEb), notturno, D; Io d'amore, o Dio, mi moro (?Metastasio), B, C; I sospiri (Ti sento, sospir) (Metastasio), C; L'addio (Dunque addio) (F. Romani), F; L'addio (Io resto), G; La gelosia (Querelle d'amour), scherzo, G, L; L'aito di Bice (F. Puoti), notturno, D

La passeggiata al lido (Ch: bel mar), J; L'aurora (Tarantini), notturno, D; La voce del core (T'intendo, si, mio cor) (Metastasio), C; Les napolitains (Crevel de Charlemagne), nocturne; L'incostanza di Irene (Metastasio), 1826, added to E; L'ultimo rimprovero (O crudel che il mio pianto), I, J; Lumi rei del mio martire, canzonetta, private collection of Marchesa Medici, Rome; Non mi sprezzar Licori (Metastasio), I-BGi; Pr-destinazione (Guaita), H; Quegli sguardi e quegli accenti, BGi; Se mai turbo il tuo riposo (Metastasio), Nc

Sempre più t'amo, mio bel tesoro, F-Pc; Sempre sarò costante (Metastasio) (Rome, n.d.); Se tu non vedi tutto il mio cor (Metastasio), copies Pc,J-Nc; Si soffre una tiranna (Metastasio), BGi; Sull'onda cheta e bruna, barcarola (Milan, 1838); Uno sguardo ed una voce (Une nuit sur l'eau) (Palazzo), notturno, D; Vedi là sulla collina, Mc; Vuoi casa ti, duetto buffo, 2B

(3-5vv)

Ah che il destino (Metastasio), (S, S, T)/(S, S), BGi; Cede la mia costanza, Irene, al tuo rigor (Metastasio), S, A, T, B, 1820, F-Pc; Clori infedel, S, A, B, I-Rsc; Di gioja di pace la dolce speranza, Moldenhauer Archive, Seattle; Finchè fedele tu mi sei stata, canzonetta, 4vv, 5 May 1817, F-Pc; Io morrò, sonata è l'ora, 3vv, Pc; La campana, T, T, B, B, G Lumi rei del mio martire, madrigale, 4vv, 12 June 1817, I-BGi; Qui s-a il male, trio, Nc; Rataplan (La partenza del reggimento), T, T, B, B, G, K: Se schiudi il labbro, divertimento, S, S, T, T, B, unacc.. B: Strofe di Byron, S, A, B, B, Mc; Sien l'onde placide, Per noi la vita Ma pci passati stragi e orror

ORCHESTRAL

Sinfonias: C, 12 June 1816, *I-Bc*; Sinfonia concertante, D, 17 Sept 1816, ed. G. Piccioli (Milan, 1937); C, 24 Nov 1816, *BGi*; D, 29 March 1817, *F-Pc*; g, wind insts, 19 April 1817, ed. D. Townsend (New York, 1967), ed. B. Päuler (Zürich, 1970); D, 10 Sept 1817, *Pc*; 'La partenza', 25 Oct 1817, *Pc*; D, 17 Dec 1817, *Pc*; d, on death of A. Capuzzi, 1818, *Pc*; 'L'incendio', perf. Bergamo, 19 March 1819, *Pc*; D, ?1832 or 1833, inc., *I-BGi* [incl. themes used in Il furioso and L'elisir d'amore]; on themes by Bellini, 1836, *F-Pc*, arr. pf (Milan, 1836); D, 25 non-autograph pts. *I-BGi*; Adagio and Minuet from a sym., *F-Pc*

Sinfonia to the cantata In morte M. Malibran, perf. Milan, 17 March 1837, other movts by Pacini, Mercadante, Coppola, Vaccai; *I-Mr*, vs (Milan, 1837 or 1838) 127

Concs.: Concertino, G, eng hn, orch, perf. Bergamo, 19 June 1817, ed. R. Meylan (Frankfurt am Main, 1966); Cl Conc., Eb, private collection A. Marinelli, Bergamo; Conc., vn, vc, orch, *F-Pc*; Conc., for unspecified inst, *Pc*; untitled work, Bb, cl, small orch, *I-BGi* 133

Other works: Introduzione, str orch, 1829, ed. U. Schaffer (London and Davos, 1975); Gran marcia militare imperiale, for the Sultan of Turkey, arr. pf (Paris, n.d.), arr. sym. band by D. Townsend (n.p., 1967); March, Aug 1840, *F-Pc*; Preludio, for an opera, *Pc*; Rataplan, *I-Mr*

CHAMBER

Str qts: no.1, Eb, 26 Dec 1817; no.2, A; no.3, c; no.4, D, 27 July 1818; no.5, e; no.6, g; f, 6 May 1819; Bb, 26 May 1819; d, 22 Jan 1821; g, 26 Jan 1821 (without 4th movt); C, 12 March 1821; C, 15 March 1821; A, 19 April 1821; D, 1825; e, 1836; D, F, b, all dated 1819-21 by Zavadini; all in Gaetano Donizetti: 18 quartetti, ed. Istituto italiano per la storia della musica (Rome and Buenos Aires, ?1948) [defective edn.]; C, *F-Pc* (without last movt); inc. 1st movt, a, *Pc*, both dated 1819-21 by Zavadini

Other works: Sextet, 2 vn, va/vc, fl, 2 hn, lost; Qnt, C, 2 vn, 2 va, vc, 1st movt *I-BGi*; Qnt (Introduzione and Largo affettuoso), 2 vn, va, vc, db, MS property of Donizetti heirs; Qnt, C, 2 vn, va, vc, gui, *Nc*; Pf Trio, Eb, 12 Nov 1817, copy *BGi*; Fl Sonata, c, 15 May 1819, ed. R. Meylan (Frankfurt am Main, 1969); Vn Sonata, f, 26-7 Oct 1819, *BGi*; Vc Sonata, D, copy *BGi*; Ob Sonata, ed. R. Meylan (Frankfurt am Main, 1966); Variations, Db, vn, pf, *BGi*; Scherzo, D, vn, pf, 1826, on 27 themes from Donizetti operas, *BGi*; Larghetto and Allegro, g, vn, harp, ed. R. Meylan as Sonata (Frankfurt am Main, 1970); Largo, vn, vc, pf, d, copy *BGi*; Larghetto, fl, bn, pf, ed. B. Päuler as Trio (Zürich, 1971); Larghetto and Polonaise, vn, acc. inc., *F-Pc*; Largo, g, vc, pf, ed. U. Schaffer (London and Davos, 1975); untitled work, Bb, wind insts, org, *I-BGi*; Studio no.1, Bb cl, 1821, ed. R. Meylan (Frankfurt am Main, 1970); Duetto, Bb, 2 cl, ed. B. Päuler (Zürich, 1971)

PIANO

Pastorale, E, 1813, *I-BGi*; Sinfonia no.3, A, 22 Oct 1813, *BGi*; Sinfonia, C, 19 Nov 1816, *Bc*; Un capriccio in sinfonia, e, 15 Aug 1817, *BGi*; 2 motivi del celebre Mo Paer messi in suonata, 7 Oct 1817, *BGi*; Variazioni sopra la canzonetta del bardo nell'Alfredo di Mayr (Milan, 1820); Rondò, D, Feb 1825, *BGi*; Larghetto, C, 30 Dec 1834, *Mc*; La vénitienne, waltz (Milan, 1843)

Undated: Adagio e Allegro, G; Allegro, f, ed. R. Meylan (Frankfurt am Main, 1971); Allegro vivace, C; Allegro vivace, G; Fugue, g; Invito, waltz; Larghetto, theme and variations, Eb; Piece on theme of 'Una furtiva lagrima', g; Presto, F; La ricordanza, adagio sentimentale, Eb; Sinfonia, D; Waltz; Variations. G; Variations. E: all *BGi*; Sinfonia. D, *Nc*; Waltz, *F-Pc*; Giuseppina, polka-mazurka (Naples, n.d.)

4 hands: Il Capitan Battaglia, sonata, Eb, 1819; Polacca, D, 1819; Sonata, C, 31 March 1819; Sonata, D, 12 Oct 1819; Sinfonia no.2, d, 28 March 1820; Sonata, a, 25 April 1820; Una delle più matte, C, 17 May 1820; untitled piece, C, 25 Feb 1821; Waltz, 1844: all *I-BGi*

4 hands, dated 1813-21 by Zavadini: 2 Allegro, D, E; Allegro moderato, A; Allegro vivace, C; Il genio di GDM, G; L'inaspettata, Eb; La lontananza, e; Larghetto, G; Marcia lugubre, f; La solita sonata, F; Sonata no.3 a 4 sanfe, F; Sonata, Bb; Sonata, D; Sonata no.3, F; all *BGi* 94, 127, 133

OTHER WORKS

Student vocal essays, etc: Ah! quel Guglielmo, sextet, S, S, T, T, B, B, orch, 1812, *Nc*; Ognun dice che le donne, aria, solo B, orch, 20 March 1815, *F-Pc*; Guarda che bianca luna (J. Vittorelli), anacreontica, v, orch, 30 March 1815, *Pc*; Perchè quell'alma ingrata, duet, S, T, orch, 27 Sept 1816, *I-Nc*; Amor mio nume, aria, 1816; Ti sovvenga amato bene, aria, S, orch, 10 May 1817, *Nc*; Isabella ormai mi rendi, trio, T, T, B, orch, 1818, *Nc*; Se bramate che vi sposi, duet, MS property of Donizetti heirs; Taci, tu cerchi invano, duet, S, S, orch, *Nc*; Sposo lo so, recit, Da quel piano difendemi, duet, S, B, small orch, *Nc*; Che avenne che fu, recit, Solo per te sospiro, romanza, T, small orch, *BGi*

Student exercises: Fugues and counterpoint exercises, some 1815-17, *BGi*, *Nc*

Didactic: Solfeggi, Mez, pf, *Nc*; Vocalizzi o gorgheggi, *F-Pc*

BIBLIOGRAPHY

CATALOGUES

Ricordi di Gaetano Donizetti esposti nella mostra centenaria tenutasi in Bergamo nell'agosto–settembre 1897, raccolti da Giuseppe e Gaetano Donizetti, collezione di proprietà dei fratelli Giuseppe e Gaetano Donizetti (Bergamo, 1897, enlarged 2/1897)

C. Malherbe: *Centenaire de Gaetano Donizetti: catalogue bibliographique de la section française à l'exposition de Bergamo* (Paris, 1897)

G. Zavadini: *Catalogo generale: Museo donizettiano di Bergamo* (Bergamo, 1936)

V. Sacchiero and others: *Il Museo donizettiano di Bergamo* (Bergamo, 1970)

LETTERS

A. Eisner-Eisenhof, ed.: *Lettere di Gaetano Donizetti* (Bergamo, 1897)

F. Schlitzer: 'Curiosità epistolari inedite nella vita teatrale di Gaetano Donizetti', *RMI*, 1 (1948), 273

G. Zavadini: *Donizetti: vita, musiche, epistolario* (Bergamo, 1948)

G. Barblan and F. Walker: 'Contributo all'epistolario di Gaetano Donizetti: lettere inedite o sparse', *Studi donizettiani*, i (1962)

F. Speranza, ed.: *Studi donizettiani*, ii (1972)

'An Unpublished Donizetti Letter', *Journal of the Donizetti Society*, ii (1975), 271

J. Commons: 'Una corrispondenza tra Alessandro Lanari e Donizetti (45 lettere inedite)', *Studi donizettiani*, iii (1978), 9–74

F. Lippmann: 'Autographe Briefe Rossinis und Donizettis in der Bibliothek Massimo, Rom', *AnMc*, no.19 (1980), 330

LIFE AND WORKS

F. Regli: *Gaetano Donizetti e le sue opere* (Turin, 1850)

G. Bonetti: *Gaetano Donizetti* (Naples, 1926)

G. Donati-Pettèni: *Donizetti* (Milan, 1930, 3/1947)

G. Gavazzeni: *Gaetano Donizetti: vita e musiche* (Milan, 1937)

G. Monaldi: *Gaetano Donizetti* (Turin, 1938)

G. Zavadini: *Donizetti: vita, musiche, epistolario* (Bergamo, 1948)

L. Bossi: *Donizetti* (Brescia, 1956)

A. Geddo: *Donizetti: l'uomo, le musiche* (Bergamo, 1956)

H. Weinstock: *Donizetti and the World of Opera in Italy, Paris and Vienna in the First Half of the Nineteenth Century* (London, 1964)

W. Ashbrook: *Donizetti* (London, 1965)

G. Barblan: 'Donizetti', *LaMusicaE*

W. Ashbrook: *Donizetti and his Operas* (Cambridge, 1982) [incl. full bibliography]

Donizetti

BIOGRAPHICAL STUDIES AND MEMOIRS

L. Stierlin: *Biographie von Gaetano Donizetti* (Zurich, 1852)

T. Ghezzi: 'Ricordi su Donizetti', *Omnibus* (Naples, 7 March 1860)

L. Escudier: *Mes souvenirs* (Paris, 1863)

F. Cicconetti: *Vita di Gaetano Donizetti* (Rome, 1864)

A. Bellotti: *Donizetti e i suoi contemporanei* (Bergamo, 1866)
Cenni biografici di Gaetano Donizetti raccolti da un vecchio dilettante di buona memoria (Milan, 1874)

F. Alborghetti and M. Galli: *Gaetano Donizetti e G. Simone Mayr: notizie e documenti* (Bergamo, 1875)

P. Cominazzi: 'Sorsa attraverso le opere musicali di Gaetano Donizetti: reminiscenze', *La fama* (1875), no.35, p.137; no.36, p.141; no.37, p.149; no.38, p.149; no.39, p.153; no.40, p.157

G. Duprez: *Souvenirs d'un chanteur* (Paris, 1880)

E. Branca: *Felice Romani ed i più riputati maestri di musica del suo tempo* (Turin, Florence and Rome, 1882)

G. Cottrau: *Lettres d'un mélomane* (Naples, 1885)

G. Capeli: 'La calotta cranica di Donizetti', *Archivio italiano per le malattie nervose e più particolarmente per le alienazioni mentali* (1887)

A. Gabrielli: 'Le case di Donizetti a Napoli', *Fanfulla della domenica*, liii (1893)

E. Verzino: *Contributo ad una biografia di Gaetano Donizetti* (Bergamo, 1896)

C. Ricci: 'Donizetti a Bologna: appunti e documenti', *Gaetano Donizetti: numero unico nel primo centenario della sua nascita 1797–1897*, ed. P. Bettòli (Bergamo, 1897), 10

A. Cametti: *Un poeta melodrammatico romano: appunti e notizie in gran parte inedite sopra Jacopo Ferretti e i musicisti del suo tempo* (Milan, 1898)

D. G. Antonini: 'Un episodio emotivo di Gaetano Donizetti', *RMI*, (1900), 518

A. Gabrielli: *Gaetano Donizetti* (Rome and Turin, 1904)

A. Cametti: *Donizetti a Roma* (Turin, 1907)

A. Pougin: 'Donizetti', *Musiciens du XIXe siècle* (Paris, 1911)

U. Riva: 'Un bergomasco (Giuseppe Donizetti pascià), riformatore della musica in Turchia', *Rivista di Bergamo*, i (1922), 349

G. Caversazzi: *Gaetano Donizetti: la casa dove nacque, la famiglia, l'inizio della malattia* (Bergamo, 1924)

A. Codignola: *I fratelli Ruffini: lettere di G. e A. Ruffini alle madre dall'esilio francese e svizzero* (Genoa, 1925–31)

G. Caversazzi: *Gaetano Donizetti: discorso a cura della Congregazione di carità* (Bergamo, 1926)

Bibliography

F. Abbiati: 'La musica in Turchia con Giuseppe Donizetti, pascià, *Bergomum*, xxii (1928), Nov

G. Donati-Pettèni: 'Attraverso le biografie donizettiane', *Rivista di Bergamo*, viii (1929), 389

——: *Studi e documenti donizettiani* (Bergamo, 1929)

G. Rota-Basoni Scotti: 'Le memorie donizettiane della Baronessa Basoni Scotti', *Rivista di Bergamo*, viii (1929)

T. Oliario: 'La malattia ed i medici di Gaetano Donizetti', *Minerva medica*, xxix (1938)
Donizetti l'uomo: Bergamo 1946–8

O. Tiby: 'Gaetano Donizetti a Palermo', *Annuario dell'Accademia di Santa Cecilia* (1949–51); pubd separately (Rome, 1951)

F. Schlitzer: *L'ultima pagina della vita di Gaetano Donizetti da un carteggio inedito dell'Accademia Chigiana*, Quaderni dell'Accademia Chigiana, xxviii (Siena, 1953)

A. Damerini: 'Vita tragica di Donizetti', *Melodramma*, i–ii (1954)

F. Schlitzer: *Donizetti, G.: episodi e testimonianze F. Fiorentino* (Naples, 1954)

——: *Mondo teatrale dell'ottocento* (Naples, 1954), 49

——: *L'eredità di Donizetti: da carteggi e documenti dell'archivo dell'Accademia Chigiana*, Quaderni dell'Accademia Chigiana, xxx (Siena, 1954)

O. Tiby: *Il Real Teatro Carolino e l'ottocento musicale palermitano* (Florence, 1957)

G. Zavadini: *Donizetti l'uomo* (Bergamo, 1958)

A. Geddo: 'Para una iconografia de Donizetti', *Boletin de programas*, xx (1961), 86

F. Walker: *The Man Verdi* (London, 1962)

H. Weinstock: 'Chi era Marianna Donizetti?', *Studi donizettiani*, ii (1972), 41

G. Barblan: 'Donizetti in Naples', *Journal of the Donizetti Society*, i (1974), 105

L. Mikoletzky: 'Gaetano Donizetti und der Kaiserhof zu Wien: neue Dokumente', *AnMc*, no.14 (1974), 411

J. Allitt: *Donizetti and the Tradition of Romantic Love: a Collection of Essays on a Theme* (London, 1975)

G. Pillon: 'I diarii della follia di Gaetano Donizetti', *Il borghese* (31 July 1977), 1073, 1085

SPECIALIZED CRITICAL STUDIES

H. Berlioz: '"La fille du régiment"', *Journal des débats* (16 Feb 1840); repr. in *Les musiciens et la musique* (Paris, 1903), 145

P. Scudo: 'Donizetti et l'école italienne depuis Rossini', *Critique et*

147

littérature musicales (Paris, 1850), 75

H. F. Chorley: 'Donizetti's Operas', *Thirty Years' Musical Recollections*, i (London, 1862), 153

P. Bettòli: 'Le opere di Gaetano Donizetti: errori e lacune', *Gaetano Donizetti: numero unico nel primo centenario della sua nascita 1797–1897*, ed. P. Bettòli (Bergamo, 1897), 26

A. Calzado: *Donizetti e l'opera italiana in Spagna* (Paris, 1897)

A. Centelli: 'La musica di Donizetti a Venezia', *Gaetano Donizetti: numero unico nel primo centenario della sua nascita 1797–1897*, ed. P. Bettòli (Bergamo, 1897), 13

C. Malherbe: 'Le centenaire de Donizetti et l'exposition de Bergame', *RMI*, iv (1897), 707

A. Pougin: 'Les opéras de Donizetti en France', *Gaetano Donizetti: numero unico nel primo centenario della sua nascita 1797–1897*, ed. P. Bettòli (Bergamo, 1897), 20

E. C. Verzino: *Le opere di Gaetano Donizetti: contributo allo loro storia* (Bergamo and Milan, 1897)

E. Prout: 'Auber's "Le philtre" and Donizetti's "L'elisir d'amore": a Comparison', *MMR*, xxx (1900), 25, 49, 73

W. J. Kleefeld: *Don Pasquale von Gaetano Donizetti* (Leipzig, 1901)

A. Lazzari: 'Giovanni Ruffini, Gaetano Donizetti e il *Don Pasquale*', *Rassegna nazionale* (1, 16 Oct 1915)

L. Miragoli: *Il melodramma italiana nell'Ottocento* (Rome, 1924)

A. Cametti: *La musica teatrale a Roma cento anni fa: 'Olivo e Pasquale' di Donizetti* (Rome, 1927)

G. Donati-Pettèni: 'Una visita al Museo Donizettiano di Bergamo', *Emporium*, lxv/2 (1927), 17

——: *L'Istituto musicale Gaetano Donizetti* (Bergamo, 1928)

——: *Studi e documenti donizettiani* (Bergamo, 1929)

R. Barbiera: 'Chi ispirò la "Lucia" ', *Vite ardenti nel teatro (1700–1900)* (Milan, 1930)

A. Cametti: 'La musica teatrale a Roma cento anni fa: "Il corsaro" di Pacini, il "Furioso" e "Torquato Tasso" di Donizetti, "La sonnambula" di Bellini, la "Norma" di Bellini', *Reggia Accademia di Santa Cecilia, Roma: annuario* (1930–31), 445–89; (1933–4), 365–421

C. B. Micca: 'Giovanni Ruffini e il libretto del Don Pasquale', *Rivista di Bergamo*, x (1931), 537

E. Appelius: 'Il centenario dell' "Elisir d'amore" ', *Rivista di Bergamo*, xi (1932), 195

G. Gavazzeni: 'Donizetti e l'Elisir d'amore', *RaM*, vi (1933), 44

G. Roncaglia: 'Il centenario di "Lucia" ', *RMI*, xl (1936), 119

G. Pinetti: *Le opere di Donizetti nei teatri di Bergamo* (Bergamo, 1942)

I. Pizzetti: 'Un autografo di Donizetti', *La musica italiana dell' Ottocento* (Turin, 1947), 231 [on *Lucia di Lammermoor*]

Bibliography

M. Baccaro: 'Lucia di Lammermoor' prima al S. Carlo di Napoli (Naples, 1948)

G. Barblan: 'La "Messa di Requiem" di Gaetano Donizetti', RaM, xviii (1948), 192

——: L'opera di Donizetti nell'età romantica (Bergamo, 1948)

M. Rinaldi: 'Antonio e Pasquale', La Scala (1950), July

A. Capri: 'Linda di Chamounix', La Scala (1952), May, 46

A. Pironti: 'Duca d'Alba', La Scala (1952), no.34, p.38

N. Gallini: 'Inediti donizettiani: ultima scena dell'opera "Caterina Cornaro" ', RMI, lv (1953), 257

B. Dal Fabbro: 'Donizetti e l'opera buffa', I bidelli del Valhalla (Florence, 1954)

A. della Corte: 'Un secolo di critica per l'opera di Donizetti', Melodramma, i–ii (1954)

F. Sacchi: 'Sensazionale tragedia in Scozia', Melodramma, i–ii (1954)

F. Schlitzer: Mondo teatrale dell'ottocento (Naples, 1954)

B. Becherini: 'Il "Don Sebastiano" di Donizetti al XVIII maggio musicale fiorentino', RBM, ix (1955), 143

E. Dent: 'Donizetti: an Italian Romantic', Fanfare for Ernest Newman (London, 1955), 86; repr. in Journal of the Donizetti Society, ii (1975), 249

M. P. Boyé: 'Donizetti et l'opéra italien', Revue de la Méditerranée (1956–8), nos.73–83

A. Geddo: 'Donizetti: ordine fra i suoi quartetti', La Scala (1956), no.77, pp.63, 111

M. Ballini: 'Ritorno dell' "Anna Bolena" ', La Scala (1957), no.89, p. 17

U. Cattini: 'Note sul Roberto Devereux', Ricordiana (1957), Nov

G. Barblan: 'Un personaggio di Cervantes nel melodramma italiano: "Il furioso all'isola di San Domingo" ', Musicisti lombardi e emiliani, Chigiana, xv (1958), 85

F. Walker: 'The Librettist of "Don Pasquale" ', MMR, lxxxviii (1958), 219

G. Barblan: 'Il "Giovedì grasso" e gli svaghi "Farsaioli" di Donizetti', Musicisti piemontesi e liguri, Chigiana, xvi (1959), 109

P. Berri: 'Il librettista del "Don Pasquale": leggende, ingiustizie, plagi', La Scala (1959), no.110, p.19

J. Commons: 'An Introduction to "Il duca d'alba" ', Opera, x (1959), 421

——: 'Emilia di Liverpool', ML, xl (1959), 207

G. Roncaglia: 'Ricuperato anche "Il furioso all'isola di S. Domingo" ', La Scala (1959), no.115, pp.34, 69

G. Barblan: 'Una donizettiana farsa di costume: "Le convenienze e le inconvenienze teatrali"', Le celebrazioni del 1963, Chigiana, xx (1963), 217

Donizetti

H. Liebsch: 'Eine Oper – zwei Texte: textkritische Bemerkungen zu Donizettis "Don Pasquale" ', *Musik und Gesellschaft*, xiii (1963), 91

G. Barblan: 'Alla ribalta un'ottocentesca tragedia lirica: "Parisina d'Este" di Donizetti', *Chigiana*, xxi (1964), 207–38
——: 'Características corais do "D. Sebastiano" de Donizetti', *Estudos italianos em Portugal*, xxiii (1964), 203
——: 'Attualità di Donizetti', *L'opera italiana in musica . . . in onore di Eugenio Gara* (Milan, 1965), 59
——: *La favorita: mito e realità* (Venice, 1965)

F. Cella: 'Indagini sulle fonte francesi dei libretti di Gaetano Donizetti', *Contributi dell'Istituto di filologia moderna*, Fr. ser., iv (1966), 343–590

F. Lippmann: 'Die Melodien Donizettis', *AnMc*, no.3 (1966), 80–113

G. Barblan: 'Lettura di un'opera dimenticata: "Pia de' Tolomei" di Donizetti (1836)', *Chigiana*, xxiv (1967), 221

R. Celletti: 'Il vocalismo italiano da Rossini a Donizetti', *AnMc*, no.5 (1968), 267; vii (1969), 214–47

F. Lippmann: 'Gaetano Donizetti', *Vincenzo Bellini und die italienische opera seria seiner Zeit*, AnMc, no.6 (1969), 304

E. de Mura: *Enciclopedia della canzone napoletana* (Naples, 1969)

P. Rattalino: 'Il processo compositivo nel "Don Pasquale" di Donizetti', *NRMI*, iv (1970), 51, 263

E. H. Bleiler: *Lucia di Lammermoor by Gaetano Donizetti* (New York, 1972) [incl. lib and trans., introductory essays]

W. Dean: 'Some Echoes of Donizetti in Verdi's Operas', *3° congresso internazionale di studi verdiani: Milano 1972*, 122

J. Freeman: 'Donizetti in Palermo and *Alahor in Granata*', *JAMS*, xxv (1972), 240

F. Speranza, ed.: *Studi donizettiani*, ii (1972) [incl. W. Ashbrook: 'La composizione de "La favorita" '; P. Rattolino: 'Unità drammatica della "Linda di Chamounix" '; H. Weinstock: 'Chi era Marianna Donizetti?']

P. Schmid: '*Maria Stuarda* and *Buondelmonte*', *Opera*, xxiv (1973), 1060

W. Dean: 'Donizetti's Serious Operas', *PRMA*, c (1973–4), 123

F. Lippmann: 'Der italienische Vers und der musikalische Rhythmus: zum Verhältnis von Vers und Musik in der italienischen Oper des 19. Jahrhunderts', *AnMc*, no.12 (1973), 253–369; no.14 (1974), 324–410; no.15 (1975), 298–333

L. Mikoletzky: 'Gaetano Donizetti und der Kaiserhof zu Wien: neue Dokumente', *AnMc*, no.14 (1974), 411

Journal of the Donizetti Society, i (1974) [incl. J. Schaap: 'Il burgomastro di Saardam'; J. Watts: 'L'ajo nell'imbarazzo']

Journal of the Donizetti Society, ii (1975) [incl. G. Barblan: 'Maria di

Bibliography

Rohan'; J. Commons: 'The Authorship of "I piccioli virtuosi ambulanti"', 'Unknown Donizetti Items in the Neapolitan Journal "Il sibilo"'; J. Guaricci: 'Lucrezia Borgia'; R. Leavis: '*La favorite* and *La favorita*: One Opera, Two Librettos'; M. F. Messenger: 'Donizetti, 1840: 3 "French" Operas and their Italian Counterparts']

F. Lippmann: 'Verdi und Donizetti', *Opernstudien: Anna Amalie Abert zum 65. Geburtstag* (Tutzing, 1975), 153

I° convegno internazionale di studi donizettiani: Bergamo 1975 [incl. R. Angermüller: 'Gli anni viennesi di Donizetti'; F. L. Arruga: 'La drammaturgia donizcttiana'; W. Ashbrook: 'La struttura drammatica nella produzione di Donizetti dopo il 1838'; L. Baldacci: 'Donizetti e la storia'; G. Bezzola: 'Aspetti del clima culturale italiano nel periodo donizettiano'; B. Cagli: 'Sui testi poetici della produzione vocale di camera'; G. Carli Ballola: 'Lettura del "Torquato Tasso"'; P. Cattaneo: 'Contributo per un'analisi della produzione sacra di Donizetti'; C. Casini: 'Il decennio della fortuna critica di Donizetti a Parigi'; F. Cella: 'Il donizcttismo nci librctti di Donizctti'; J. Commons: 'Donizctti c la censura napoletana'; S. Döhring: 'La forma dell'aria in Gaetano Donizetti'; P. Gossett: 'Anna Bolena e la maturità di Donizetti'; A. Gazzaniga: 'La produzione musicale donizettiana nel periodo napoletano'; F. Lippmann: 'Donizetti e Bellini: contributo all'interpretazione dello stile donizettiano'; P. Rattalino: 'Trascrizioni, riduzioni, trasposizioni e parafrasi del "Don Pasquale"'; B. Zanolini: 'L'armonia come espressione drammaturgica in Donizetti'; A. Zadda: 'Caratteristiche della strumentazione nell'opera teatrale di Gaetano Donizetti']

G. Barblan: 'Gaetano Donizetti mancato direttore dei conservatori di Napoli e di Milano', *Il melodramma italiano dell'ottocento, ii: Da Rossini a Puccini*, ed. M. Mila (Turin, 1977)

G. Gavazzeni: 'Brogliaccio donizettiano', ibid

B. Sarnaker: 'Chi cantò l'*Esule di Roma*? ovvero, Parti in cerca di cantanti', ibid

Journal of the Donizetti Society, iii (1977) [incl. J. Commons: 'Maria Stuarda and the Neapolitan Censorship'; ——: 'Giuseppe Bardari'; J. Commons, P. Schmid and D. White: '19th century Performances of *Maria Stuarda*']

J. N. Black: 'Cammarano's Libretti for Donizetti', *Studi donizettiani*, iii (1978), 115

D. White: 'Donizetti and the "Three Gabriellas"', *Opera*, xxix (1978), 962

A. Gazzaniga: 'Un intervallo nelle ultime scene di "Lucia"', *NRMI*, xiii (1979), 620

Journal of the Donizetti Society, iv (1980) [incl. J. N. Black: 'Cammarano's Notes for the Staging of Lucia di Lammermoor';

——: 'Cammarano's Self-Borrowings: the Libretto of Poliuto'; T. G. Kaufman: 'L'esule di Roma: a Performance History'; ——: 'Italian Performances in Vienna 1835–1859'; F. Lo. Presti: 'La fortuna di Donizetti oggi in Inghilterra'; A. Weatherson: 'Donizetti in Revival'] W. Ashbrook: '*L'ange di Nisida* di Donizetti', *RIM*, xvi (1981), 96

VINCENZO BELLINI

Friedrich Lippmann

CHAPTER ONE
Life

I Education and early career (1801–26)

Vincenzo Bellini was born in Catania on 3 November 1801. He was the eldest of seven in a family of musicians. His grandfather, Vincenzo Tobia Bellini, a native of the Abruzzi, had studied at one of the Naples conservatories and from 1767 or 1768 had worked in Catania as an organist, composer and music teacher. Bellini's father, Rosario, was also a composer, *maestro di cappella* and music teacher in Catania. Vincenzo gave signs of a receptive intelligence at a very early age and was given piano lessons by his father long before normal school age; a priest taught him the rudiments of school learning. According to an anonymous manuscript in the Museo Belliniano, Catania, Bellini could already play the piano marvellously at little more than five years of age; he also gave proof of an excellent ear and musical memory. At six he wrote his first composition, a *Gallus cantavit*, and at seven, according to the same source, he received private instruction in Latin, modern languages, rhetoric and philosophy. In fact, he did not even learn correct Italian (his letters prove this), to say nothing of foreign languages; these studies probably served only to develop his innate feeling for good poetry. In music – meaning by this time, above all, composition – his principal teacher after his seventh year was his grandfather. Bellini was now writing much sacred music (the manuscripts of those works still extant, most of which cannot be precisely dated, have been listed by Francesco Pastura, on p.710 of his *Bellini secondo la storia*, 1959). The handsome, good-natured boy was well known in Catania. Soon it was not only in churches that his compositions were heard, but also in the salons of the aristocrats and patricians, for which he wrote his first ariettas and probably some instrumental pieces as well.

His grandfather having taught him all he could, Bellini went to Naples in June 1819 to study at the conservatory (the municipal government of Catania provided him with the means). His first teacher there was Giovanni Furno; Carlo Conti supervised him as a *maestrino*. In counterpoint he was instructed, probably from 1821 on, by Giacomo Tritto. In 1822, according to Florimo, Bellini entered the class of the director of the conservatory, Niccolò Zingarelli, studying strict composition complemented by exercises in solfège. With him Bellini also studied the masters of the so-called Neapolitan school and the instrumental works of Haydn and Mozart. Bellini's interest in Mozart is known from some editions of Mozart's works in the Naples Conservatory bearing autograph evidence of Bellini's ownership. The exercises he did at the conservatory, especially after 1822, were directed towards the composition of a series of sacred and instrumental pieces. About 1824 he wrote a wedding cantata for some friends; in addition, he composed a number of ariettas (the romanza *Dolente immagine di Fille mia*, the first work of Bellini's to be printed, was published about 1824 by Girard & C. in Naples).

It was a custom at the Naples Conservatory to introduce a composition student who had completed his studies to the public at large with a dramatic work. Thus, early in 1825 Bellini and a cast of male pupils of the conservatory performed *Adelson e Salvini*, his *opera semiseria*, in the conservatory's theatre. Its success led to a commission to write an opera for a gala evening at the Teatro S Carlo. *Bianca e Fernando*, renamed *Bianca e Gernando* out of consideration for the late king, met with good success in May 1826. His hopes for a performance at the Teatro del Fondo of his reworking of *Adelson e Salvini* came to nothing (manuscripts in the Naples Conservatory show that Bellini modified the work for singers of that theatre). He was similarly disappointed in his hope of marrying a Neapolitan girl Maddelena Fumaroli. Thus his good fortune was all the more appreciable when he received from the impresario Barbaia a *scrittura* for an opera for La Scala, Milan.

II Operatic success (1827–33)

In Milan, between May and October 1827, Bellini composed his third opera, *Il pirata*, which at once laid the foundation of his career. He achieved the sort of success with the public that came to Donizetti only after more than 30 operas (*Anna Bolena*, 1830). With *Il pirata* Bellini began his extremely fruitful collaboration with the librettist Felice Romani, who was also to write the librettos for the operas *La straniera, Zaira, I Capuleti e i Montecchi, La sonnambula, Norma* and *Beatrice di Tenda*. No other Italian opera composer of the time showed such attachment to a single librettist. It was founded not only on the sonorousness of the poet's verses and their elegance, frequently reminiscent of Metastasio, but also on the friendship that united Bellini

13. Vincenzo Bellini: portrait (1832) by Giuseppe Patania

158

and Romani up to the time of their estrangement over the preparation of *Beatrice di Tenda*. 1827 also marked the beginning of his close working relationship with the tenor G. B. Rubini (who had already appeared in *Bianca e Gernando* in 1826). This association, which was to continue until *I puritani* (1835), was no less fruitful for the singer than for the composer. Later Bellini was to work just as closely with Giuditta Pasta (in *La sonnambula*, *Norma* and *Beatrice di Tenda*). Early in 1828 *Il pirata* was performed in Vienna; already Bellini was attracting attention abroad.

Between 1827 and 1833 Bellini lived mostly in Milan. He quickly made his entrée into the higher social circles, becoming popular with Princess Belgioioso, Count Barbò, Duchess Litta, Countess Appiani and others. He made his living solely from opera commissions and, unlike his colleagues Rossini, Donizetti, Pacini and Mercadante, never held any official position, such as conservatory teacher or artistic director of an opera house. Instead he was able to ask a higher price for his works than had hitherto been usual in Italy, and for months he lived at the country residences of his friends, the Cantù and Turina families. Bellini had a passionate love affair, lasting until 1833, with Giuditta Cantù, who was unhappily married to the landowner and silk manufacturer Ferdinando Turina. It began in April 1828 in Genoa, where the second version of *Bianca e Gernando* was enjoying a success as the opening production of the Teatro Carlo Felice. The second important landmark in his artistic career (the first having been *Il pirata*) was the opera *La straniera*, performed in February 1829, again at La Scala. Its success with the public exceeded even that of *Il pirata*, but it also gave rise to lengthy debates among music critics (Cambi, 1943, reprinted them in part), some of whom saw dangers in the work's genuinely novel style. In May 1829 Bellini opened a second theatre: the new Teatro Ducale in Parma. However his *Zaira* was a failure, partly caused by ill-feeling in Parmesan theatrical circles (where it was thought that Bellini showed too little enthusiasm for the undertaking). All the more marked, therefore, was the success, barely a year later, of *I Capuleti e i Montecchi* at the Teatro La Fenice in Venice.

Bellini knew that he had reached his years of mastery. With self-assurance he wrote on 28 March 1830: 'My style is now heard in the most important theatres in the world . . . and is heard with the greatest enthusiasm'. Early in 1830 he first experienced in a serious form the illness of which he was to die five years later – a violent attack of gastro-enteritis. He spent the summer convalescing on Lake Como (as a guest of the Cantù and Turina families). In August he directed rehearsals of *La straniera* in Bergamo and in the autumn began the composition of *Ernani*. Felice Romani had already adapted part of Hugo's famous play as a libretto, but the project was abandoned because of fears of censorship difficulties. Instead of *Ernani* he wrote *La sonnambula*, performed with enormous success at the Teatro Carcano in Milan in March 1831. *Norma*, which opened the 1831–2 Carnival season at La Scala, did not at first fare as well. 'Fiasco, fiasco, solenne fiasco' reported Bellini after the first performance. In the course of the subsequent performances, however, the public began to understand the worth of this masterpiece. It was with an easy mind that he was able, on 5

January 1832, to set out on a long journey to Naples and Sicily which became a veritable triumphal procession when he reached his native island. His return journey to Milan took him through Naples, Rome and Florence. He did not reach Milan until the end of May. His next major tasks were to direct rehearsals of *Norma* in Bergamo and Venice (August and December 1832). *Beatrice di Tenda*, the new opera he then wrote for Venice, was a failure, but Bellini himself considered *Beatrice* 'not unworthy of her sisters'.

III Final operas: London and Paris (1833–5)

About February 1833 Bellini concluded a contract to rehearse three of his operas in London. In April he travelled there via Paris. *Il pirata, Norma* and *I Capuleti e i Montecchi* (with Giuditta Pasta as principal) were highly successful at the King's Theatre, and *La sonnambula* (with Maria Malibran in the title role) was equally well received at Drury Lane. In August Bellini went to Paris. Negotiations with the Opéra came to nothing, but he came to terms with the Théâtre-Italien, where *Il pirata* and *I Capuleti e i Montecchi* were staged successfully in the autumn. Since negotiations over a new opera were long drawn out (only early in 1834 did he receive a definite commission), Bellini had time to devote himself to social life, for which he had also shown much enthusiasm in London. He formed a closer acquaintance with Rossini, who became a fatherly friend to him, and also got to know Chopin, Carafa, Paer and other musicians. In the salon of Princess Belgioioso, who had emigrated to Paris, he met Heinrich Heine. Of the musical impressions he received in Paris, the strongest was of performances of Beethoven at the

Conservatoire: 'È bel comme la nature', Bellini cried to Ferdinand Hiller after he had heard the Sixth Symphony.

Finally in April 1834 Bellini began work on *I puritani* to a libretto by the Italian émigré Count Carlo Pepoli – 'after a year of real solid rest', as the composer put it. At about the same time as the commission from the Théâtre-Italien, he received from Naples an invitation to write a new opera. He declined for reasons of insufficient time; however, he remained in touch with the directors of the Teatro S Carlo. The outcome of numerous proposals and counter-proposals was a second version of *I puritani*, adapted to the voices of Malibran, Duprez and Porto; this, however, was not performed, since the score did not arrive in Naples by the agreed deadline. With the Paris version of *I puritani*, the only one to be published, Bellini celebrated a genuine triumph in January 1835, a few months after *La sonnambula* had scored a great success in the same theatre. He was appointed a Chevalier of the Légion d'honneur. Bellini found he had arrived at the point to which his ambition had always led him, 'namely, [in a position] second only to Rossini'. Bellini decided to remain in Paris. During the early months of 1835, once again without a commission for an opera, project succeeded project in his head. These plans concerned a hoped-for marriage, his career in general and certain operas in particular. Negotiations with the Opéra and with the Opéra-Comique dragged on for a long time. None of the projects was accomplished. At the end of August he fell ill and on 23 September died alone at a country house in the Paris suburb of Puteaux, apparently kept in isolation because of suspected cholera. The post-mortem gave the true cause of death: 'It is clear that Bellini succumbed to an acute inflammation of the large intestine, complicated by an abscess of the liver'. The requiem was at the Invalides Cathedral on 2 October. 'Paer, Cherubini, Carafa and Rossini each held one corner of the shroud', according to one report of the ceremony. The remains rested in the Père Lachaise cemetery until 1876, when they were moved to the cathedral of his native town, Catania.

IV Character

The most celebrated literary portrait of Bellini is that by Heinrich Heine (*Florentinische Nächte*, 1837). But Heine's amusing portrayal lays bare at the most one side of Bellini: the somewhat dandyish aspect, which was probably characteristic of him, at least during his Paris period. Even so, Heine noted 'that his character was thoroughly noble and good. His soul certainly remained pure and unsullied by anything hateful'. That Bellini retained an essential integrity is also testified to by other observers whom there is no reason to disbelieve. His lifelong friend Francesco Florimo spoke of an 'animo candido'. Rossini said to the painter Guglielmo De Sanctis: 'He had a most beautiful, exquisitely humane soul'. Ferdinand Hiller wrote: 'His personality was like his melodies – it was captivating – just as charming as it was sympathetic'. Hiller also said: 'His thinking was acute and his feelings animated. ... He knew very well what he wanted, and was far from being the kind of purely instinctive artist that many like to portray him as'. This reflective side of Bellini's personality is much in evidence in a number of letters in which he spoke about his art.

'Animo candido' – but not 'angelico': darker sides to Bellini's nature were not lacking. Not infrequently he reacted to his fellow composers with mistrust, envy and even malevolence. Much of this may have been occasioned by the inevitable rivalries that were a feature of operatic life at the time. But Bellini often went to needless lengths, as in his relationship with Donizetti. One need only compare his thoroughly spiteful derogation of *Marino Faliero* (letter of 1 April 1835) with Donizetti's ungrudging admiration of *Norma* (Donizetti's letter of 31 December 1831). Negative aspects of his character are also unmistakable in his dealings with women. That he did not take very seriously his minor love affairs (whose frequency has certainly been exaggerated in popular literature) will bring reproaches only from strict moralists. But it is less easy to condone the fact that even when – as in his relationship with Giuditta Turina – he was seized by an ardent passion, he was still capable of cold calculation (letter to Florimo, 27 September 1828). Bellini did not emerge blameless from this relationship with a woman who was seriously in love with him. His marriage plans of 1834–5 were as egotistical as they were vague (his letters mention no names, but speak much of a dowry).

Bellini was in no sense a delicate, melancholy being without strong masculine qualities. Florimo described his character as not only 'sincere, amiable, appreciative, modest', but also 'passionate, inflammable, bold'. Giovanni Ricordi even spoke of a 'volcanic character, quick to erupt'. In Parisian theatrical circles Bellini was considered, as he himself wrote to Florimo in 1835, 'a little haughty and full of vanity'.

CHAPTER TWO
Works

I Origins of Bellini's style

While Rossini and Verdi are regarded as composers not only of operas but also of extremely important sacred music, the non-theatrical works of Bellini are mere side-products, which one can ignore without great loss. To speak of Bellini is to speak of his operas, and further – apart from the *opera semiseria Adelson e Salvini* – it is to speak of *opere serie* (*La sonnambula* inclines towards the *semiseria* genre, but has no single scene that is explicitly comic). His first influences were Rossini, the teaching of Zingarelli and the folk music of his native Sicily and of Naples. As Florimo reported to Scherillo, during his time at the conservatory Bellini enjoyed making music out of an 'anthology [zibaldone] of Sicilian poetry'. Much of Sicilian folk music may have found its way into his music, for example his preference for melodies that move in small intervals and for 6/8, 9/8 and 12/8 metres. But no direct influence is demonstrable, since, long before 1825, Sicilian folk music had already rubbed off on art music. From present knowledge the influence of Neapolitan folk music is even harder to verify; however, certain affinities at least are evident. Among the doctrines passed on by Zingarelli was that which holds that melody is the central element of music and that it must be conceived in the simplest way possible. Zingarelli, however, could not prevent Bellini from falling under the influence of Rossini, with his vital melodies and rhythms and also his superabundance of coloratura, which went against all 'simplicity'. The Naples performance of *Semiramide* in 1824 was one of the most decisive musical experiences of Bellini's student period.

Adelson e Salvini shows the young composer combining all these tendencies and influences. In several parts of the score there are echoes of Rossini: in the crescendos of the *introduzione* and the first finale, in numerous orchestral motifs, in the part of the *buffo* character Bonifacio, but also in a number of cantilenas in the *parti serie* (like the beginning of Adelson's entrance aria 'Obliarti! abbandonarti!'). But side by side with the Rossinian passages, this first opera also presents much evidence of an entirely independent cast of expression: a genuinely Romantic feeling for sound, evident in major–minor shifts and in the emphatic élan of certain melodies. Such exuberant effusions represented something quite new in Italian – and indeed in European – opera. It is misleading to relate Bellini's novel lyrical style to the tradition of the 'Neapolitan school', as has frequently been done. Historically more correct is the affirmation that it represented a sentimentalization and heightening of Rossinian lyricism. But this too neglects one essential feature: the spontaneity with which a new, profoundly Romantic form of expression here sprang into being. In this first work, and also in the two versions of *Bianca e Gernando*, passages of strongly individual expression are still very much in the minority, compared with those typical of any respected Italian composer of the time. In *Il pirata*, however, an original style is more apparent and in consequence the work is more tightly and impressively integrated. Thereafter Bellini was one of Italy's most influential composers, particularly after Rossini's early decision to write no more operas. Certain quintessential features of Italian operatic music after Rossini can be traced back to Bellini. Donizetti and Pacini, Mercadante and Verdi all learnt from him.

II Words and music

Foremost among the essentials of Bellini's music (the operas of 1827 – 35 will be discussed here synoptically rather than chronologically) is the close relationship of music and text. This so impressed his contemporaries that they often called his music 'filosofica'. It even won the approval of Wagner: 'Bellini's music comes from the heart, and it is intimately bound up with the text', he told Florimo in 1880. The new seriousness with which Bellini treated his text represented a reaction against Rossini's rather frequent nonchalance in this respect. In Bellini's melodies the text is precisely de-claimed, and with relatively few exceptions the verbal and musical accents coincide. Moreover, the intellectual content and mood of each scene are given thorough-going musical interpretation. Bellini, however, did not put into practice any pervasive and systematic musical delinea-tion of character. His operas, in common with Italian opera in general between about 1815 and about 1850, present a sequence of scenes depicting particular emo-tions, not always psychologically connected. No regard was paid to whether a good or a bad character was expressing these emotions: villains (like Filippo in *Beatrice di Tenda*) sing in the same beautiful cantabile style as the purer souls. A love-aria is a love-aria, no

167

matter who sings it. Real musical characterization of individuals entered Italian opera only with middle- and late-period Verdi.

Associated with the new seriousness with which Bellini confronted his text was a lessening in both the number and the extent of coloratura passages. In *La straniera* he restricted coloratura to such a degree that contemporary Italian critics spoke of 'declamazione cantata, o canto declamato' (see ex.1, from the cabaletta of the duet between Arturo and Alaide in the first act of

Ex.1

Allegro moderato

Un ul - ti-mo ad-di - o   ri - ce-vi, in-fe - li - ce,   di

più non pos-s'i - o, di   più non ti   li - ce,

La straniera). This radical approach was bound up with Bellini's determined efforts to break free from the Rossinian style, 'to introduce a new genre and a music which should express the text as closely as possible, making of song and drama but a single thing' (cf Cicconetti). From *La sonnambula* on he again gave somewhat more space to coloratura, but often integrated it thematically (as for instance in ex.2, from the second duet between Elvino and Amina in the first act of *La sonnambula*, or Norma's 'Casta diva').

Bellini needed a good libretto and good verses to fire his imagination. For him a good libretto was one with numerous thrilling 'situations' and with verses 'designed to portray the passions in the liveliest manner' (letter to Florimo, 4 August 1834). 'Opera, through singing, must make one weep, shudder, die', he wrote to Count Pepoli early in 1834. In his demands for dramatically tense situations (he praised the far-fetched plot of *La straniera* as 'full of situations, all of them new and magnificent', letter to Florimo, August 1828) Bellini resembled Verdi in his early and middle periods. Bellini, however, was more fastidious than Verdi or, probably, than any other Italian composer of his time in his feeling for the poetic merits and deficiencies of verse. He knew himself to be 'very fond of good words' (letter to Florimo, September 1828), and for this reason he adhered with great fidelity to the librettist Romani, the best versifier of the time. However, it is hard to believe in a supposed remark of Bellini's transmitted by Florimo: 'Give me good verses and I will give you good music'.

A similar naivety, which one also cannot believe Bellini capable of, is apparent in a so-called letter to Agostino Gallo (published in Florence in 1843, reprinted in Cicconetti, Pastura and elsewhere). Here the process of composition is set forth in such an unprofessional manner that the 'letter' must be considered at most no more than a later and distorted rewording of authentic remarks. Bellini was far too good a musician to have been able to follow the principle of composition expounded in this 'letter', accord-

Ex.2

169

ing to which the composer works through the following
stages: study of the characters; declamation of the
verses and attention to their 'speech melody'; translation
of the speech melody into musical melody; trying-out on
the piano. In fact, Bellini's melodies arose in the most
varied ways: often, certainly, as the 'letter' has it,
through ·the inspiration of a specific text; but equally
frequently in 'daily exercises', as Bellini termed them.
These consisted in sketching out melodies at random,
partly with a general idea of a scene in mind, and partly
even without this support. A fair number of Bellini's
scenes are provisioned from stocks of such melodies (a
number of these sketches are in the Museo Belliniano,
Catania) and from parodies of earlier pieces (in
Bellini's operas such reworkings are proportionally no
less numerous than they are in those of Rossini). Moreover, it is by no means only in subsidiary scenes that
Bellini made use of melodies already to hand, but also in
central ones, as in the worship scene in *Norma*, the duet
of Adalgisa and Pollione, or the first-act finale in *I
Capuleti e i Montecchi*.

III Melody and sonority

In a letter to Camille Bellaigue (2 May 1898), Verdi
praised Bellini in particular for the broad curves of his
melody: 'there are extremely long melodies as no-one
else had made before him'. This was indeed one of
Bellini's greatest contributions, and it is all the more
remarkable because these melodic curves are built up of
small (generally two-bar) units of the same rhythmic
types used by his Italian contemporaries and corresponding to the various Italian verse forms. Seen as a
whole, Bellini's works belong to that phase of Italian

operatic music entirely characterized by melodic correspondence and symmetry (there are very few metrically irregular melodies). But Bellini succeeded in building from these relatively small, standardized units melodic curves of wide span which can still impress as much as they did Verdi. To achieve this he employed a variety of techniques: for example, pitch climaxes in which the melody forces its way systematically upwards, as in 'Casta diva', the avoidance of accentuated harmonic cadences over long periods, as in Amina's 'Ah! non credea mirarti' (*La sonnambula*), or the combination of melodic gesture and dynamic intensification. In addition to the passages from *Norma* and *La sonnambula* already mentioned, the second-act finale of *Norma* (particularly the E major section) and the Larghetto from the quintet in Act 2 of *Beatrice di Tenda* are in this respect worthy of attention.

In these passages, as in 'Casta diva', the melodic climax comes at the end – a striking innovation for Italian opera around 1830. Bellini exerted a strong influence on Verdi in his use of this device (as, for example, in Leonora's *preghiera* 'Madre, pietosa Vergine' in the second act of *La forza del destino*).

A second new feature is sonority used to ecstatic effect. At the climax of 'Casta diva' Bellini luxuriates in sound in an unprecedented manner. This happens to an even more marked degree in the closing scene mentioned above. Here Bellini's tendency towards an ecstatic unfolding of sonorities reaches its highest expression. The way in which the sequential motif in the E major section screws itself up to the harmonically accented (tritone) climax through a considerable number of bars is all truly intoxicating in its effect, and in 1831 it was new. These sequences also influenced Wagner, an influence that can still be felt in the mounting sequences of *Tristan*. The novelty of Bellini's climaxes lies in part in the treatment of dissonance. In the sequences in the Act 2 finale of *Norma* the dissonances at the outset are resolved on notes of crotchet length, though, notably, on weak beats of the bar (ex.3). In the bars that follow Bellini gives the consonances less and less room: almost without exception they occur only as semiquaver passing notes. In this way the tension is immensely strengthened, to find its resolution in an E major chord on the strong beat of a bar.

Ex.3

It is above all in this ecstasy of sound that the Romanticism of Bellini's music is grounded. A Romantic approach to sound is also apparent in his preference for small intervals. Bellini liked to write melodies that gain intensity and, frequently, a curious sweetness by sliding over semitonal steps. Examples of these are, again, 'Casta diva', the first part of Isoletta's aria in the second act of *La straniera* and the passage at 'Prendi, l'anel ti dono' in the first duet between Amina and Elvina in *La sonnambula* (ex.4). Melodies like these are wholly typical

Ex.4

Andante sostenuto

Pren - di, l'a - nel ti do - no che un

dì, che un dì re-ca-va al - l'a - - - ra

of Bellini, though he by no means left off writing melodies with large intervals – consider, for instance, the wide pitch range of the final number of *La straniera* (cabaletta 'Or sei pago, o ciel tremendo'). For Berlioz, Bellini's melodic style was characterized by the predominance of the third degree of the major scale; Federico Ricci thought so too. Neither writer took into consideration the fact that a predilection for the 3rd (often reached by way of an upwards leap of a 6th), not infrequently associated with a suspended 4th, is a hallmark of the Romantic operatic style in general. But without doubt Bellini's melodies of this type are among the most convincing examples of that kind of Romantic exuberance. Even more typically Romantic than melodies with an accented 3rd degree are those characterized by a double leap, as for instance in ex.5 (the cabaletta from Elvino's second-act aria in *La sonnambula*). The leap of a

Ex.5

Allegro moderato

Ah! per-chè non pos - so o - diar - ti

173

14. Two pages from the finale of Bellini's opera 'La straniera' (first performed 14 February 1829) showing the opening of the cabaletta 'Or sei pago'

174

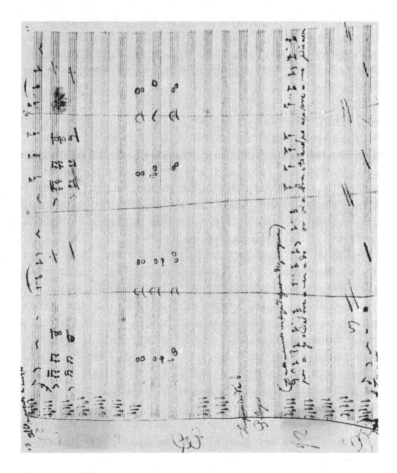

6th to the 3rd above the bass at the beginning is eclipsed by the emphasis given in the following bar to the rise to the 6th above the bass, which functions as a suspension to the 5th. This fundamentally Romantic type of melody, with the double ascent, is often found in Bellini's work.

IV Other aspects of style

Bellini's treatment of rhythm lacks the individuality of his melodic style (this is also true of Donizetti and early Verdi). Certain formulae are all too frequently met within the orchestral accompaniments. In the rhythmic construction of his vocal lines, Bellini, like Donizetti and Verdi in his early works, inclined towards isorhythm: a rhythmic model chosen for the composition of the first verse is readily retained throughout the whole piece, or a large part of it. This tendency to isorhythm is closely allied to the hyperperiodicity of the melodic phrases mentioned above. On the other hand those melodies in which Bellini breaks through this hyperperiodicity merit attention; they are frequently those in which he strives for 'melodie lunghe lunghe lunghe' (Verdi). In Amina's 'Ah! non credea mirarti' none of the first 11 bars matches any of the others rhythmically.

With regard to Bellini's harmonic style, his fine treatment of dissonance should be mentioned again, as should the frequent interchange of major and minor. *La straniera* is rich in harmonic shifts into remote keys, and colourful modulations appear in *I puritani* especially. Bellini's orchestra, like Donizetti's, accompanies vocal lines of markedly cantabile characters with great reticence; in other words, chordally. Sometimes, however, as in the middle sections of arias, it comes to the fore with vivid motifs. Not infrequently, in choruses and dialogues, it actually dominates, imparting unity and continuity to the musical scene through the use of a single motif. In the operas from 1831 and later the instrumentation becomes here and there more highly coloured, most notably in *I puritani*.

One might suppose that a composer who took a strong sensual delight in sound, and who in passages of ecstatic sonority proved himself a Romantic *par excellence*, would incline towards a lack of formal clarity, even a total disregard of it. With Bellini the opposite is true. His luxuriance in sound is combined with a strict economy of formal layout and occurs within extremely confined limits. His favourite aria form is A^1 (= lines 1 and 2 of the first stanza), generally four bars in all; A^2 (= lines 3 and 4 of the first stanza), again generally four bars; B (= lines 1 and 2 of the second stanza), generally four bars; A' + coda (= lines 3 and 4 of the second stanza), where an increase in content is possible (this is also the place for longer coloratura passages). Such a concise form was not favoured by Rossini, and even Donizetti inclined towards greater breadth.

In general, Bellini held to the musical layout of scenes that had become standard in Italy from about 1820 on. The arias and ensembles are much subdivided, the arias being usually in two and the duets often in three sections or movements ('tempi'). The big finales (usually ending the first act) and the *introduzioni* are even more subdivided. Following the model of Rossini and *opera buffa* the main structural elements of the finale consist of a slow lyrical ensemble and the dramatic closing *allegro* with its stretta. The chorus plays an important part in all

177

these forms, even in the aria, sometimes with dramatic justification and sometimes merely to achieve a fuller body of sound or to create a contrast between solo and tutti. Nowhere is the drama forgotten (as it often was in arias of the settecento); at most it is suspended for a short while. The use of multi-partite forms calling on varied performing forces enables the dramatic action to be propelled from one closed form to the next (and these are often not genuinely 'closed'); such forms are thus well suited to the Romantic spirit of the librettos with their frequently adventurous, rapidly changing situations. Bellini followed the general practice, but not without individual nuances and innovations. More than any other Italian composer of the years round 1830, he minimized the differences between aria and recitative. He achieved this bringing together of 'closed' and 'open' forms mostly by introducing a very large number of cantabile, indeed aria-like, passages into his recitative. What was new in this was the frequency of these passages, and also their style, which goes far beyond the traditional ariosos. Often the ear cannot distinguish the point in the scene at which the actual aria begins. Thus, for example, when listening to a scene like that of Riccardo's entry in *I puritani*, one imagines that the aria is beginning as early as the start of the arioso 'O Elvira, o mio sospir', when in fact it does not begin until the words 'Ah! per sempre io ti perdei'.

The delicate, elegiac aspects of Bellini's art have been hitherto overemphasized, as they have in his character. The notion, one that leaves its mark on practical interpretation, that he was able to express in a personal way only the more delicate, elegiac emotions – that he was

178

fundamentally an 'elegist', a 'gentle Sicilian', as Wagner called him – is absolutely wrong. It is true that many of his melodies are bathed in a current of melancholy. But he was also exceptionally well able to portray emotions other than the gentle ones. For proof of this one need refer only to Norma's songs of vengeance ('I romani a cento' and 'Già mi pasco' in the second-act duet with Pollione), to the war chorus of the Gauls in the same opera, to the warlike melody 'Suoni la tromba' in the second-act finale of *I puritani*, to the almost overflowing joyfulness of the cabaletta 'A quel nome' in the duet of Elvira and Giorgio at the beginning of the same opera, and to Alaide's aria of defiance at the conclusion of *La straniera* (cabaletta). How then does one account for the one-sided pronouncement that Bellini's style is 'delicate', 'elegiac' or simply 'lyrical'? For one thing, of course, by the strong impression created by those melodies of Bellini's that are genuinely elegiacal in tone. Another reason, however, lies in stylistic developments subsequent to Bellini's work; the passion and the pathos of Verdi made Bellini's expression of the more violent emotions seem pale to many listeners, and even exposed it to the danger of not being noticed at all.

In order to perform Bellini in a suitable way, it is necessary to find a style of singing that achieves the proper balance between bel canto and dramatic tension, much the kind of style that Bellini's favourite tenor Rubini must have found. Bellini's music cannot be sung as one sings that of a master of pure bel canto. The soprano in the part of Norma who reduces the dramatic features, which anticipate the way in which many of Verdi's heroines sing, merely to a melliflous bel canto, falsifies Bellini in much the same way as does the music critic who refers to him one-sidely as 'delicate' and 'lyrical'.

Bellini's greatness is accepted unquestioningly. After a period of exaggerated popularity about the middle of the 19th century and a period of unduly severe neglect at the beginning of the 20th, he now appears to be receiving fairer treatment. From about 1950 the number of performances has again increased; great singers, with Maria Callas foremost among them, have sung his operas. Musicologists have at last produced reliable biographies and endeavoured to analyse Bellini's style. It is to be hoped that a critical edition of his major works will not be long in appearing.

WORKS

Numbers in the right-hand column denote references in the text.

OPERAS

Title and genre	Acts, librettist	First performance	Sources and remarks	
Adelson e Salvini, semiseria	3, A. L. Tottola	Naples, S Sebastiano Conservatory, early 1825	inc. autograph *I-CATm*	157, 165, 166
2nd version	2	made for Naples, Fondo, 1826, not perf.	autograph frags. *F-Pn*, *I-Baf*, *Nc*, copies *GB-Lbm*, *I-Nc*; vocal score (Paris, n.d.; Milan, 1903)	
Bianca e Gernando, seria	2, D. Gilardoni	Naples, S Carlo, 30 May 1826	orig. compd as Bianca e Fernando; autograph frags. *Nc*, copies *CATm*, *Nc*; vocal score (Naples, 1826)	157, 159, 166
2nd version: Bianca e Fernando	2, F. Romani, after Gilardoni	Genoa, Carlo Felice, 7 April 1828	autograph frags. *Nc*, defective copy *Nc*; excerpts vocal score (Milan, 1828; Naples, 1828), complete vocal score (Milan, 1837, 2/1903)	157
Il pirata, seria	2, Romani	Milan, La Scala, 27 Oct 1827	autograph *Nc* [some pages in *US-NYpm*]; vocal score (Milan, 1827–8, 2/1903)	111, 157, 159, 161, 166
La straniera, seria	2, Romani	Milan, La Scala, 14 Feb 1829	autograph *I-Mr*, copy *Mc*; vocal score (Milan, 1829, 2/1864, 3/1902)	157, 159, 168, 169, 172, 173, 174–5, 176, 179
Zaira, seria	2, Romani	Parma, Ducale, 16 May 1829	autograph *Nc*; excerpts vocal score (Milan, 1829, c1894; Naples, 1829)	157, 160
I Capuleti e i Montecchi, seria	2, Romani	Venice, La Fenice, 11 March 1830	autograph *CATm*, autograph Introduzione *BGi*, copy *Mr*; vocal score (Milan, 1831, 2/1870–71)	157, 160, 161, 170
La sonnambula, seria/semiseria	2, Romani	Milan, Carcano, 6 March 1831	autograph *Mr*, facs (Milan, 19-5); vocal score (Milan, 1831, 2/1858, 3/1869)	31, 123, 157, 159, 160, 161, 162, 165, 168, 171, 172, 173, 176
Norma, seria	2, Romani	Milan, La Scala, 26 Dec 1831	autograph *Rsc*, facs. (Rome, 1915); score (Milan, 1915), vocal score (Milan, 1832, 2/1859, 3/1869)	125, 126, 157, 159, 160, 161, 164, 168, 170, 171, 172, 179
Beatrice di Tenda, seria	2, Romani	Venice, La Fenice, 16 March 1833	autograph *Rsc* (Rome, n.d.); vocal score (Milan, 1833, 2/c1860–70, 3/1877–3)	157, 159, 161, 167, 171
I puritani, seria	3, C. Pepoli	Paris, Théâtre-Italien, 24 Jan 1835	autograph *PLcom*, copies, with autograph markings, *CATm*, *Mr*; score (Milan, 1897/*R*197:), vocal score (Milan, 1836, 2/1870)	99, 114, 159, 162, 176, 177, 178, 179
2nd version	2, Pepoli	made for Naples, S Carlo, not perf.	autograph of nos. different from 1st version in *CATm*	160

Others: Ernani (Romani), late 1830, not completed, autograph frags. *CATm*; Il fu ed il sarà (J. Ferretti), Rome, 183: [almost certainly a pasticcio made without Bellini's participation, cf Cametti, 1900]

SACRED

(all works composed before 1825)

Compline, lost; Cor mundum crea, F, 2 solo vv, org, in *Publicazione periodica di musica sacra sotto gli auspici della S. C. di Propaganda Fide*, ii/2 (Rome, 1879), also in *Cronache musicali*, i (Rome, 1900), no.28; Credo, C, 4vv, orch; Cum sanctis, autograph *I-Nc*; De torrente, autograph *Nc*; Dixit Dominus, solo vv, 4vv, orch, inc. autograph *Nc*, facs. of pt.iii; Tecum principium, in *Composizioni giovanii inedite* (Rome, 1941); Domine Deus, autograph *Nc*

Gallus cantavit, ?autograph *I-CATc*; Gratias agimus, C, solo S, orch; Juravit, autograph *Nc*; Kyrie, autograph *Nc*; Laudamus te, autograph *Nc*; Litanie pastorali in onore della B.V., 2S, org; Magnificat, 4vv, orch, autograph frag. *F-Pn*; Mass, a–A, S, A, T, B, 4vv, orch, inc. autograph *I-CATm* (Milan, 1843); Mass (Ky–Gl), D, SSTB, orch, autograph, dated 1818, *Nc*; Mass (Ky–Gl), G, SSTB, orch; Mass, g, solo vv, vv, orch, autograph frags. *CATm*, *Nc*

Pange lingua, 2vv, org, autograph *CATm*; Qui sedes, autograph *Nc*; Qui tollis, autograph *Nc*; Quoniam, T, 4vv, orch, autographs *F-Pn*, *I-Nc*; Quoniam, S, orch [uses Aria di Cerere], autograph *Nc*; Salve regina, A, 4vv, orch, autograph *CATm*, facs. in *Composizioni giovanii inedite* (Rome, 1941); Salve regina, f–F, solo B, org (Milan, 1862)

4 Tantum ergo, 1823 (Milan, n.d.); D, solo A, orch, E, solo vv, chorus, orch, F, 2vv, orch, G, solo S, orch; 5 Tantum ergo with Genitori, probably before 1823: Bb, solo S, orch; Eb, solo S, orch [Florence and Rome, n.d.], F, 2S [4vv in Genitori], orch, F [without Genitori], solo S, orch [Florence and Rome, n.d.], G, chorus, orch; 2 Te Deum, C, Eb, 4vv, orch; Versetti da cantarsi il Venerdi Santo, 2T, orch, autograph in private collection Marusia Manzella, Rome, mentioned in F. Pastura: 'Le tre ore di agonia', *Rivista del Comune di Catania* (1953); Virgam virtutis, autograph *Nc*

OTHER VOCAL

(composed after 1825 for 1v, pf, unless otherwise stated)

6 ariette da camera (Milan, 1829 [Ricordi]; Naples, n.d. [Clausetti]; Paris, ?1831 [Launer, no copy found]; Naples, n.d. [Girard] [A]
Bellini per camera: raccolta completa delle sue ariette (Naples, n.d.) [the Girard edn. of 6 ariette da camera, enlarged by 8 additional nos.] [B]

Brezze dell'Etna: 26 ispirazioni del cigno catanese (Naples, n.d.) [all 26 nos. probably not pubd] [C]
Soirées musicales: Sammlung beliebter Arietten und Romanzen (Vienna, 1839 [Mechetti]) [D]
3 ariette inedite (Milan, 1837–8 [Ricordi]) [E]
Composizioni da camera (Milan, 1935, 2/1948 [Ricordi] [F]
Principal MS sources, some autograph: *F-Pn*, *I-CATm*, *Fn*, *Mc*, *Nc*, *Rsc*, *US-NYpm*, *Wc*

Almen se non poss'io (Metastasio), arietta, A, B, C, D, F
A palpitar d'affanno, romanza, no.270 in *Aurora d'Italia e di Germania* (Vienna, n.d.), also in *Prima ed ultima composizione di Bellini* (Turin, n.d.)
Bella Nice che d'amore, arietta, A, B, C, D, F
Chi per quest'ombre (Giudiccione), free canon, 4vv, unacc., 15 Aug 1835, facs. in *Gazette musicale de Paris*, ii (Oct 1835), also in A. Pougin: *Bellini: sa vie, ses oeuvres* (Paris, 1868), following p.228
Dalla guancia scolorita, free canon, 2vv, pf, 1835, in *Strenna letteraria artistica musicale del giornale 'Il pirata'* (Bologna 1872), also in *La musica popolare*, ii (1883), following p.145
Dolente immagine di Fille mia, arietta (Naples, c1824; Paris, n.d.), B, C, D, E, F, autograph orch pts. *I-Nc*
E nello stringerti a questo core, aria, 1v, orch, before 1825, autograph *Nc*
Era felice un di, arietta, in *Musica d'oggi*, xviii (1936), suppl. to no.4
Gioite, amiche (Aria di Cerere; used in Quoniam), S, orch, before 1825, autograph *Nc*
Il fervido desiderio, arietta, B, C, E, F
Imene, wedding cantata, S, T, T, vv, orch, ?1824, autograph frags. *I-CATm*, *US-NYpm*, trio [Ombre pacifiche] pubd (Florence and Rome, n.d.)
L'abbandono, romanza, B, C, D, F; as L'ultima veglia (Milan, 1836); as La mammoletta (Paris, n.d.)
La farfalletta, canzoncina, ?1813, F
L'allegro marinaro, ballata (Milan, 1844), B, C, F
La ricordanza (C. Pepoli), 1834, autograph *US-Wc*
Malinconia, ninfa gentile (I. Pindemonte), arietta, A, B, C, D, F

Ma rendi pur contento (Metastasio), arietta, A, B, C, D, F

No, traditor, non curo, aria, S, pf, before 1825, *I-CATm* [probably orig. with orch]

O souvenir: pagina d'album, arietta (Florence and Rome, n.d.)

Per pietà, bell'idol mio (Metastasio), arietta, A, B, C, D, F

Quando incise su quel marmo, aria, S, orch, before 1825, autograph *Nc*, with pf acc. (Milan, 1836), also as no.269 in Aurora d'Italia e di Germania (Vienna, n.d.), B, C, F [incl. introductory recit]

Si, per te, gran nume eterno, cavatina, S, orch, before 1825, autograph *I-Nc*

Sogno d'infanzia, romanza (Milan, 1835), B, C, D, F

T'intendo, si, mio cor (Metastasio), 4S, unacc., c1824, autograph *US-NYpm*

Torna, vezzosa Fillide, romanza, *I-Mc*, F

Vaga luna che inargenti, arietta, no.246 in Aurora d'Italia e di Germania (Vienna, n.d.), B, C, E, F

Vanne, o rosa fortunata, arietta, A, B, C, D, F

Lost: Amore, Malinconia, La speranza (C. Pepoli), 3 sonnets, 1834–5; Alla luna (Pepoli), 1834–5; Numi, se giusti siete (Metastasio), romanza, announced on title-page of C; Arietta, Milan, for Lady Christina Dudley-Stuart, 1828; Cavatina, Milan, for album of

Duchess Litta: Guarda che bianca luna, romanza, ?Palermo, 1832, mentioned in O. Tiby: *Il Real Teatro Carolino e l'ottocento palermitano* (Florence, 1957), 156

Spurious and doubtful: Ah, non pensar = section of Introduzione of Beatrice di Tenda; Se l mio nome (Berlin, n.d.), D = Rossini: Il barbiere di Siviglia; Tu che al panger, B, actually by F. Florimo; Le dernier soir, romanza (Paris, 1841) [authenticity very doubtful]

INSTRUMENTAL

Orch (all composed before 1825): Capriccio, ossia Sinfonia per studio, c; 6 sinfonie: B♭, autograph *I-CATm*, c (Milan, 1941), d-D (Milan, 1941), D, facs in Composizioni giovanili inedite (Rome, 1941) (Padua, 1959), E♭, facs in Composizioni giovanili inedite (Rome, 1941), E♭ (Milan, 1941); Ob. Conc., E♭, autograph *Nc*, facs. in Composizioni giovanili inedite (Rome, 1941) (Milan, 1961)

Kbd: Allegretto, g, pf, au ograph *I-Fn*; Capriccio, G, pf 4 hands, *Nc*; Pensiero musicale, pf, ed. F. P. Frontini (Florence and Rome, n.d.); Polacca, pf 4 hands; Sonata, F, pf 4 hands, autograph *Nc*; Org Sonata, G, autograph *US-NYpm*; Tema, f, pf, c1834, autograph *F-Pn*

Spurious: pieces for pf, vn, fl, ob

BIBLIOGRAPHY

LISTS OF WORKS

F. Pastura: 'Elenco delle opere', *Bellini secondo la storia* (Parma, 1959), 709

G. Pannain: 'Bellini: catalogo delle opere', *LaMusicaE*

F. Lippmann: 'Bellinis Opern – Daten und Quellen', *Vincenzo Bellini und die italienische Opera seria seiner Zeit*, AnMc, no.6 (1969), 365–97; rev., It. trans. in M. R. Adamo and F. Lippmann: *Vincenzo Bellini* (Turin, 1981), 523

L. Orrey: 'Catalogue of Works', *Bellini* (London, 1969), 157

H. Weinstock: *Vincenzo Bellini: his Life and his Operas* (New York, 1971), 213

BIBLIOGRAPHIES

O. Viola: 'Bibliografia belliniana', *Omaggio a Bellini* (Catania, 1901), 336; pubd separately (Catania, 1902, 2/1923)

L. Ronga: 'Note sulla storia della critica belliniana', *Bollettino dei musicisti*, ii (1934), 70; repr. in L. Ronga: *Arte e gusto nella musica* (Milan and Naples, 1956)

A. Damerini: 'Bellini e la critica del suo tempo', *Vincenzo Bellini*, ed. I. Pizzetti (Milan, 1936), 215–50

S. Pugliatti: 'Problemi della critica belliniana', *Chopin e Bellini* (Messina, 1952)

H. Weinstock: *Vincenzo Bellini: his Life and his Operas* (New York, 1971), 547

W. F. Kümmel: 'Vincenzo Bellini nello specchio dell' "Allgemeine musikalische Zeitung" di Lipsia 1827–1846', *NRMI*, vii/2 (1973), 3

LETTERS

F. Florimo: *Bellini: memorie e lettere* (Florence, 1882)

A. Amore: *Vincenzo Bellini: vita: studi e ricerche* (Catania, 1894) [incl. letters addressed to Bellini]

F. Pastura: *Le lettere di Bellini* (Catania, 1935)

L. Cambi: *Vincenzo Bellini: epistolario* (Milan, 1943)

F. Pastura: *Bellini secondo la storia* (Parma, 1959)

F. Walker: 'Lettere disperse e inedite di Vincenzo Bellini', *Rivista del Comune di Catania*, viii/4 (1960), 3

D. Musto: 'Vincenzo Bellini in due autografi inediti dell'Archivio di Stato di Napoli', *Rassegna degli Archivi di Stato*, xxi (1961), 351

L. Cambi: 'Bellini: un pacchetto di autografi', *Scritti in onore di Luigi Ronga* (Milan and Naples, 1973), 53–90

F. Lippmann: 'Belliniana', *Il melodramma italiano dell'ottocento: studi e ricerche per Massimo Mila* (Turin, 1977), 281

Bibliography

ICONOGRAPHY

B. Condorelli: 'Il volto di Bellini', *Vincenzo Bellini: numero commemorativo a cura della Rivista del Comune di Catania* (Catania, 1935), 18

O. Profeta: 'Dantan e la Parigi di Bellini', *Vincenzo Bellini: numero commemorativo a cura della Rivista del Comune di Catania* (Catania, 1935), 77

F. Pastura: *Bellini secondo la storia* (Parma, 1959)

H. Weinstock: *Vincenzo Bellini: his Life and his Operas* (New York, 1971)

LIFE AND WORKS

A. Pougin: *Bellini: sa vie, ses oeuvres* (Paris, 1868)

F. Florimo. *Cenno storico sulla scuola musicale di Napoli*, ii (Naples, 1871; rev., enlarged 2/1882 as *La scuola musicale di Napoli*, iii)
——: *Bellini: memorie e lettere* (Florence, 1882)

I. Pizzetti: 'Bellini, Vincenzo', *Enciclopedia italiana*, vi (1930)

G. T. De Angelis: *Vincenzo Bellini: la vita, l'uomo, l'artista* (Brescia, 1935)

O. Tiby: *Vincenzo Bellini* (Turin, n.d.)

F. D'Amico: 'Bellini, Vincenzo', *ES*

F. Pastura: *Bellini secondo la storia* (Parma, 1959)

R. Monterosso: 'Bellini, Vincenzo', *DBI*

L. Orrey: *Bellini* (London, 1969)

H. Weinstock: *Vincenzo Bellini: his Life and his Operas* (New York, 1971)

W. Oehlmann: *Vincenzo Bellini* (Zurich, 1974)

M. R. Adamo and F. Lippmann: *Vincenzo Bellini* (Turin, 1981)

P. Brunel: *Vincenzo Bellini* (Paris, 1981)

BIOGRAPHICAL AND CHARACTER STUDIES

H. Heine: 'Florentinische Nächte', *Salon*, iii (Hamburg, 1837; Eng. trans., 1891)

F. Cicconetti: *Vita di Vincenzo Bellini* (Prato, 1859)

A. Amore: *Vincenzo Bellini: vita: studi e ricerche* (Catania, 1894)

A. Cametti: *Bellini a Roma: brevi appunti storici* (Rome, 1900)

A. Aniante: *Vita amorosa di Vincenzo Bellini* (Milan, 1926)

G. de Gaetani: *Ipotesi sulla natura della malattia che condusse a morte Vincenzo Bellini* (Catania, 1931)

L. Cambi: *Bellini: la vita* (Milan, 1934)

G. Nataletti: '1819–1827: gli anni di Napoli', *Bollettino dei musicisti*, ii (1934), 45

F. Pastura: '1801–1819: a Catania', *Bollettino dei musicisti*, ii (1934), 41

A. della Corte: 'L'animo', *Vincenzo Bellini*, ed. A. della Corte and G. Pannain (Turin, 1935), 3

185

G. Policastro: *Vincenzo Bellini (1801–1819)* (Catania, 1935)
L. Cambi: 'La fanciullezza e l'adolescenza', *Vincenzo Bellini*, ed. I. Pizzetti (Milan, 1936), 11
J. Chantavoine: 'Bellini a Parigi', *Vincenzo Bellini*, ed. I. Pizzetti (Milan, 1936), 191
E. J. Dent: 'Bellini in Inghilterra', *Vincenzo Bellini*, ed. I. Pizzetti (Milan, 1936), 163
P. Cavazzuti: *Bellini a Londra* (Florence, 1945)
G. Roncaglia: 'Vincenzo Bellini: il musicista, quale appare dal suo epistolario', *RMI*, l (1948), 159
F. Walker: 'Amore e amori nelle lettere di Giuditta, Bellini e Florimo', *La Scala* (1959), no.112, p.13: Eng. trans. as 'Giuditta Turina and Bellini', *ML*, xl (1959), 19

GENERAL CRITICAL STUDIES

H. Berlioz: 'Bellini: notes nécrologiques', *Journal des débats* (16 July 1836); repr. in H. Berlioz: *Les musiciens et la musique* (Paris, 1903)
R. Wagner: 'Bellini: ein Wort zu seiner Zeit', *Zuschauer* (Riga, 7/19 Dec 1837); repr. in *Bayreuther Blätter* (1885), Dec; Eng. trans. in *Richard Wagner's Prose Works*, viii (1899/R1972)
A. Amore: *Brevi cenni critici* (Catania, 1877)
F. Hiller: 'Vincenzo Bellini', *Künstlerleben* (Cologne, 1880)
F. Ricci: 'Una lettera di Federico Ricci su Bellini', in F. Florimo: *Bellini: memorie e lettere* (Florence, 1882), 140ff
M. Scherillo: *Vincenzo Bellini: note aneddotiche e critiche* (Ancona, 1882)
———: *Belliniana: nuove note* (Milan, n.d.)
A. Amore: *Vincenzo Bellini: arte: studi e ricerche* (Catania, 1892)
———: *Belliniana: errori e smentite* (Catania, 1902)
I. Pizzetti: 'La musica di Vincenzo Bellini', *La voce*, vii (1915); also pubd separately; repr. in I. Pizzetti: *Intermezzi critici* (Florence, n.d.) and *La musica italiana dell 800* (Turin, 1947)
C. Gray: 'Vincenzo Bellini', *ML*, vii (1926), 49
F. Torrefranca: 'Il mio Bellini', *Bollettino dei musicisti*, ii (1934), 65
A. della Corte: 'La formazione', *Vincenzo Bellini*, ed. A. della Corte and G. Pannain (Turin, 1935), 29
D. de' Paoli: 'Bellini, musicien dramatique', *ReM* (1935), no.156, p.52
A. Einstein: 'Vincenzo Bellini', *ML*, xvi (1935), 325
G. Pannain: 'Saggio critico', *Vincenzo Bellini*, ed. A. della Corte and G. Pannain (Turin, 1935), 77–123
———: 'Vincenzo Bellini', *RaM*, viii (1935), 1, 100, 174, 237; repr. in G. Pannain: *Ottocento musicale italiano* (Milan, 1952), 16
I. Pizzetti: 'Hommage à Bellini', *ReM* (1935), no.156, p.39

Bibliography

G. Gavazzeni: 'Spiriti e forme della lirica belliniana', *Vincenzo Bellini*, ed. I. Pizzetti (Milan, 1936), 81–131

M. Mila: 'Bellini cent'anni dopo', *Cent' anni di musica moderna* (Milan, 1944)

S. Pugliatti: 'Carattere dell'arte di Vincenzo Bellini', *Chopin e Bellini* (Messina, 1952)

I. Pizzetti: 'Spiriti e forme dell'arte belliniana', *Musica d'oggi*, new ser., i (1958), 346

F. Lippmann: *Vincenzo Bellini und die italienische Opera seria seiner Zeit*, AnMc, no.6 (1969); rev., It. trans. in M. R. Adamo and F. Lippmann: *Vincenzo Bellini* (Turin, 1981)

—: 'Ein neuentdecktes Autograph Richard Wagners: Rezension der Königsberger "Norma"-Aufführung von 1837', *Musicae scientiae collectanea: Festschrift Karl Gustav Fellerer* (Cologne, 1973), 373

—: 'Belliniana', *Il melodramma italiano dell'ottocento: studi e ricerche per Massimo Mila* (Turin, 1977), 281

—: 'Donizetti und Bellini', *Studi musicali*, iv (1975), 193

WORKS: SPECIFIC STUDIES

O. Viola: 'Saggio bibliografico delle più antiche edizioni dei libretti musicati da Vincenzo Bellini', appx to O. Viola: *Bibliografia belliniana* (Catania, 1902), 57

H. de Saussine: 'L'harmonie bellinienne', *RMI*, xxvii (1920), 477

A. della Corte: 'Vicende degli stili del canto dal tempo di Gluck al 900', *Canto e bel canto*, ed. A. della Corte (Turin, 1933)

L. Tonelli: 'I libretti di Bellini', *Bollettino dei musicisti*, ii (1934), 75

B. Condorelli: *Il Museo Belliniano: catalogo storico-iconografico* (Catania, 1935)

A. della Corte: 'Il canto e i cantanti', *Vincenzo Bellini*, ed. A. della Corte and G. Pannain (Turin, 1935), 49

H. de Saussine: 'Sur Bellini harmoniste', *ReM* (1935), no.156, p.63

F. Pastura: 'Due frammenti della "Beatrice di Tenda" di Bellini', *RaM*, viii (1935), 327

—: 'Rivelazioni degli autografi musicali belliniani: varianti e temi inediti', *Vincenzo Bellini: numero commemorativo a cura della Rivista del Comune di Catania* (1935), 25

—: 'Un'arietta inedita di Vincenzo Bellini', *Musica d'oggi*, xviii (1936), 115

G. F. Winternitz: 'I cimeli belliniani della R. Accademia Filarmonica di Bologna', *RMI*, xl (1936), 104

F. Schlitzer: 'Cimeli belliniani', *Tommaso Traetta, Leonardo Leo, Vincenzo Bellini: notizie e documenti raccolti da F. Schlitzer*, Chigiana, ix (1952), 61

187

N. Gallini: 'Collana d'arie per Mademoiselle Carlier', *La Scala* (1953), no.49, p.42

F. Schlitzer: 'Vincenzo Bellini', *Mondo teatrale dell'ottocento* (Naples, 1954)

M. Rinaldi: *Felice Romani* (Rome, 1965)

F. Lippmann: 'Verdi e Bellini', *I° congresso internazionale di studi verdiani: Venezia 1966*, 184; Ger. trans. in *Beiträge zur Geschichte der Oper*, ed. H. Becker (Regensburg, 1969), 77

——: 'Pagine sconosciute de "I Capuleti e i Montecchi" e "Beatrice di Tenda" di Vincenzo Bellini', *RIM*, ii (1967), 140

——: 'Quellenkundliche Anmerkungen zu einigen Opern Vincenzo Bellini's', *AnMc*, no.4 (1967), 131

F. Cella: 'Indagini sulle fonti francesi dei libretti di Vincenzo Bellini', *Contributi dell'Istituto di filologia moderna*, Fr. ser. (Milan, 1968), 449–576

R. Celletti: 'Il vocalismo italiano da Rossini a Donizetti', *AnMc*, no.5 (1968), 267; no.7 (1969), 214–47

F. Lippmann: 'Wagner und Italien', *AnMc*, no.11 (1972), 200–47

——: 'Der italienische Vers und der musikalische Rhythmus', *AnMc*, no.12 (1973), 253–369; no.14 (1974), 324–410; no.15 (1975), 298–333

WORKS: INDIVIDUAL OPERAS

A. Damerini: *Vincenzo Bellini, 'Norma': guida attraverso il dramma e la musica* (Milan, 1923)

G. Pannain: 'La Norma', *ReM* (1935), no.156, p.44

A. della Corte: 'Le prime opere', *Vincenzo Bellini*, ed. I. Pizzetti (Milan, 1936), 39–80

G. Pannain: ' "Norma": cento anni', *Ottocento musicale italiano* (Milan, 1952), 49

J. A. Borromé: 'Bellini and "Beatrice di Tenda" ', *ML*, xlii (1961), 319

V. Gui: 'Beatrice di Tenda', *Musica d'oggi*, new ser., ii (1969), 194

F. Lippmann: 'Su "La straniera" di Bellini', *NRMI*, v (1971), 565–605

P. Petrobelli: 'Note sulla poetica di Bellini: a proposito de *I puritani*', *MZ*, viii (1972), 70

R. Monterosso: 'Per un'edizione di "Norma" ', *Scritti in onore di Luigi Ronga* (Milan and Naples, 1973), 415–510

L. Orrey: 'The Literary Sources of Bellini's First Opera', *ML*, lv (1974), 24

C. S. Brauner: 'Textual Problems in Bellini's *Norma* and *Beatrice di Tenda*', *JAMS*, xxix (1976), 99

F. Degrada: 'Prolegomeni a una lettera della *Sonnambula*', *Il melodramma italiano dell'ottocento: studi e ricerche per Massimo Mila* (Turin, 1977), 319

Bibliography

L. Gherardi: 'Varianti ne "I puritani" ', *Chigiana*, xxxiv (1977), 217

P. Petrobelli: 'Bellini e Paisiello: altri documenti sulla nascita dei *Puritani*', *Il melodramma italiano dell'ottocento: studi e ricerche per Massimo Mila* (Turin, 1977), 351

Atti del Convegno di studi sull'opera 'Bianca e Fernando' di Vincenzo Bellini (Genoa, 1978)

G. Spina: 'Origine di "I puritani"', *NRMI*, xii (1978), 29

Atti del simposio belliniano celebrato in occasione del 150° anniversario della 1° esecuzione di 'Norma' (Catania, 1981)

GIUSEPPE VERDI

Andrew Porter

CHAPTER ONE
Life, 1813–43

Verdi was born at Roncole, near Busseto, in 1813. He always observed his birthday on 9 October, the feast of S Donnino; but his baptismal record of 11 October which shows his name as Giuseppe Fortunio Francesco – refers to an 'Infantem natum heri', and the Busseto civil register of the following day to 'un Enfant . . . né le jour dix du courant'. By old Italian reckoning, a new day began officially at sunset; perhaps Verdi was born late on 9 October, and the parish priest drew up his records after sunset on the following day, technically on 11 October. This is but the first of several minor puzzles about Verdi's early days. As late as 1876 he told the Countess Maffei with apparent surprise of his discovery that he had been born in 1813, not 1814; yet passports he had been using show the correct date. He discouraged biographers, exaggerated the humbleness of his origins, liked to call himself 'a peasant from Roncole', and in later life made several misleading remarks about his youth. In 1891 he wrote: 'Alas! Born in a poor village, I had no way to teach myself anything. They put a miserable spinet under my hands, and some time later I began to write notes . . . notes upon notes. That is all'. But that is not all, as recent research (notably by Mary Jane Matz) has made abundantly clear; nevertheless, the composer's own picture of himself is still being copied from one biography to the next. He was not a peasant, but descended from two families of small landowners, taverners and tradesmen. In the parish registers of Sant'Agata (a village about 4 km north of Busseto, where Verdi bought property in 1848 and became in time a very large landowner) his forebears have been traced to the mid-17th century. His grandfather, another Giuseppe, moved in the early 1780s to Roncole (about 4 km south-east of Busseto) to open a tavern there. Giuseppe's youngest son Carlo (1775–1867) succeeded to the family business. In 1805 Carlo married Luigia Uttini, daughter of a tavern-keeping family long established in Saliceto di Cadeo (a hamlet about 8 km west of Busseto). They had two children, the composer and his sister Giuseppa Francesca (1816–33).

The young Giuseppe's ability was recognized early and sedulously fostered. When he was three, the precocious child began studies with Don Pietro Baistrocchi, *magister parvulorum* and organist at Roncole. He was provided with a spinet, which accompanied him through life and at his death accompanied him to the Casa di Riposo in Milan (it is now in the Scala Museum), and the first written testimony to Verdi's musical gifts is the inscription tacked inside its lid by the craftsman who, in 1821, renewed and repaired its mechanism 'free of charge, in view of the young Giuseppe Verdi's eagerness to learn to play this instrument'. Probably in 1822, when Baistrocchi died, Verdi, aged nine, assumed some of his teacher's duties, and he won some local fame as the *maestrino* of Roncole. The following autumn his father sent him to study in Busseto. When he was 11 he entered the *ginnasio*, where he received a humane classical education; several of his school companions achieved distinction in academic and medical fields. At the same time he was taught counterpoint and composition by Ferdinando Provesi, director of the municipal music school and philharmonic society and organist of S Bartolomeo, Busseto's principal church. Verdi remained in Busseto until 1832, composing a quantity of sacred and secular music. He made his début with an overture to Rossini's *Il barbiere di Siviglia*, played before a local performance of the opera in 1828. In 1831 he went to live in the house of the merchant and musical patron Antonio Barezzi, who became to him as a second father, and in time his father-in-law. That year, Carlo Verdi petitioned the Monte di Pietà for a grant for his son's further musical education. No scholarship was available before 1833, and Barezzi undertook to finance Verdi's first year of study in Milan.

In June 1832 Verdi applied for admission to the Milan Conservatory. He was rejected, and in later life recalled this rejection with bitterness and inaccuracy. The examiners' report sounds reasonable enough: faulty piano technique; a promising composer with 'genuine imagination' but in need of contrapuntal discipline; a 'foreigner' (a Parmesan, in Lombardy); at a time when the school was already overcrowded, not qualified for the special dispensation needed by a pupil who, at 18, was already four years over the usual age of entry. Verdi became a private pupil of Vincenzo Lavigna (a composer who had had some Scala successes early in the century). 'In the three years I spent with him, I did nothing but canons and fugues, fugues and canons, served up in every fashion [*in tutte le salse*]. No-one taught me orchestration or how to handle dramatic music.' That declaration of 1871 must, like all Verdi's

15. Autograph MS of the opening of Verdi's aria 'Io la vidi', probably written during his student years in Milan, ?1832–5

late claims to being largely self-taught, be handled with care. In an 1853 account of these student years in Milan he spoke of 'various pieces, mostly comic, which my master made me do as exercises and which were not even scored'. One aria probably from this period, *Io la vidi*, survives in score (see fig.15), its instrumentation corrected in another hand. There is little in Verdi's earliest works to suggest any special mastery of counterpoint, yet one anecdote is revealing. Arturo Basily, one of the conservatory examiners who had turned Verdi down, visited Lavigna and complained that none of the candidates for the post of organist of Monza Cathedral had been able to provide a decent fugue on Basily's set subject. Lavigna handed the theme to his pupil, and while the two professors continued their conversation Verdi wrote a fugue that excited Basily's admiration. 'How come that you have made a double canon of my subject?' – 'Well, I found it a little thin and wanted to give it some richness.'

The well-paid Monza post could probably have been his but instead, under local pressure and through loyalty to his patron Barezzi, Verdi returned to Busseto to become, at a much lower salary, the town's *maestro di musica*. The appointment was not made without incident. Provesi had died in 1833; in Lavigna's opinion, Verdi was not yet equipped to succeed him, and he continued his studies in Milan. A year later, one Giovanni Ferrari was nominated *maestro di cappella* at S Bartolomeo, without the customary competitive examination. There followed a long and heated town quarrel – lampoons, street brawls, arrests and prosecutions were involved – between Ferrari's champions and Verdi's, the ecclesiastical and the secular parties. The

Bishop of S Donnino (now Fidenza; it resumed its ancient name in 1927), in whose diocese Busseto was, weighed in in favour of Ferrari, 'a grown man . . . more to be depended on than a beardless youth who learnt music in a populous city where the young are attracted by the scandalous goings-on that swarm there in public', and he told the Parma home secretary that 'the civil and military authorities should be ordered to watch attentively, to crush the rebellion at birth'. Dragoons stood by. Eventually Ferrari was confirmed in the sacred post and Verdi appointed to the secular. He returned to Busseto in 1835. He was examined in Parma in February 1836 (Ferrari did not compete) by Giuseppe Alinovi. Again there is evidence – this time more than anecdotic – about the esteem accorded to his contrapuntal ability. After scanning the final exercise, a four-part fugue, Alinovi

rose to his feet and said to Verdi: 'So far I have played the part of a rigorous examiner; now I play that of an admirer. This fugue is worthy of a consummate master. You have knowledge enough to be *maestro* in Paris or London, rather than at Busseto.

Verdi's contract with the *comune*, dated 20 April 1836, required him to reside in Busseto ten months of the year, to give lessons at the music school in vocal and instrumental music (harpsichord, piano, organ), singing, counterpoint and free composition, and to conduct the concerts of the philharmonic society. His salary was 657 lire a year (later raised by the society to 1000); after three years either party could break the nine-year contract at six months' notice. His position assured, Verdi married Barezzi's eldest daughter, Margherita (*b* May 1814; *d* June 1840), in May. They had two children, Virginia Maria Luigia (*b* 26 March 1837; *d* Aug

1838) and Icilio Romano Carlo Antonio (*b* 11 July 1838; *d* 22 Oct 1839). From the scanty documentation of Verdi's three years as Busseto's *maestro di musica* there emerges a portrait of a musician restless with his municipal duties, eager to make his way in a larger world, irked by his obligations towards the community who, having once supported his studies, never let him forget it. There is consistent testimony, starting with the reminiscences of those who had known him as a small child and continuing throughout his life, of his proudly independent spirit, self-reliance, and impatience with any public claims made upon him.

In 1853 Verdi recalled:

Back again in my home town, I began to write marches, *sinfonie* [overtures or short orchestral movements], a complete mass, a complete set of vespers, three of four settings of *Tantum ergo*, and other church music that I don't recall. Among the vocal pieces there were choruses from the tragedies of Manzoni for three voices, and *Il cinque maggio* for solo voice.

Programmes of the Busseto *accademie* confirm this activity. That for 25 February 1838, for example, contained a capriccio for horn, a recitative and aria, an introduction, variations and coda for bassoon and a *buffo* duet all by Signor Maestro Verdi; the evening began with Rossini's overture to *Semiramide*, ended with a Meyerbeer overture, and had Scribe's comedy *The Artists' Garret* as its central panel. One *Tantum ergo* survives; some fragmentary duets for two tenors and organ, once ascribed to Verdi, prove to be a copy of Bellini's Good Friday music. In 1838 Verdi's first songs were published in Milan. He was also at work on the opera that, in his words, 'became *Oberto, Conte di San Bonifacio*'. Whether it was a lost *Lord Hamilton* or an all-but-lost *Rocester* that became *Oberto*, and how much the three may have had in common, has not been established (see Walker, 1962, pp.24ff; Budden, 1973, pp.45ff). In November 1837 Verdi's hopes that *Rocester* would be staged in Parma were dashed. He spent his 1838 leave in Milan, trying to place his opera, and evidently received encouragement, for on his return to Busseto he tendered his resignation. In February 1839 he moved with his family to Milan. In November, *Oberto* was produced at La Scala, with fair success. Ricordi bought the rights in it for 2000 Austrian lire, and Bartolomeo Merelli, the director of the theatre, commissioned three more operas.

The first of these was a comedy, *Un giorno di regno*, to a slightly revised version of a libretto, *Il finto Stanislao*, that Felice Romani had written for Adalbert Gyrowetz in 1812. It was a failure, and withdrawn after a single performance (5 September 1840). In an 1881 memoir, Verdi recalled that during the composition of this merry piece his daughter, son and wife had died within the space of some two months. In fact, as shown by the dates above, Virginia had died before the family left Busseto, and Icilio before the production of *Oberto*. It is not the only instance of Verdi's rearranging his memories in a more strikingly dramatic form. Yet the facts themselves are sad enough. Rejected by the audience he had hoped to conquer, lonely in his Milan lodgings, Verdi sank into depression and vowed to write no more. By a blend of tactful encouragement, persuasion and stratagem, the astute Merelli induced him to return to composition, and Verdi's third opera, *Nabucodonosor* (its unwieldy title soon shortened to *Nabucco*), was born almost against his will, as desolation was penetrated by returning hope and new-found strength. Merelli had thrust upon him a libretto by Temistocle Solera intended for but, fortunately for posterity, rejected by Otto Nicolai. According to Verdi's own account, his eyes fell first on the chorus of Hebrew exiles, 'Va, pensiero, sull'ali dorate', which left an indelible impression: 'I was much moved, because the verses were almost a paraphrase from the Bible, the reading of which had always delighted me'. He spent a sleepless night reading and rereading the whole libretto. In succeeding months 'one day one line, another day another ... little by little the opera was composed'. In autumn 1841 he took it to Merelli – but the repertory for the following season had already been settled, and it needed Verdi's angry insistence to bring *Nabucco* to performance. Self-doubt had been replaced by self-confidence – a recurrent pattern in his life (sensitively traced in Franz Werfel's novel, 1925).

The confidence was justified. *Nabucco*, produced at La Scala in spring 1842, was an outstanding success, and a triumph when it was revived in the autumn season for 57 more performances – a figure unmatched before or since in the Scala annals. The work swiftly carried Verdi's name throughout Italy and then through the world. In 1843 it reached Vienna and Lisbon; in 1844, Barcelona, Berlin, Corfu, Stuttgart, Oporto and Malta; in 1845, Paris, Hamburg, Marseilles and Algiers; in 1846, Copenhagen, Constantinople, Budapest and London; in 1847, Havana and Bucharest; in 1848, New York and Brussels; in 1849, Prague; in 1850, Lemberg (Lwów) and Buenos Aires; in 1851, Zurich and St Petersburg. Similar accounts – but this one may stand for all – could be provided to show how rapidly and widely all his other successful operas were disseminated.

As Henry F. Chorley remarked in 1862, 'Signor Verdi is . . . the only writer of his country representing, during the last 15 years, that Maestro of better days [Rossini], whose music was heard from one end of Europe to the other'.

Solera drew his libretto from a Scala ballet of 1838, itself based on a French play. He was a composer, a poet and an Italian patriot who had brushed with the Austrian police; the strong sense of national identity in *Nabucco* was largely his own contribution to his sources. Verdi, in turn, insisted that a love-duet should be replaced by the Hebrew leader's sombre, then fiery, *profezia*. In the large *I lombardi alla prima crociata*, produced at La Scala the following year, the two men aimed to repeat their earlier triumph, and succeeded. Their source was an epic poem by Tommaso Grossi; the big choruses are now sung by Italians.

CHAPTER TWO

The patriotic element in the operas

Verdi's early biographer 'Folchetto' (Jacopo Caponi, 1881; see Pougin) put it well. With *Nabucco* and *I lombardi*, he said:

Verdi began – I would say at first instinctively – to instigate political action with his music. Foreigners will never be able to understand the influence exerted, for a certain period, by the ardent, blazing melodies that Verdi conceived when the situations, or even isolated lines of verse, recalled the unhappy state of Italy, or her memories, or her hopes. The public saw allusions everywhere, but Verdi found them first and shaped them to his inspired music, which often ended by causing a revolution in the theatre.

In *Ernani*, the 'horrid embrace' (of an elderly guardian) from which Elvira cries to be rescued was equated with Austrian dominion. In *Attila*, the stirring lines 'Avrai tu l'universo, Resti l'Italia a me' ('You may have the universe, So long as I keep Italy') roused immense enthusiasm, even though in context they are uttered by an Italian traitor proposing a deal with the Hun. *La battaglia di Legnano* is in effect a Risorgimento call to arms. The *Nabucco* chorus of exiles yearning for their homeland and the parallel *Lombardi* chorus of Italian crusaders yearning for their native fields and vineyards, 'O Signore, dal tetto natio' – that chorus which, in the words of the Risorgimento poet Giuseppe Giusti, 'has shaken and intoxicated so many hearts' – gave rise, Folchetto claimed, to 'the first political demonstrations that signalled the reawakening of Lombardy and the Veneto'.

Verdi was an emotionally committed patriot; of that his letters leave no doubt. All of his operas before *Aida* were composed in the shadow of impending or actual revolution and war in his country, and, as Luigi Dallapiccola wrote (1965), 'the phenomenon that is Verdi is unimaginable without the Risorgimento. Whether or not he played an active part in it is unimportant; he absorbed its air and its tone' and in words and music 'formulated a style through which the Italian people found a key to their dramatic plight and vibrated in unison with it'. At the same time, the composer must have been well aware that this appeal to patriotic emotions helped to ensure a popular success for his works. New topical allusions are found in them still. Yet, beyond any specific 'relevance', there was and is the power of Verdi's melodies and strong, slow-surging rhythms to generate mass emotion. It is an important element in his works, a reason for their immediate and their continued hold on the large public. Even people who have lived comfortable, untroubled lives can be moved to 'vibrate in unison' with the Hebrews' cry (in *Nabucco*) of 'O mia patria, sì bella e perduta' or the Scottish exiles' lament (in *Macbeth*) for their 'Patria oppressa'. In the late 1850s, the composer's name was seized on as an acronym for *V*ittorio *E*manuele, *Re D'I*talia; a shout of 'Viva VERDI!' could also be one for an Italy united under that monarch.

CHAPTER THREE

The 'four periods'

Ernani, Verdi's next opera after *I lombardi alla prima crociata*, was composed for Venice (1844), and with it the composer entered what he called his 'years in the galley'. (In fact, he claimed there were 16 'galley years', from *Nabucco* onwards; the phrase occurs in an 1858 letter to Clarina Maffei.) During the nine years that followed, 14 more operas came from his pen. For Rome he produced *I due Foscari* (also 1844), *La battaglia di Legnano* (1849) and *Il trovatore* (1853); for Milan, *Giovanna d'Arco* (1845); for Naples, *Alzira* (1845) and *Luisa Miller* (1849); for Venice, *Attila* (1846), *Rigoletto* (1851) and *La traviata* (1853); for Florence, *Macbeth* (1847). *Il corsaro* (1848) and *Stiffelio* (1850) had their first performances in Trieste. Commissions from abroad resulted in *I masnadieri* (London, 1847) and *Jérusalem* (an elaborated reworking of *I lombardi*; Paris, 1847).

The pace slackened only when, in October 1853, after *La traviata*, Verdi settled in Paris and spent nearly two years on the composition of *Les vêpres siciliennes* (produced June 1855). He remained in Paris most of the time until 1857. In that year, returning to Italy, he produced *Simon Boccanegra* in Venice and *Aroldo*, a reworking of *Stiffelio*, in Rimini – neither with much success. Then *Un ballo in maschera*, composed for Naples in 1858, ran into censorship troubles there and was eventually given in Rome the following year. It was acclaimed, but the performance left Verdi dissatisfied.

16. *Giuseppe Verdi: photograph by A. A. Disderi, 1850s*

His distaste for the conditions of Italian operatic life grew. He cultivated his estates, and was drawn back into the theatre only by three handsome foreign commissions, *La forza del destino* (St Petersburg, 1862), *Don Carlos* (Paris, 1867) and *Aida* (Cairo, 1871). His two final masterpieces were composed at leisure and then brought to the stage of La Scala, *Otello* in 1887 and *Falstaff* in 1893.

Abramo Basevi, in the earliest (1859) and still one of the most penetrating studies of Verdi's music, proposed a division into four periods or manners: the 'grandiose', as far as *La battaglia di Legnano*, in which the dominant influence is that of late Rossini; the 'personal', inaugurated by *Luisa Miller*, in which the characters express themselves with greater delicacy and individuality, and the composer moves closer to Donizetti; then a 'French-influenced' period introduced by *La traviata* and a 'German-influenced' represented by *Simon Boccanegra*. When Basevi's book appeared, six major operas were still to come. In the light of these, one might propose a redivision in which the second, 'personal' period culminates in *La traviata* and *Les vêpres siciliennes* begins a third, lasting some 30 years, during which the composer strove (with results that never quite satisfied him, since *Simon Boccanegra*, *La forza del destino*, *Don Carlos* and, to a lesser extent, *Aida*, were all refashioned after their premières) to create a grand opera in which lofty Meyerbeerian subject matter was brought to life by his own particular kind of Italian 'warmth'. During these years, Verdi was constantly threatening a Rossini-like retirement – and at the same time fairly constantly in touch with Paris, nibbling at subject after subject, rejecting all that did not excite him and longing ever for the decisive, unqualified Opéra triumph that eluded him until, under his direction, *Aida* was produced there in 1880.

By that time the seeds of *Otello* had been planted. In revisions of *Simon Boccanegra* (1880–81) and of *Don Carlos* (1882–3) he flexed his muscles to meet the challenge of composing that work. *Otello*, in which there is no musical or dramatic maladroitness, and the miraculous envoy that is *Falstaff* constitute a fourth and final period.

CHAPTER FOUR
Towards maturity

Verdi, aged 26 in 1839, was a late starter, and
had no regular conservatory training. Rossini, Donizetti
and Bellini were the best of the composers performed at
La Scala during his student years in Milan, but there
were many others whose works were played there with
success. In 1834 Verdi directed a performance of
Haydn's *Creation*; by then, however, Haydn was a classic, not the model that he had been for the student
Rossini and Donizetti. In 1845 Verdi set his pupil
Emanuele Muzio to the study of 'all the Classical music
of Beethoven, Mozart, Leidesdorf, Schubert, Haydn,
etc; and then we shall come to the moderns'; in later life,
the composer kept at his bedside pocket scores of
Haydn's, Mozart's and Beethoven's string quartets. But
it is hard to point to any specific influence on his first
two operas beyond the general 'Code Rossini' in force at
the time. It is easy for anyone wise after the event to
discern the specifically Verdian energy that informs
both *Oberto* and *Un giorno di regno*. *Nabucco* is clearly
modelled on Rossini's *Moïse* (which played at La Scala
during 1840), both in its general scheme and in the
formation of some individual numbers. Much about *I
lombardi* is also Rossinian, and another influence is
Mercadante, whose 'reform' opera *Il giuramento* appeared at La Scala in 1837, followed by *Il bravo* in
1839. Mercadante aimed to diversify the traditional
structure and sequence of numbers, to increase dramatic

209

directness and to handle the orchestra in less conventional ways, thus taking a stage further 'reforms' that already engaged the attention of Rossini, Bellini and Donizetti. The first act, in particular, of *I lombardi* suggests that Verdi listened to Mercadante's music attentively.

Precedents for Verdi's early procedures are readily found – for his aria, ensemble and act forms, his vigorous recitative now declamatory, now lyrically expansive, the rhythmic cut of his melodies, and his harmonic movement between keys a 3rd apart. Today, someone who hears an opera by Mercadante, Pacini or Federico Ricci is apt to be struck by its 'Verdian' features. It is useful to turn to a critic of the time who heard those composers first and could assess the newcomer against common stock. When Chorley declared that Verdi was the only Italian of his day having, for better or worse, a personal style, he continued:

> Yet many salient features of this style are not Signor Verdi's own. The crescendo and the use – not abuse – of unison, had been suggested by Donizetti; the form of the cabaletta, in which the phrase leaps and starts, rather than flows, by Federico Ricci; the employment of syncopation, by Signor Pacini; the excess of appoggiatura, by Bellini. No matter: by new combination known materials make a new whole.

Correctly, Chorley noted as the dominant features of Verdi's personal new combination a fondness for 'ferocious and gloomy stories'; an increasing solicitude to vary, enrich and temper 'the naked ferocity of instrumentation' found in his first pieces; much broad cantabile in 9/8 and 12/8, apt to heavy, long-breathed voices; frequent 'incitements for the singer to use the utmost force of his voice'; and, above all, 'an earnestness in attempting dramatic expression', an aspiration, that distinguished him from the men who, having found a successful formula, were content to continue exploiting it for others' diversion and their own profit.

The genesis of *Ernani*, conceived and largely composed in Milan while its librettist was in Venice, is well documented. In his letters of the time Verdi formulated, as early as 1843, articles of operatic belief that were to guide him throughout his career. Ideas, precepts, very phrases from them recur constantly over the next 40 years. And so *Ernani* can well be the starting-point for a 'thematic' survey of how Verdi's operas were written, avoiding the repetitions that a work-by-work chronicle would necessitate.

CHAPTER FIVE

Choice of subject

Singers, censors and local susceptibilities had all to be considered in the choice of subject. For the matter of his first Venetian opera, Verdi regretfully dismissed *King Lear* and Byron's *The Corsair* as needing more forceful male leads than the Venice company could provide that season. Such practical considerations were always important. Florence, for example, lost *I masnadieri* because Verdi's favoured tenor, Gaetano Fraschini, was not available to create – and have created for him – the role of the impetuous Karl Moor, and gained *Macbeth* because the excellent baritone Felice Varesi was in the company. With increasing stringency, Verdi made the engagement of particular singers or, at the least, singers of a particular calibre a condition of his accepting a contract. The unwritten *King Lear* that runs through his biography like a King Charles's Head might more than once have been composed if artists embodying the Lear and Cordelia of his dreams had been at hand. (But perhaps not; for more than one great composer a *Lear* opera has remained an unrealizable vision.) The composition of a *Ruy Blas* after Victor Hugo, which he long wanted to write, was foiled in 1857 when Filippo Coletti, the principal baritone of the Naples company, was deemed unsuitable for either Dom César or the title role. Four years later *Ruy Blas* was blocked again, but for different reasons: the matter, a queen's love for a lackey, was deemed unsuitable for presentation in St Petersburg (and *La forza del destino* was chosen instead).

Something similar had happened in 1843, during the genesis of *Ernani*. After dismissing *King Lear* and *The Corsair*, Verdi toyed with a *Bride of Abydos* after Byron, a *Catherine Howard*, a *Rienzi* and a *Fall of the Longobards*; for various reasons all were rejected, and then Verdi put forward Byron's *The Two Foscari* as the ideal subject – Venetian, passionate, and most apt for music. But the idea was vetoed, since descendants of the families concerned were still alive. Verdi set it aside for later use elsewhere; as ever, when a subject had truly seized his imagination, the opera that could be made from it had taken shape and 'colour' in his mind although not a line of the libretto or a note of the music had yet been written. For Venice he at first accepted, with no great enthusiasm, a *Cromwell* by a young poet named Francesco Maria Piave, thereby inaugurating a collaboration that lasted for nearly 20 years, until *La forza del destino*. But the text did not arouse him:

This *Cromwell* is certainly of no great interest, considering the requirements of the theatre. It is well ordered, clear, and admirably put together, but wretchedly uneventful. The first act convinced me but the second, instead of being a crescendo, as I had hoped, is a diminuendo. . . . Oh, if only we could do *Hernani*, that would be something great. . . . Tomorrow I will write at length to Signor Piave, setting out all the scenes that seem to me suitable. I have already seen how all the first act could be drawn together in a magnificent *introduzione*, and end where Don Carlos demands Hernani, who is hidden behind his portrait, from Silva. Act 2 is made from Act 4 of the French play. Act 3 ends with the magnificent trio in which Hernani dies.

That immediate 'seeing' how a play could take musico-dramatic shape is characteristic. *Cromwell* was dropped and *Ernani* was composed. It was as if subjects chose

213

Verdi as much as he chose them. *Nabucco* had already provided one example. In 1852, after rejecting two Scribe texts for his forthcoming Opéra commission, he told the playwright that he could not begin to consider an opera until he had 'a poem that sets me on fire and makes me shout "That's it! That's the one! To work at once!"'. In 1865, during the negotiations that led to *Don Carlos*, he exclaimed 'A libretto, just give me a libretto – and the opera is written!'. In 1870, after dallying with subject after subject, he leapt with undisguised relief on the *Aida* scenario when it reached him.

In March 1844, the month of *Ernani*, Verdi began keeping his *Copialettere*, volumes containing copies or drafts of his principal letters. The first page records his terms for composing an opera for Naples (among them, that a libretto by Salvatore Cammarano should reach him seven months before the opera was due, and that he would choose his own cast from a troupe which in any event would include Eugenia Tadolini, Fraschini and Coletti). On another page he jotted down a list of possible opera subjects. It begins with *King Lear*, *Hamlet* and *The Tempest* and includes Byron's *Cain*, Victor Hugo's *Le roi s'amuse*, *Marion de Lorme* and *Ruy Blas*, the elder Dumas' *Kean*, and two Spanish plays. These are authors and kinds of play to whom and which he was to devote his long career – Shakespeare, and the Romantics who looked to Shakespeare as their master. Less characteristic, in veins that he did not explore, are a *Phaedra* after 'Euripides–Racine', an *Annia* to be drawn from Tacitus's *Annals*, and a *Giacomo di Valenza* (the 14th-century Bolognese youth whose execution incited a student revolt) to be drawn from Sismondo Sismondi's great history of the Italian republics. One major name alone is missing, that of

Schiller, whose collected works still stand beside Shakespeare's in the shelf by Verdi's bed in Sant'Agata. *Giovanna d'Arco* (1845) represented little more than a first brush with the German playwright; Solera even denied, unconvincingly, that his libretto had anything to do with *Die Jungfrau von Orleans*. Verdi's first real Schiller opera and his first Shakespeare opera, *I masnadieri* and *Macbeth*, were conceived during July 1846, spent at a spa with Andrea Maffei, the translator of Schiller and (later) of Schiller's version of *Macbeth*.

Schiller's first play, *Die Räuber*, which yielded Verdi's *I masnadieri*, is a flamboyant document of early Romanticism. It appeared (1782) at the time when Shakespeare was first being played on German stages; Verdi's earliest Shakespeare and Schiller operas to some extent reflect not only his own but also Italy's discovery of Shakespeare – and the popularity in Italy of Schiller's plays. It is not surprising that for subject matter Verdi turned to Schiller more often than to any writer (and more fruitfully than to any other but Shakespeare). Between the artistic careers of the two men there are striking parallels; sentences about Schiller in A. W. Schlegel's *Lectures on Dramatic Art and Literature* (1809, 2/1811) apply with equal force to Verdi, who also

made his appearance, a man endowed with all the qualifications necessary to produce a strong effect on the multitude, and on nobler minds; . . . and although a genius independent and boldly daring, he was nevertheless influenced in various ways by the models which he saw in [the works of elder colleagues], and in Shakespeare, so far as he could understand him without an acquaintance with the original.

In his early work there is crudity and extravagance as well as power, but 'so noble a mind could not long persevere in such mistaken courses . . . and therefore,

215

17. *Stage design by Giuseppe and Pietro Bertoja for Act 3 scene i (the encampment of Count Luna) of 'Il trovatore', as performed at La Fenice, Venice, 1853–4: pen and ink drawing with wash*

with incredible diligence and a sort of passion, he gave himself up to artistic discipline'. In the works of his middle period 'we observe a greater depth in the delineation of character; yet the old and tumid extravagance is not altogether lost, but merely clothed with choicer forms'. Later works are 'planned and executed with more artistic skill, and also with greater depth and breadth'.

Schiller's *Kabale und Liebe* is a 'middle-class tragedy' and *Luisa Miller*, the opera based on it, reflects Verdi's new concern with 'ordinary' – but interesting – people in interesting predicaments. Verdi turned only twice to modern plays (which had appeared only a year before he made operas from them) and 19th-century settings: in *Stiffelio* (1850), which is about divorce, and *La traviata* (1853), which reflected his own situation at the time, living with a talented, experienced and attractive woman to whom he was not married. Between *Stiffelio* and *La traviata* there were *Rigoletto* and *Il trovatore*. Verdi liked to vary his genres. Patriotic 'spectaculars' by Solera and 'intimate' dramas by Piave alternate. The city of first performance had to be considered. Salvatore Cammarano, the doyen of Neapolitan librettists, fashioned traditional subject matter in *Alzira* (after Voltaire, with the sharp criticism of Christian morality much softened) and in *Il trovatore*, and he drew the political teeth of *Kabale und Liebe*. But, for production in a Rome on the point of declaring itself a republic, he and Verdi sounded the revolutionary clarions of *La battaglia di Legnano*, an opera that proved unperformable elsewhere until it had been tamed.

One of my ideas is to set *The Tempest* to music, and to do the same with all the principal plays of the great tragedian. (1850)

217

Le roi s'amuse is the greatest subject and perhaps the greatest play of modern times. Triboulet [Rigoletto] is a creation worthy of Shakespeare. . . . You know that six years ago, when Mocenigo suggested *Ernani* to me, I exclaimed 'Yes, by God, that can't go wrong'.

Today, while I was considering various subjects, *Le roi* flashed into my mind like lightning, an inspiration, and I said the same thing: 'Yes, by God, that can't go wrong'. (1850)

I want subjects that are novel, big, beautiful, varied and bold – as bold as can be. (1853)

Ten years ago I would not have dared to tackle *Rigoletto*. . . . Today I would refuse subjects of the kind of *Nabucco, Foscari*, etc. . . . They harp on one chord, elevated, if you like, but monotonous . . . I prefer Shakespeare to all other dramatists, the Greeks not excepted. I think the best, the most effective subject I have so far set to music . . . is *Rigoletto*. It has very powerful situations, variety, brio, pathos. All the sudden changes of fortune are brought about by the lighthearted, libertine character of the Duke, who arouses Rigoletto's fears, Gilda's passion, etc, which form many excellent dramatic points, among them the quartet. (1853)

The last quotation is from a letter to Antonio Somma, who wrote a *Lear* libretto for Verdi and rewrote Scribe's *Gustave III* as *Un ballo in maschera*. Verdi went on to explain to Somma that in his view a drama could not be animated by the simple provision of festivities, banquets or tourneys; variety of situation was indeed necessary but had to spring from the characters themselves. Increasingly, he was drawn to dramas whose eventfulness had a focal point in a divided character. A common operatic conflict of the day was between love and patriotic duty (it is prominent, for example, in Rossini's three *grands opéras*); Verdi touched on it in some early pieces and returned to it in *Aida*, which in point of situations and subject matter has the most conventional of all his librettos. But more singular are the plights of Stiffelio, the pastor who preaches

Christian forgiveness yet cannot bring himself to forgive his errant wife, and Azucena, the gypsy torn between filial vindictiveness and maternal affection. Many of Verdi's heroes are rulers upon whom public cares weigh heavy. If one sought to derive a moral from the sum of the subjects he set, it might be this: that honour and duty prompt an upright man to make a choice which conflicts with his hopes of personal happiness. A similarly sombre view of life is often expressed in his letters. His second opera and his last were comedies; of the others, only *Oberto* and the exceptional *Stiffelio/Aroldo* do not end with a death scene.

Verdi sought subjects that were unconventional and that would yield, not simply a sequence of events lending themselves to effective musical treatment, but a dramatic progression towards a climax. Once a subject was settled, and had been accepted by the theatre concerned, the opera was, in his words, 'as good as written'.

CHAPTER SIX
Libretto, forms

But the words themselves still remained to be written, and getting a libretto into shape generally proved to be a longer task than composing the music. When the first instalment of the *Cromwell* text reached Verdi, he replied: 'I'm putting this first act aside, because I do not want to begin work until I have all the libretto. That's my usual way, and I find it best, because, when I have an idea of the whole text, the notes always find themselves'. The general structure of *Cromwell* had already been discussed with Piave. For *Ernani*, a careful groundplan of the numbers was sent to him. That was Verdi's usual procedure, often extensively documented when the composer and his librettist were in different towns, and to be presumed when, for example, Verdi visited Paris for five months in 1865–6 to discuss the text of *Don Carlos* with Méry and Du Locle or when Du Locle visited him in Sant'Agata in 1870 to plan *Aida*. At this stage the basic form and sequence of numbers were defined:

At the moment of Carlos's entrance, I would have a very little tender duet. . . . Then, at Ernani's entrance a little later, I would plunge into the stretta of that piece [i.e. a trio closing-section to what had begun as a duet; Rossini, Bellini and Donizetti had already made striking use of the device]. Afterwards, with a sort of recitative, I would have a servant or Giuseppa announce Ruy's arrival; after a few words of surprise, he would launch the *adagio* of the final ensemble.

If all the large-scale Italian operas of the 19th century, in four acts or in a prologue and three, were superimposed, the resultant 'image' might have the fol-

220

lowing features: an *introduzione* in which one of the characters has a solo framed by choruses; heroine introduced in the second or third scene, often with an aria of narrative character, a dream, a memory, and often preceded by a women's chorus; large concerted finales to Acts 2 and 3 (or perhaps a rousing duet as one of the finales); an extended three-movement duet within one of the central acts; a *preghiera* for the heroine near the start of the last act; a final death scene for the hero or else, particularly in a prima donna opera, a so-called 'rondo finale' for the heroine. In three-act and two-act operas the scheme is condensed. There are countless variations, in the works of Verdi's predecessors as in his, but features of the basic scheme can be observed in all his operas, from *Oberto* to *Otello* and *Falstaff*. When conventions served his dramatic and musical purposes he was content to use them, but he was always happy to break with them, and insistent on doing so if they might obscure the singularity of his chosen drama. 'I have no detestation of cabalettas', he wrote in 1870, 'but I want them to be about something and to have a reason. In the *Ballo in maschera* duet there was a splendid reason; after all that scena, love had, so to speak, to burst forth.'

Piave was told that *Ernani* should 'end with a magnificent trio' (September 1843). 'For God's sake, don't end Act 4 with a rondo, but do a trio; what's more, this trio should be the best piece in the opera' (October 1843). (Magnificent trios also end *Luisa Miller* and the revised version of *La forza del destino*.) *Luisa Miller* represents a very close collaboration, amply documented, between the composer and his librettist. At one point Cammarano wrote: 'If I were not afraid of being thought Utopian, I should be tempted to say that, to

221

achieve the peak of perfection in an opera, the same mind should be responsible for both the words and the music' (that was in 1849, a year before the production of *Lohengrin*). In 1851, when *Il trovatore* was under discussion, Cammarano was told:

As for the arrangement of numbers, I assure you that when I am presented with poetry that can be set to music, every form, every arrangement is good, and the more novel and bizarre they are, the happier I am. If only in opera there could be no cavatinas, no duets, no trios, no choruses, no finales, etc, and if only the whole opera could be, so to speak, all one number, I should find that sensible and right. So I say, if you can, avoid beginning this opera with a chorus (all operas begin with a chorus); skip Leonora's cavatina and go straight into the troubadour's song, and join the first two acts together if you can, since these isolated numbers, with a scene-change for each, make on me the effect of concert pieces rather than an opera.

Verdi followed these general instructions with his own detailed, number-by-number groundplan, since he felt that the scenario Cammarano had sent him lacked 'all the novelty and strangeness of the Spanish play'. Among other things, he prescribed the conjunction of Leonora's aria, the troubadour's song from the tower and the 'Miserere' chant as a single number, and repeated his request for 'free, novel forms'. When he came to set the libretto, after Cammarano's death, he removed the stretta of the second finale ('perhaps Cammarano put it in only because it's traditional') in order to close the act with a series of excited cries ('That way, the form seems to me more novel'). Similarly, at the very end he scrapped 12 lines of verse in favour of the abrupt exclamations that now finish the opera.

Changes of this kind can be paralleled in the creation of all Verdi's operas whenever the evidence survives. It was not only to the pliant Piave that he dictated. To Scribe he prescribed metres that he required in *Les vêpres siciliennes*, and even suggested lines. For sections of *Don Carlos*, both in 1866 and again when revising it in 1883, he wrote (in French) the verses that he required and submitted them to Du Locle only for polishing. The most detailed series of letters is that written to Antonio Ghislanzoni about *Aida*; Verdi explained not only what he wanted but also why he wanted it; he revealed his concern both for forceful passing effects and for the part these must play in the whole drama. The correspondence is a major document of operatic literature. The basic plot of *Aida*, set out in a 23-page pamphlet by Auguste Mariette, had been elaborated into a scenario by Verdi and Du Locle; Ghislanzoni was then engaged to turn the result into the Italian verses which Verdi would set. On 14 August 1870 Verdi received the poet's first attempt at the consecration scene, and he wrote:

If I must tell you my frank opinion, it seems to me that this consecration scene has not attained the importance I expected. The characters don't always say what they should say, and the priests are not *priests* enough. Moreover, it seems to me that the *parola scenica* is either lacking or, when present, buried beneath the rhyme or the versification so that it does not leap, sharply and plainly, in the way it should. . . . This scene must be given all possible importance and solemnity.

The *parola scenica* was a concept that had long been with him, instinctively at first, and in a later letter defined as 'the words that cut through and give precision and immediacy to the situation'. Verdi rewrote some of Ghislanzoni's regular verses as brusque, exclamatory exchanges, and continued:

I know well that you'll say: And what of the verse, the rhyme, the strophe? I don't know what to answer; but, when the action calls for it, I would straightway abandon rhythm, rhyme and strophe; I would make irregular lines so as to say clearly and precisely what the action demands. Unfortunately, the theatre requires that on occasion poets and composers should have the ability to create neither poetry nor music.

223

On 16 August he returned to the consecration scene. 'We must study it again to give it greater character and greater scenic importance. It must not be a chilly hymn but a true scena. I enclose a copy of the French scenario, which reveals all the importance of this tableau.' Even an episode with no action in it, he explained, such as, in *Don Carlos*, that of the ladies awaiting the queen outside the convent, can become 'a true scena' if the words have sufficient character and colour. The scene for Amneris and her tirewomen (Act 2 scene i) must also be such a scena. On 22 August he wrote:

I have found something for the consecration scene. If it seems to you unsatisfactory, let us go on looking. Meanwhile it seems to me that in the following way a musical scena of some effect could be created. The number would consist of a litany intoned by the priestesses, to which the priests respond; a sacred dance with slow, sad music; a short recitative, energetic and solemn as a biblical psalm; and a prayer in two strophes, given out by the priest and taken up by everyone. And I should like it to have a pathetic, serene character, especially in the first strophe, so as to avoid any resemblance to the other choruses that end the introduction and Act 2, which are rather *Marseillaise* in manner.

It seems to me that the litanies (and for the thousandth time, excuse my presumption) should be little strophes of one long and one five-syllable line; or – and perhaps this would be better, so that everything could be said – there could be two eight-syllable lines. The five-syllable line would be the *ora pro nobis* [the 'Noi t'invochiamo' refrain of the finished score]. Thus there would be little strophes of three lines each; and there should be six of them, more than enough to create a number with.

Such examples of verbal and musical advance planning, determining form and dramatic tone, could be multiplied a hundredfold. In any listing of Verdi's operas the words 'and the composer' could justly be added to every librettist's name. Music began to form during this preparatory process – on surviving draft librettos there are some 'shorthand' annotations sugg-

18. *A page of the 'skeleton score' (vocal line and some instrumentation) of Carlos' monologue intended to open Act 5 of 'Don Carlos', with the words adjusted when Verdi assigned the music to Elizabeth; it was never completed, and staves 11–19 were used to sketch the viola d'amore (later violin) solo in the ballet music*

225

esting musical treatment – but as a rule it was not until he had a complete libretto, more or less in the form he wanted, that Verdi turned in earnest to the process of setting down the notes. Then, of course, there began a second round of libretto revisions. Sometimes they were slight, a simple matter of verbal adjustment to a striking musical idea, and sometimes they drastically affected the form of an act. (Instances of the latter in *Il trovatore* have already been cited.) When, during the composition of *Don Carlos* in 1866, Verdi reached Eboli's air, the libretto draft before him began 'Que de larmes brûlent ma paupière! O don fatal et détesté'; it was his idea to attack the piece with the more arresting second phrase. Rehearsals of that opera had already begun when he decided to change the form of the last act by adding Elizabeth's extended air 'Toi qui sus le néant', which in its central strophes incorporates a monologue for Carlos that had originally opened the act (see fig.18, p.225).

CHAPTER SEVEN

Composition, style

In his comments to the Venice impresario on the 1843 draft contract for the opera that became *Ernani*, Verdi said that he could not deliver the full score at the date specified because 'it is my custom to do the orchestration during the piano rehearsals, and the score is never completely finished before the pre-dress rehearsal'. The bulk of Verdi's sketches remain unavailable for study at Sant'Agata, but some have found their way into public collections, and those for *Rigoletto* have been published in facsimile (1941). Carlo Gatti, who saw the Sant'Agata archives, spoke of cabinets filled with sketches, amounting to 'continuity drafts', for the operas from *Luisa Miller* onwards, growing ever more elaborate from the time of *Les vêpres siciliennes*. Verdi's mature practice is deducible: sketching and shaping ideas (to watch those for the 'maledizione' motif of *Rigoletto*, the Rigoletto–Sparafucile dialogue and 'La donna è mobile' taking form is an enthralling study), proceeding to continuity draft and then moving into full score – but, at this stage, setting down only the vocal lines, the bass and a few striking instrumental cues. From this skeleton full score the singer's parts were then prepared, and once they were made rehearsals could begin. Meanwhile the pages were returned to Verdi to be completed as full score, and any changes he introduced at this stage were entered as corrections in the singers' copies. Surviving first-performance material in the Paris

227

Opéra archives shows the process plainly. Until more sketches become available, Verdi's early practice can be only a matter of speculation, but the evidence both of his expressed intentions and of the works themselves suggests that almost from the first he cared about continuity and a long dramatic line. Act 4 of *Ernani* (see Kerman, 1973) shows the results of such concern in action; and his scorn for operas that are merely one number after another, 'cavatina operas', was often expressed.

One method of achieving continuity was through harmonic organization. But about Verdi's feeling for large-scale harmonic structure there has been disagreement. Because a sketch may be in one key and the finished number in another – or because in 1867 the Andante of the final duet of *Don Carlos* is in B♭ and the close of the opera in A, while in the 1883 revision both keys are B – some have argued that precise tonality was a matter of indifference to him, and others that the changes between sketch and final product indicate precisely that key did matter. Practical considerations also enter into it. Eboli's Veil Song, originally composed in G for a mezzo, was lifted to A when a singer with a higher voice was chosen to create the role. (Ingenious harmonic analysis can demonstrate either G or A to be structurally the 'right' key.) Verdi's stipulation in several contracts that a company practising any cuts or transpositions should pay a large penalty fee can be considered evidence of a feeling for pitch and for tonal structure. Certainly in *Macbeth*, in *Il trovatore* and in *Simon Boccanegra* keys are associated with dramatic ideas, and the later operas show an increasing concern for harmonic architecture. (See in particular, for *Nabucco*, Lawton, 1972; for *Ernani*, Kerman, 1973; for

Composition, style

La traviata, Chusid, 1972; and for *Falstaff*, Sabbeth, 1972 – an example of 'harmonico-psycho-dramatic' argument carried to extremes.)

On the small scale, within numbers, Verdi's harmonic movement is generally, in a minor key, to the tonic or relative major, with an effect of increased emotional intensity; and, in a major key, to keys a 3rd away, achieved by treating the tonic as the mediant of the new key (ex.1, from the love-duet of *Un ballo in maschera*),

Ex.1

or vice versa, or by isolating the mediant and treating it as a dominant to the new key. These are common enough procedures of the time, as are Verdi's other devices of diminished-7th pivots and of chromatic sequences – short, repeated figurations set to climb up or down as many steps as are needed to reach the new key or its dominant. Ex.1 demonstrates one characteristic way of reaching D♭ major, a key much favoured by Verdi; *Il trovatore* can provide three others. The Act 1 trio, the baritone's scena in Act 2, and the tenor's aria (not its cabaletta) all end in D♭, though none begins in it. In the trio, Di Luna strikes into the key from the tonic minor, by attacking a high F♮, *tutta forza*, after a series of phrases containing an emphatic F♭. The aria of his

229

scena begins in B♭ ('Il balen'); from a cadence in that key, a chromatic sequence settles on E♭, treated as the dominant of a little A♭ chorus, whose final notes are then reiterated as a dominant to the D♭ cabaletta ('Per me l'ora fatale'). Manrico's 'Ah si, ben mio' begins in F minor and then makes 3rd moves to A♭, F♭, then A♭ again as dominant to the D♭ final section.

These uncomplicated, securely achieved key changes produce a powerful effect in the theatre. But sometimes in the early operas the 'surprise effect' of mediant modulation is worked so hard that it ceases to be surprising. There are also, even as late as *Luisa Miller*, some laboured, clumsy progressions that suggest no more than a striving for novelty. Verdi's development is towards a stronger, simpler mastery. In *Otello*, chromatic slithering is used in Iago's music for characterizing effect. Basically, the 3rd relationships remain prominent. The use of passing chromatic enrichments becomes ever more delicate. The 'kiss' motif of *Otello* turns on an unprepared C major triad, in 6-4 position, within the E major context (ex.2). Other examples in

Ex.2

G♯° ___ E ___ G♯⁺ ___ B⁷ ___ E

Otello are 'Ora e per sempre' (which bursts out in A♭ after a long chain of dominant- and diminished-7th chords has pointed towards F minor) and the duet 'Sì, pel ciel'. Othello begins this duet in A; his line descends to a low mediant, which is treated as a C♯ tonic, and three bars later to a high mediant in the new key, to which the orchestra supplies F major harmony. Othello ends his strophe in F, but with his voice on the mediant, A, which Iago and the orchestra at once take up in an A major cadence, completing the chain of 3rd moves. Iago then sings the bass line that had accompanied Othello, but harmonized now with an effect of 6-4 on its recurrent A. 6-4 is a propellant chord, which Verdi favoured for exclamations. The correspondent of the *Allgemeine musikalische Zeitung* (1840) noted its use as early as *Oberto*; there are striking examples in *Rigoletto* and *Falstaff* (ex.3).

Ex.3

(a)

Spa - ra - fu - cil   mi   no - mi - no

Eb ♭♮   C♯   D   D♭ ♮

(b)

Ca - ro Sig - nor Fon - ta - na

G♯

When Verdi told Venice, in 1843, that he would supply, not a fully orchestrated score, but one 'finished *as regards the composition* and in such a way that the singers' parts and the choruses can be extracted', the italicized phrase makes his priorities plain. His early scoring was functional. The voice usually begins with string accompaniment. Melodic wind lines are added progressively as the vocal melody reaches its climax, and sustaining wind underlines any harmonic interest; as Budden has noted, 'at the first accidental, woodwind (usually clarinets and bassoons) will add sustaining chords'. In martial or otherwise vigorous movements, brass may double both the accompaniment figures and the vocal line. All this is standard. But in each of the early operas there is usually one number set apart from the rest by the singularity and delicacy of its orchestration. Examples are Zaccaria's *preghiera* in *Nabucco* (six solo cellos, three arco and three pizzicato, and double bass; ex.4), Giselda's *preghiera* in *I lombardi* (eight

Ex.4

violins, two violas, bass, solo flute and clarinet), and Odabella's romance in *Attila* (english horn, flute, harp, cello, and pizzicato double bass; ex.5; while moonlight sparkles on the stream, Odabella sings of evanescent shapes in the clouds). The dagger monologue and the sleepwalking scene in *Macbeth*, the Rigoletto–Sparafucile encounter (muted cello and double bass rising above an accompaniment of wind and strings in carefully specified numbers), Gilda's 'Lassù in cielo' (flute arpeggios and trills, and six solo strings above soft pizzicato chords; incidentally, another D♭ major passage exquisitely approached) and Amelia's cavatina in *Simon Boccanegra* (strings and woodwind picturing sunrise over the rippling sea) may also be cited. Such passages become less and less exceptional. There are many in *Don Carlos*, still more in *Aida*; the score of *Falstaff* can be opened at almost any page to provide an example. Subtlety of scoring becomes not a special ef-

Ex.5

fect but part of the tissue of the music drama; instrumentation is no longer something added later to a score 'already finished as regards the composition'.

The baptism scene of *I lombardi* and the overture to *I masnadieri* contain small concerto movements for, respectively, violin and cello. In the ballet divertissements of the French operas there are prominent instrumental solos. More remarkable – not for their novelty, since the device is common enough in Verdi's predecessors, but for their eloquence – are the instrumental solos that wind through some vocal scenes: the poignant cello of Rigoletto's 'Miei signori, perdono' (yet another emotional passage in D♭ major) and the clarinet that sounds in much of *Luisa Miller*, in Violetta's scena after. the duet with Germont, and in Alvaro's romance in *La forza del destino*.

An analysis of Verdian melody would have to start with the conventions of his day, the rhythmic and melodic formulae implicit in the metre of the verses being set. (They are codified in Lippmann's long study 'Die italienische Vers und der musikalische Rhythmus', *AnMc*, 1973–5.) Standard forms were similarly predetermined – and it was in order to avoid formulae that Verdi constantly urged on his librettists novel, irregular, even bizarre metres and irregular stanza forms. He enjoined them to be brief, to say directly only just as much as was necessary and to strike out any words that were there merely for purposes of scansion and rhyme. Towards the end of his career he recommended the abandonment altogether of regular versification.

In rough and ready summary, the aria form Verdi inherited was *AABA* or, particularly when there is a change of key in the final section, *AABC*. Grand arias conclude with a cabaletta of two identical verses, the second of which is (or should be) graced and varied by the individual singer. Grand duets are in three parts, introduced and linked by recitatives: solo statements of opposed sentiments, often to the same music; at a slower tempo and in a different key, a reflective passage, ending in chains of 3rds, 6ths or 10ths and a double cadenza; a fast section in which the melody is sung first by one voice, then by the other, and then by both together. Ensembles, particularly mid-opera act finales, are launched expansively by a single voice (sometimes after a fast introductory section); other soloists, and then the full chorus, join in, and there is a concluding section in fast tempo. Verdi's predecessors all made notable departures from the standard forms. So did he. It need only be remarked what is particularly individual about his practices.

In duets, more consistently than Donizetti, Verdi liked to give the singers different material. In *Il trovatore*, when Manrico and Azucena, and later Leonora and Di Luna, join in octaves in the concluding sections of their duets, the effect is, for Verdi, curiously old-fashioned. The Violetta–Germont duet shows the standard form completely freed of melodic convention, each line being motivated by individual emotions. On the other hand, the final Violetta–Alfredo duet returns to the old pattern (with a foreshortened first section), and in this duet of eager reunion it is not dramatically unapt for the lovers to sing the same lines. A Verdian speciality often remarked is the extended duet for a soprano and a baritone who are father and daughter or in a similar relationship. The combination regularly

235

inspired him; the oft-contemplated duet for Cordelia
and Lear must be counted one of music's great might-
have-beens.

Verdi's particular developments of aria form, linked to
his maturing melodic practice, are hard to describe,
since two contradictory forces seem to be at work. On
the one hand, the long, non-repetitive, rhapsodic periods
of his earlier operas (Rossinian or Bellinian) tend to
yield to a melody organized in smaller units, capable of
plastic transformation (Donizetti affords a precedent).
'La donna è mobile' is a simple example, and the succes-
sion of 'Sì, la stanchezza', 'Riposa, o madre' and 'Ai
nostri monti' in the last scene of *Il trovatore* (solo
statements in a finale of intricately lapped duos and
trios) one less simple. 'Urna fatale' (Carlo's aria in *La
forza del destino*) and 'Celeste Aida' are highly
developed examples. With such units, larger and more
intricately developed structures could be built. But
analysis yields so many different patterns of aria that
any general observations break down, beyond that of
remarking the increasing employment of large-scale ternary structures, as distinct from the small-scale *AABA*
forms.

On the other hand, there is Verdi's fondness for free,
dramatic declamation moulded only by the progress of
the text. There is precedent in things like Assur's hal-
lucination in Rossini's *Semiramide* and the long melodic
periods found in recitatives by Bellini, but there is nothing in earlier operas quite like Macbeth's dagger speech,
the latter part of Francesco Moor's vision of the Last
Judgment (in *I masnadieri*) or Rigoletto's 'Pari siamo'.
Macbeth's monologue is headed 'gran scena',
Francesco's 'sogno', and Rigoletto's 'scena'; they are

larger examples of lyric outpouring within recitative
such as Leonora's 'Come d'aurato sogno' (before her
first aria in *Il trovatore*) and Violetta's 'Amami,
Alfredo', but they are more than merely long accompanied recitatives. Basevi termed this kind of writing
Verdi's 'dialectical' manner. When practised within a
more regular 'number' it could produce an aria form
without precedent, such as that of Stiffelio's 'Vidi
dovunque gemere' (Act 1), where each interjection of
the soprano sets the tenor's music on a new tack. It is
often found in Verdi's duets. But in the operas of the
third period, from *Les vêpres siciliennes* to *Don Carlos*,
this particular kind of direct lyric impulsiveness is
increasingly subordinated to formal considerations.
Aida marks the beginning of a new synthesis, perfected
in *Otello* and *Falstaff*.

Some astonishingly close resemblances between
Verdi and Donizetti have been remarked, not just of
melody but also of key and accompaniment in response
to similar dramatic situations (see Dean, 1972 and
1973–4; Lippmann, 1975). Basevi placed the main
force of Donizettian influence in Verdi's second period.
It becomes strong in *Macbeth* and extends right up to
La forza del destino, and it would indeed be strange if
Verdi had not sought to learn from the most 'Verdian' of
his elder colleagues. Yet one must try to distinguish –
though often it is hard to do so – between coincidence,
commonplace of the day, unconscious reminscence, and
deliberate, 'creative' imitation. The ideas concerned are
sometimes too arresting to be considered mere current
formulae. If Verdi had remembered that ex.6 occurred
in Donizetti's *Pia de' Tolomei*, would he have dared to
use the melody so prominently in *La traviata*? Or could

he have wanted to show, almost as if in tribute, how much more could be made of what in Donizetti is a passing, though powerful, moment?

Ex.6

Moderato assai
con grande espressione

Oh Pia men - da - ce,   o - v'è,   ov'è il ri - go - re

In the men of *Ernani*, Verdi established his basic vocal types: the vigorous baritone, centre of energy, forceful, determined, with his voice pitched about a tone higher than Donizetti's *basso cantante*; the ardent, lyrical, brave but often despairing tenor; the severe, unyielding bass, usually (though not in *Ernani*) voicing his sorrow only in soliloquy. '*Ernani* is the first opera of what might be called vocal *scontro*, an opera whose dramatic force and musical interest derive from the clashing of characters embodied in vocal archetypes' (Budden). Verdi's sopranos are more various. Joan of Arc is the first of them to be convincingly individual, not merely a prima donna, in everything that she sings. From *Simon Boccanegra* to *Aida* a similar kind of soprano voice is used consistently, which needs to be pure, full, delicate yet powerful, and capable of long, smooth phrasing. Verdi's first important mezzo-soprano is Azucena, descended from Fidès in Meyerbeer's *Le prophète*. Eboli and Amneris, rivals to the soprano, and female counterparts to the Verdian baritone in their dramatic forcefulness, were later discoveries, though Lady Macbeth (a role not infrequently tackled by mezzos) is to some extent their ancestress. In his letters Verdi declared again and again that spirited, powerful

declamation of the words and a vivid stage presence
were qualities in a singer more important to him than a
polished vocal technique. To Felice Varesi, the first
Macbeth, he wrote: 'I shall never cease recommending
you to study closely the dramatic situation and the
words; the music comes of itself'. On the other hand, he
was quick to denounce technical shortcomings, and the
gramophone records of singers he admired (Adelina
Patti, Gemma Bellincioni) and wrote for and worked
with (Francesco Tamagno, Victor Maurel, Eduard de
Reszke) show very high vocal accomplishment coupled
with that feeling for character on which he was insistent.
It has been noted how the presence or absence of
particular singers in a company might determine the
subject of his next opera. Individual singers could also
determine, to some extent, the music that he wrote.
Varesi was sent alternative settings of a Macbeth phrase
and asked which suited him better. Verdi's admiration
for Fraschini is reflected in a long series of tenor parts
reaching from Zamoro in *Alzira* (1845) to Riccardo in
Un ballo in maschera (1859) and even to Radamès
(1871), since Verdi hoped to secure Fraschini for the
Aida première. The soprano solos of the Requiem en-
shrine the vocal prowess of Teresa Stolz, the first Italian
Elizabeth (*Don Carlos*) and Aida. The title role of *Otello*
(1887) predicates the stentorian utterance of Tamagno,
with whom Verdi had worked when producing the
revised versions of *Simon Boccanegra* (1881) and of
Don Carlos (1884).

Composition proceeded right up to the first performance of an opera – and sometimes beyond that. Verdi
personally supervised the creation of all his works except *Il corsaro*, the revised *Macbeth* and *Aida* (though in

19. Libretto of *'Aida'*, *Act 2 scene ii* (*The Triumph Scene*), with Verdi's annotations for its staging

the last case he clearly regarded the Cairo première in the nature of a try-out and the Scala performance, which he did supervise, as the 'real' première). Marianna Barbieri-Nini, the first Lady Macbeth, left a vivid account of the 'more than 150 rehearsals' he demanded for the Act 1 duet, and the 151st he insisted upon while keeping an invited dress-rehearsal audience waiting.

I can still remember the black look Varesi shot at Verdi as he followed the Maestro into the foyer. With his hand on the pommel of his sword he seemed about to murder Verdi even as later he would murder King Duncan. But even Varesi gave in, and the 151st rehearsal took place, while the impatient audience made an uproar in the theatre.

There is abundant evidence of Verdi's concern for the staging as well as the singing, playing and acting of his operas, in the form of detailed descriptions, stage plans and sketches in his own hand, and angry complaints when things went wrong. His musical effects were often composed with their precise visual accompaniment in mind. About *Simon Boccanegra* he wrote:

Take great care over the staging. Although the directions [in the score and libretto] are fairly precise, let me add some notes. In the first scene, if the Fieschi palace is to one side, it must be in full view of the public, since it is essential that everyone should see Simone when he enters the house, and when he comes out on the balcony and takes down the lantern; here, I believe, I have achieved a musical effect that I do not want ruined by the staging.

For the next scene he described the curtains and gauzes that should be used to portray moonlight shimmering on the sea. In the final scene, on a distant backcloth the illuminations of Genoa *en fête* should be clear and brilliant, and then go out one by one until, at the death of the Doge, all is dark – 'a powerfully effective moment, I believe, and it would be a disaster if the staging were not good'. For all his operas from *Les vêpres siciliennes*

241

to *Otello*, production books based on performances that he supervised were published. That for *Les vêpres* he sent to Venice with instructions that it should be followed in detail. These production books contain descriptions of scenery, costumes and properties, move-by-move stage directions (often with the 'motivation' of the gestures explained), details of how to set up the successive scenes so that changes can be quick, lighting cues, stage plans that show the blocking during the progress of each scene, and lists of the extras and supers required, with instructions how they should be clad and used. Verbally, musically and visually at once an opera took shape in Verdi's mind. During his work on the libretto, and then on the score, that shape became more and more clearly defined, often with the timbres and personalities of particular singers and with precise theatrical images in his ear and eye.

This survey has ranged beyond Verdi's 'second period', but if a pause be made at *La traviata*, a retrospect will show that the dividing line between 'first' and 'second' periods is indistinct. The shift from 'grandiose' to 'personal' is gradual, although by *Luisa Miller* it is fully achieved. In every one of Verdi's operas there are innovations, and there is little without precedents and consequents; it has been justly observed that any of his pieces can correctly be called transitional. His work shows a steadily increasing mastery of techniques, and the subsequent application of those techniques both to new and to earlier, proved kinds of subject matter. In *Macbeth* and *I masnadieri* he rose to a greater literary challenge than he had known before and was inspired to make notable advances in form, in expressive declamation and in his handling of the orchestra. *Jérusalem* brought the direct experience of the Paris Opéra, and its immediate successors, *Il corsaro* and *La battaglia di Legnano*, two of Verdi's most 'experimental' scores, are French-influenced in their detailed working, their use of 'thematic development' and their avoidance of simple repetition.

From early days, Verdi had made use of recurring themes (see Kerman, 1968), associated with nations (the Assyrian and the Israelite marches of *Nabucco*), objects (Silva's horn, in *Ernani*) or individuals (in *I due Foscari* there are recurrent melodies identifying Lucrezia and Jacopo Foscari, and the Council of Ten). In later operas, Violetta's love for Alfredo, Monterone's curse on Rigoletto and Othello's kiss (ex.2) provide memorable recurrent motifs. Similar situations in different operas would sometimes evoke similar musical responses. From *Nabucco* onwards, a prayer ascending to Heaven often prompts a flute solo rising through high strings. When, in *Luisa Miller*, the heart-broken Luisa is compelled to write a lying letter, to persuade Rodolfo that she is false to him, the clarinet plays ex.7*a*; and when, in *La traviata*, the heart-broken Violetta embarks on a similarly hateful letter, to persuade Alfredo that she is false to him, the clarinet plays ex.7*b*. A recurrent motif

Ex.7

(a) Adagio

(b) Adagio

in many operas (and in the 'Lacrimosa' of the Requiem) is the *come un lamento* figure (ex.8), usually syncopated, piercing the texture like a cry of grief. It is used extensively in several numbers of the sombre *Don Carlos* (the discarded prelude to that opera began with 20 bars dominated by the figure).

Ex.8

The 'thematic developments' of the French-influenced *Il corsaro* and *La battaglia di Legnano* were carried further in their successor, *Luisa Miller*; many of that opera's themes are derived, whether consciously or not, from a single basic idea. The overture is monothematic, and ex.9*a* is its theme. Ex.9*b*, which begins the last section of the *introduzione*, may bring no more than a rhythmic reminiscence, but in ex.9*c*, which opens Act 3, exx.9*a* and *b* are joined in a triple-time transformation. Ex.9*d* is a clarinet solo during the dialogue that precedes the first finale; exx.9*e* and *f* are the melodies from which that finale is built. These are not the only, but merely the most striking, examples of the opera's thematic relationships. In *Luisa Miller* and its successors, the new musical ideas from France were brought to the enrichment of a more traditional, more Donizettian kind of opera. *Rigoletto*, the 'grandiose' *Il trovatore* and the 'intimate' *La traviata* mark the secure achievement of most of what Verdi had until then been striving for.

The outstanding operas of this decade are those that have always been acknowledged as such: the three just mentioned, and the earlier *Nabucco* and *Macbeth*. (Strictly speaking, the success of *La traviata* should be dated from its second production, with a slightly revised

Ex.9

(a) Allegro

(b) Allegro brillante

(c) Andante sostenuto

(d) Adagio

(e) Allegro moderato

(f) Allegro assai sostenuto

score, in May 1854; the première had not gone well, and Verdi withdrew the opera for 14 months.) *Nabucco* caught the first full fire of Verdi's genius. In *Macbeth*, his response to Shakespeare inspired music of rare force and subtlety. Of the others, *Ernani* has been fairly often played whenever a vigorous, powerful cast was available, and the remainder have been revived from time to time – all save *Oberto, Un giorno di regno, Alzira* (apart from a 1936 broadcast), *Il corsaro* and *Stiffelio*, which were unheard in this century until the 1960s. They all have merits, all show ambition, but they need skilled advocacy in performance. The popular trio, however, has proved well-nigh performer-proof, and marks a climax in Verdi's career. After *La traviata* he left Italy for a long period; his pace of production slackened, and a new ambition was formed.

CHAPTER EIGHT

Life, 1843–80

Verdi's life for the decade 1843–53, his 'galley years' after *Ernani*, reads like a travel diary – a timetable of visits, made from a Milanese base, to bring new operas to the stage or to supervise local premières. In Milan he mingled with the intellectuals of his day. The poet Andrea Maffei and the Countess Clarina Maffei, who led a lively salon, were among his friends. (The Maffeis were amicably parted; Verdi was a witness to their deed of separation.) His companion, amanuensis and pupil was Emanuele Muzio (1825–90), a red-headed youth from Busseto who, like Verdi himself, had studied with Provesi and been taken up by Barezzi, sent on a grant to study in Milan and rejected by the conservatory. Like Verdi, he went to a private teacher instead – in this case, Verdi himself. Muzio's letters to Barezzi provide a vivid, intimate picture of Verdi's life during these years of travel. The 'years in the galley' soon began to take their toll on him, physically – for many years he was plagued with recurrent stomach and, particularly, throat troubles – and mentally. In 1845 he wrote: 'My mind is black, always black and will remain so until I have finished with this career that I abhor', and 'I look forward to the passing of the next three years. I must write six operas – and then farewell to everything!'. That year he bought the Palazzo Dordoni (now Orlandi) in Busseto.

Verdi set an increasingly high price on his work. For

247

Un giorno di regno and *Nabucco*, his first commissioned operas, he had received 4000 lire (plus 2500 for the sale of the *Nabucco* score to Ricordi); for composing *Ernani* and mounting it and *Il lombardi* in Venice, 12,000; for *Attila* and *Macbeth*, 18,000 each. *I masnadieri*, in London, brought him 20,000 francs (the franc and the lira were more or less equivalent). The salary he then proposed for becoming musical director of Her Majesty's and spending six months a year in England was 90,000 (60,000 for an annual new opera and 30,000 for directing all performances at the theatre), plus a country house and a carriage; the proposal was not accepted. Paris paid him 5000 francs for *Jérusalem*, plus *droits d'auteur* as if for a newly composed work, and he sold all but the French and English rights in that opera to Ricordi for 8000, plus royalties of 500 per production for five years and 200 for the next five. Ricordi told him he had priced the opera out of the Italian market, and subsequent contracts are more moderate, based on the expectation (usually well justified) of a large number of performances and frequent revivals. In an 1847 draft contract with Ricordi, for example, Verdi agreed that for his next opera he would receive 12,000 for all printed arrangements of the score (a successful opera yielded a very large crop of arrangements for various instruments), 4000 for the first production, which he would supervise, and thereafter 400 per production for two years, 300 for the next three, and 200 for the next five; after ten years the work would become Ricordi's property. It is interesting to note his stipulation that the first performance should be in any leading Italian theatre 'except La Scala', and that La Scala should never be permitted to perform the piece without his express permission. (He never forgave the Milanese their reception of *Un giorno di regno*, and between *Giovanna d'Arco* in 1845 and the revised *Forza del destino* in 1869 would have nothing to do with La Scala.) Another clause specifies a penalty of 1000 francs if any cut, transposition or even the slightest change of instrumentation is made. (Later, Verdi modified this to apply only to major theatres; Ricordi should threaten smaller houses with the penalty, but not insist on it.)

Verdi drove himself hard, and he drove hard bargains, but in 1847 a mellowing influence entered his life. Back in Milan in 1839, the advocacy of the soprano Giuseppina Strepponi had helped to ensure the production of *Oberto*. In 1842, Strepponi was the Abigaille of the first *Nabucco* (but had small success in it; she was not engaged for the autumn revival of the opera). She retired from the stage in 1846 and set up in Paris as a singing teacher. Here Verdi met her again, in 1847, when he came to prepare *Jérusalem* for the Opéra. One of the more romantic discoveries of recent years has been Ursula Günther's of a 'dialogue' between Strepponi and Verdi in the love-duet of *Jérusalem*. In a passage of the autograph their hands alternate, and the following exchange can be read:

G.S.: Alas! Hope is banished. My glory has faded! Family . . . fatherland
. . . all I have lost!
G.V.: No I still am left you! And it will be for life!
G.S.: Angel from heaven! . . .
May I die in the arms of a husband!
G.V.: Let me die with you! My death will be . . .
G.S.: . . . sweet.
a due: With you beside me, death will be sweet!

It was indeed to be for life. Verdi and Strepponi lived together in Paris until August 1849. In 1848, on a visit

20. Giuseppe Verdi: photograph

to Italy, he bought a house and land at Sant'Agata, whence his forebears had come. On his return to Italy the following year he was joined, first at Busseto and then at Sant'Agata, by Strepponi. At first they lived in retirement, and there was evidently town tattle. Barezzi, Verdi's father-in-law, was rash enough to mention the fact in a letter of 1852, and received a stern reply:

You live in a town where people have the bad habit of prying into other people's affairs and of disapproving of everything that does not conform to their own ideas. It is my custom never to interfere, unless I am asked, in other people's business, and I expect others not to interfere in mine. ... What harm is there if I choose to live in isolation? if I choose not to pay calls on titled people? ...

I have nothing to hide. In my house there lives a lady, free, independent, a lover of solitude, as I am, possessing a fortune that shelters her from all need. Neither I nor she owes to anyone at all any account of our actions. On the other hand, who knows what relationship exists between us? what affairs? what bonds? what claims I have on her, or she on me? Who knows whether or not she is my wife? and if she is, who knows what the particular reasons are for not making the fact public? ...

With this long rigmarole, I mean to say no more than that I demand liberty of action for myself, since all men have that right and since my nature rebels against conformity; and that you, so good, just and generous at heart, should not allow yourself to be influenced or absorb the ideas of a town that – it must be said! – once did not consider me worthy of being its organist, and now murmurs and mutters about my actions and affairs. That cannot go on. .... The world is wide, and the loss of 20 or 30 thousand francs will never stop me from finding a home elsewhere.

Verdi's unforgiving nature is clear. Ferrari's appointment as organist, back in 1834, still rankled. The feud against Busseto continued: Verdi refused to become patron of its philharmonic society, and made great difficulties before he allowed the new municipal theatre to bear his name. He resented all suggestions that the town might have any claim on its most famous son. In 1865 a list of grievances against Busseto was drawn up; it includes: 'Old Frignani [a doctor] tries to find out, by direct question, how and by what means my wife lives, because the town is not clear about that', and 'I am Liberal to the utmost degree, without being a Red. I respect the liberty of others and I demand respect for my own. This town is anything but Liberal. It makes a show of being so, perhaps out of fear, but it is of clerical tendencies'. A reconciliation with Barezzi, however, was soon effected, and 'Signor Antonio' took Giuseppina Strepponi to his heart as his 'quasi-daughter'. She began to travel with Verdi as his wife, although it was not until 29 August 1859, in a private ceremony at the church of Collonges-sous-Salève, in Savoy, that they were wed. No convincing reasons have been found for the long delay, or why they suddenly got married when they did. But it is evident that Strepponi, who had borne two illegitimate children, in 1838 and 1841 (Walker (1962) thought the tenor Napoleone Moriani was their father; De Angelis's researches (1982) point to the theatrical agent Camillo Cirelli), considered herself unworthy of Verdi. Some of her letters to him have a tone that Violetta might have used to Alfredo:

O my Verdi, I am not worthy of you, and the love that you bear me is charity, balsam, to a heart sometimes very sad beneath the appearance of cheerfulness. Continue to love me, love me also after death, so that I may present myself to Divine Providence rich with all your love and your prayers, O my Redeemer!

Other letters bear witness to the tempering, stabilizing influence that she brought into his life. She urged him not to drive himself so hard, to accept fewer commissions, to compose operas for his own satisfaction and only then think about placing them. In 1853 she wrote:

Sometimes I fear that the love of money will reawaken in you and condemn you to many further years of drudgery. My dear, you would be very wrong. Don't you see. A great part of our lives has gone by, and you would be quite mad if, instead of enjoying the rewards of your glorious and honoured labours in peace, you were to sweat to accumulate money. . . . We shall have no children (since God, perhaps, wishes to punish me for my sins, in depriving me of any legitimate joy before I die). Well, then, . . . without children you have a fortune more than sufficient to provide for your needs and a little bit of luxury besides. We adore the country, and in the country one lives cheaply – and enjoys oneself so much.

Nevertheless, it was in and outside Paris, far from Busseto gossip, that the couple spent most of their first years together. Verdi had lived there, as noted, from July 1847 to August 1849, and there were many subsequent visits. During three months in 1852–3 Verdi saw *La dame aux camélias*. A long stay from October 1853 (for *Les vêpres siciliennes*) to January 1857 was broken only by a return to Italy for Christmas and spring, 1855–6. Verdi and Strepponi were in Paris again from March to July 1863 (when Verdi flirted with the possibility of becoming director of the Théâtre-Italien, and had a stormy scene with the Opéra orchestra over a *Vêpres* revival), from November 1865 to March 1866 (when the libretto of *Don Carlos* was planned), and from July 1866 to March 1867 (when *Don Carlos* was completed and produced). It was not until 1857 that Verdi could be said to have settled at Sant'Agata.

His return to Italy was clouded by the disappointing outcome of *Simon Boccanegra* and of *Aroldo* (the revised *Stiffelio*), and the following year by the Neapolitan censors' rejection of *Un ballo in maschera*. Verdi had already compromised to the extent of relocating Scribe's drama (based on the assassination of Gustavus III of Sweden) in 12th-century Pomerania and turning the historical monarch into an imaginary duke.

253

The censor demanded further changes, which made non-sense of the plot and the personages, and, although rehearsals had already begun, Verdi withdrew his opera. It was given in Rome the following year, with the setting transferred to colonial Boston but the action and motivation left more or less intact. (Outside Italy, *Ballo* was sometimes played – for example at its Covent Garden première, in 1861 – in a Neapolitan setting, which may have pleased the composer. Edward Dent's English version of 1952 returned the action to Stockholm, and several later productions have followed suit.) Verdi had often brushed with censorship, political and ecclesiastical, before. The Archbishop of Milan had deplored the stage representation of a sacrament, baptism, in *I lombardi*. In the adaptation of Hugo's *Le roi s'amuse* as *Rigoletto*, François I had become an anonymous duke. At the first performance of *Stiffelio*, the climactic line 'Ministro, confessatemi' was changed to the meaningless 'Rodolfo, ascoltatemi'. In papal Rome, the *Macbeth* witches become gypsies, whom Banquo recognized as coming from 'another country', not 'another world'. In Italy before the Unification *Les vêpres siciliennes* was given a Lisbon setting, and fiery words such as 'liberté' were quenched in the Italian translation. But the refusal to license *Un ballo in maschera* and the crassness of the objections made to it proved to be a last straw. Censorship was not the only reason but it was one of the reasons why after *Ballo* Verdi never again accepted a commission from an Italian company.

In 1861 Verdi became, at Cavour's persuasion, a member for San Donnino in the newly formed Italian parliament. He took his seat in the Chamber of Deputies in February. But Cavour died in June 1861, and (in Giuseppina's words) 'Verdi wept as at the death of his mother.... He knew intimately that extraordinary, fascinating, marvellous man, that statesman who had conserved (unique privilege) a heart in the midst of diplomacy and politics'. The tenor of the political comments scattered through Verdi's correspondence could almost be summarized by Posa's impassioned plea to King Philip II (in *Don Carlos*) for tolerance, generosity and humanity. Qualities of heart were more important to him than those of head. Verdi came to share in the common disillusion with the new Italian kingdom to which the former heroic idealism of the Risorgimento had led. When unification was finally achieved in 1870, by the absorption of the Patrimony of St Peter, he wrote to Clarina Maffei: 'It's a great event, but it leaves me cold ... I cannot reconcile parliament and the College of Cardinals, freedom of the press and inquisition, the civil code and the Syllabus ... *Pope* and *King of Italy* – I can't see them together even on the paper of this letter'. Rome had been, in effect, a neutral Italy's prize for having abandoned France in the Franco-Prussian war; and while 'it is true that the French are ... insupportable, it was, after all, France that gave liberty and civilization to the modern world', whereas Germans are 'immeasurably proud, hard and intolerant ... men with heads but no hearts; a strong but uncivilized race ... I should have preferred to sign peace after defeat beside the French to this inertia that will make us despised one day'.

After Cavour's death, Verdi rarely appeared in the Turin chamber, though it was not until 1865 that he resigned his seat. Early in 1861 he accepted an offer to compose an opera, which became *La forza del destino*, for St Petersburg. Giuseppina was eager to visit Russia, expensive alterations and new building had been undertaken at Sant'Agata, and the fee offered was handsome (60,000 francs for the Russian rights alone, and all expenses). He was in St Petersburg in December, but owing to illness in the cast the production was postponed. In April 1862, after three months back in Paris, he visited London as Italy's representative to the International Exhibition, for which he composed his *Inno delle nazioni* to a text by Arrigo Boito. The commissioners rejected the piece on the grounds of insufficient rehearsal time; it was performed at Her Majesty's Theatre on 24 May. That summer he scored *La forza del destino*, at Sant'Agata, and brought it to the St Petersburg stage in November. In 1864 he was elected to the late Meyerbeer's chair at the Académie des Beaux Arts. From 1865 to 1867 he was occupied with *Don Carlos*, and from 1870 to 1871 with *Aida*, comissioned for the Cairo Opera. In those three operas, *La forza del destino*, *Don Carlos* and *Aida*, he believed he had done something new. He called them 'operas made with ideas', as opposed to 'operas made of duets, cavatinas, etc'. He supervised the Italian première of *Aida* at La Scala in 1872, and later that year he went to Naples to direct, of *Don Carlos* and *Aida*, what he hoped would be 'an accurate execution embodying all the reforms demanded by modern art'. The heroine of these performances, as of the Scala *Aida* and later of the Requiem, was Teresa Stolz. On inadequate evidence it has been both asserted and denied that she and Verdi became lovers; all that is sure is that, on occasions between 1872 and 1876, Giuseppina Strepponi resented the attentions that Verdi paid to the soprano and that in the latter year there was a crisis, resolved soon afterwards by the good sense and generous nature of both women.

The Naples performances did not reach the level that Verdi had hoped for. He was famous, he was rich, he was applauded, but he was not content. On the one hand, the big operatic public, as ever, was more interested in tunes and in singers than in 'modern art'. On the other, by a new generation his work was not considered to be 'modern art' at all; that was represented by Wagner. He complained of 'stupid criticism and praise more stupid still! Not a single elevated or artistic idea! No-one has wished to point out my intentions'. Back in 1863 Arrigo Boito, prominent in the new Milanese intellectual set, had published an ode, *All'arte italiana*, in which he expressed the hope that Italian music, so much debased since 'the holy days of Pergolesi and Marcello', would be cleansed by a new generation of composers; 'Perhaps the man is already born who will elevate chaste, pure art on that altar now soiled like the wall of a brothel'. Understandably enough, Verdi, the leading Italian composer, took this as a personal insult. For years it rankled. An outburst to Giulio Ricordi, of 1875, is typical:

Then you talk of results obtained!!!!!!!!! What results? I'll tell you. After 25 years' absence from La Scala, I was hissed after the first act of *La forza del destino*. After *Aida*, endless chatter: that I was no more the Verdi of *Un ballo in maschera* (that *Ballo* that was hissed at its Scala première); that I *didn't know how to write* for the singers; . . . that I was an imitator of Wagner!!! A fine result, after a career of 35 years, to end up as an *imitator*!!! . . . I can't take as anything but a joke your sentence. 'The whole salvation of the theatre and of art is in your hands!!' Oh no! . . . I will repeat what Boito said: 'Perhaps the man is born who will sweep the altar'. Amen!

257

And three years later, to Clarina Maffei:

Why on earth should I write music? What have I to gain from it? . . . I should be told all over again that I *don't know how to write*, that I have become a *follower of Wagner*. A fine sort of glory! After a career of almost 40 years to end up as an *imitator*!

In 1868 Verdi proposed that the anniversary of Rossini's death should be commemorated by a collaborative requiem to which several of Italy's leading composers should contribute movements. The score was ready the following year (Verdi's share was the 'Libera me') but for various reasons the performance did not take place. In 1873, in Naples, while *Aida* rehearsals were held up by Stolz's illness, Verdi composed a string quartet – for his private diversion, he said, though three years later he allowed it to be published. Later that year Alessandro Manzoni, the author of *I promessi sposi* and one of the few human beings whom Verdi revered, died in Milan, and for the anniversary of his death Verdi composed the 'Manzoni' Requiem, embodying the 'Libera me' of the requiem for Rossini. It was first performed in Milan, in the church of S Marco, in May 1874, and then repeated at La Scala. Manzoni was a devout Catholic while Verdi, an unbeliever, had a long record of antagonism to the church. He insisted that his religious belief, or lack of it, was no concern to anyone but himself, but since attempts have been made to claim him for Catholicism, at any rate in his later days, and letters bolstering that claim have actually been forged (see Walker, 1958–60), it may be worth glancing at that record. Verdi himself used to recount how, as a lad serving Mass, he had once been forgetful, had been kicked by the priest, and had cursed him with the peasant oath 'Dio t'manda na sajetta!' ('May God strike you with lightning'). (In 1969 Matz published a startling postscript to the story; some years later the priest concerned *was* struck by lightning, and killed; so were two members of the choir in the organ loft where Verdi himself would have been had he arrived in time for the service.) In 1834 he was the candidate of the 'advanced', secular party in Busseto, while the Church party supported Ferrari. In 1865 (the year after the pope had proclaimed his deeply reactionary Syllabus of Errors), to the *Don Carlos* scenario he himself added Philip's interview with the Grand Inquisitor, 'who should be exceedingly old, and blind (for reasons which I won't set down on paper)'. The ecclesiastical cruelty given such detailed utterance in that opera, the maledictory relish of the monks in *La forza del destino*, and Amneris's outbursts against the priests in *Aida* ('And they call themselves ministers of Heaven! ... Evil race, a curse upon you!') – these vivid passages seem to be charged with Verdi's own feelings as well as those of the stage personages. But there is also evidence more definite, such as Giuseppina's remarks in a letter of 1872 to Clarina Maffei:

Verdi is busy with his grotto and his garden. He is very well and in the best of spirits. Happy man! and may God keep him happy for many long years to come! There are some virtuous natures that need to believe in God; others, equally perfect, that are happy not believing in anything, and simply observing rigorously every precept of strict morality. Manzoni and Verdi!

Giuseppina's own faith was scarcely orthodox. From her notebooks one learns that she believed in 'God, the first, unknown, unique, omnipotent source of all creation' and had 'a certain attachment, almost childlike, to the religion in which I was born – going back, however,

259

21. *Verdi (seated) in the garden of Sant'Agata with (from left to right) ?Giulio Ricordi, the artist Metlicovitz and Giuseppina Strepponi*

to the Gospel of Christ. I would not change, because I dislike apostasy in religion, in politics, in everything else'. Nevertheless she believed that a priesthood 'originally convinced, exalted' had become 'materialized . . . corrupt, cunning, venal'. It should be added that several individual priests, men of frank, generous, and liberal spirit, were exempted from the Verdis' general disapproval of the *empia razza*. The last word can be left with the man who knew Verdi best in his later years. In 1910 Boito wrote to Camille Bellaigue:

This is the day, of all days of the year, that he loved best. Christmas eve reminded him of the holy marvels of childhood, the enchantments of faith that is truly celestial only when it attains to belief in miracles. That belief, alas, he lost early, like all of us, but perhaps more than the rest of us he retained all his life a keen regret for it.

He provided an example of Christian faith by the moving beauty of his religious works, by observing rites (you must remember his beautiful head bowed in the chapel of Sant'Agata), by his illustrious homage to Manzoni, by the directions for his funeral found in his will: 'one priest, one candle, one cross'. He knew that Faith was the sustenance of hearts. To the workers in the fields, to the unhappy, the afflicted who surrounded him, he offered himself as an example, unostentatiously, humble, severely, to be useful to their consciences.

And there the inquiry must stop: to pursue it further would take me far into the mazes of psychological research, where his great personality would have nothing to lose but I should fear to lose my way. In the ideal moral and social sense he was a great Christian, but one should take care not to present him as a Catholic in the political and strictly theological sense of the word: *nothing could be further from the truth.*

In 1874 Verdi was elected to the Italian senate, as a mark of honour; he played no active part in its deliberations. In 1875 he led a triumphal 'tour' of the Manzoni *Requiem* to Paris, London and Vienna. In 1876 he conducted it with great acclaim at the Cologne Festival. In 1880 there came the enormous success of *Aida* at the Paris Opéra, under his direction. He then began to lead a very retired life, tending his estates at Sant'Agata, and spending the winters in Genoa where, since 1867, he had maintained an apartment. He deplored the increasing influence of German ideas on Italian music; 'Honour the old Italian masters' is a refrain in his declarations of these years. His own creative life seemed to have ended, in 1874, with the Requiem.

CHAPTER NINE

The grand operas

The Opéra (or Académie Royale de Musique), for which Rossini and Donizetti wrote their last large works, was a magnet for the serious Italian composer. It had a stable, salaried company of singers and a large regular chorus and orchestra. It offered rehearsal periods and production budgets undreamt of in Italy. It played a long season, and a successful opera was assured of many performances. It also paid its composers handsomely. On the debit side, it was run as a bureaucracy (being indeed a government department), most efficiently in some respects but also in ways irksome to a composer who expected his interpreters to be fired by a sense of artistic adventure. Intrigues flourish everywhere in the operatic world, but the Parisian performers were perhaps more capricious, conceited and uncooperative than most.

Verdi, who lived so long in Paris and had amplified *I lombardi*, as *Jérusalem*, for the Paris Opéra, knew all this well. He was at once attracted to and exasperated by what, in irritated moments, he referred to as 'la grande boutique'. To turn its unparalleled resources to the creation of a great opera such as could not be achieved in the hurly-burly of Italian theatrical life was a challenge that long occupied him. In 1850, before *Rigoletto*, *Il trovatore* and *La traviata* had brought his Italian period to a close, he was already in negotiations about a *grand opéra* to be mounted by the Opéra in 1855, the year of the Universal Exhibition. He stipulated that the libretto should be by Eugène Scribe, Meyerbeer's regular collaborator. At first Scribe tried to palm off on him two pieces, *Les circassiens* and *Vlaska*, that Meyerbeer had rejected. Verdi sent them back: 'Before writing expressly for the Opéra, I want – in fact, I must have – a grandiose, impassioned and original subject. In my mind's eye I see constantly those many, many magnificent scenes to be found in your librettos – among others, the Coronation Scene of *Le prophète*'. Time was running short when he agreed to tackle a Scribe text that Donizetti had left incomplete – *Le duc d'Albe*, now expanded and reworked for Verdi as *Les vêpres siciliennes.* (Verdi later said he had not known at the time that he was being offered second-hand goods, but correspondence of 1853 suggests that his memory was at fault.) *Les vêpres siciliennes* was accepted *faute de mieux.* The opportunities it offers for spectacle are not great, even though there are multiple, contrasting choruses in the Meyerbeer manner. Verdi played his usual part in refashioning the libretto, and in particular he made drastic structural changes in the form of Acts 4 and 5. But he could not achieve the results he had hoped for. *Les vêpres* lacks the impetuous surge of his earlier pieces, although its individual numbers reveal a new care for large-scale construction and a new mastery of massed choral and instrumental forces. After *Les vêpres* Verdi began to recast the unsuccessful *Stiffelio* as *Aroldo*, so that in medieval dress it might have wider currency, and composed for it a new last act. Then he embarked on *Simon Boccanegra*, which, particularly in its earlier, unrevised form (1857), is an Italian *melodramma* with *grand opéra* features, a successor to *I due*

Foscari painted with an ampler brush and in the fuller, richer and subtler colours that he had learnt to use. Scribe–Meyerbeer operas, it might be said, are concerned with pasteboard characters involved both in large political actions and in passionate personal plights; Verdi aimed to transform the pasteboard to flesh and blood. In *Les vêpres* he did not quite succeed; with the figure of Boccanegra – lover, popular leader, tender father – he did, although he and Piave were unable to fashion their drama, which Boito and he later compared to a rickety table, into a convincing shape. In his next opera he returned to a more limited theme: *Un ballo in maschera* (1859) is a *grand opéra* (Scribe's and Auber's *Gustave III*, of 1833, which remained in the Opéra repertory until 1859) condensed and recomposed by an Italian, for Italy. The pageantry of the French original – a mimed rehearsal of the king's own opera, *Gustaf Wasa*, in the first act, a ballet in the last – is removed. The rest is largely Scribe translated. In Verdi's setting it moves swiftly; *Un ballo* is the earliest of his pieces that is regularly played uncut, a distinction it shares only with *Aida* and *Falstaff* (*Otello* often suffers mutilating cuts in the ensembles of Acts 2 and 3). Ensembles and solos alternate, and *Un ballo* is unique among Verdi's operas in containing but one duet. The forms are closely controlled. It is as if Verdi were deliberately trying out a new way of handling *grand opéra* material, reacting against Auber's large, leisurely scheme and entrenching on the 'Italian' side of his final objective. That objective was an opera on the Meyerbeer scale yet one in which huge spectacle is not mere decoration but essential to the drama, in which the musical and theatrical lines remain taut, in which the characters still sing as warmly, passionately and personally as in *Il trovatore*. Oscar, the page of *Un ballo*, has his ancestry in Urbain of *Les Huguenots*, the conspirators recall those of Meyerbeer's opera, and Ulrica has the tones of Fidès in *Le prophète*. But both Riccardo and Renato sing phrases that recall Donizetti. A Verdian synthesis is complete. This is the most shapely of his third-period operas, and the only one that needed no subsequent revision. Its successor, *La forza del destino* (1862), is the most sprawling. *La forza* does have a theme – or, rather, two related themes, the predicament of a hero compelled by a series of mischances to commit just those actions against which his noble spirit rebels, and the vanity of hoping to find peace by retiring from the world into a cloister. The first exemplifies the regular attraction for Verdi of a rent character forced into extreme situations, and it is perhaps not fanciful to discern in the second (which is explicitly restated in *Don Carlos*) a reflection of the composer's own situation, drawn back into the busy world after a silence of some years. The financial and touristic inducements for his accepting the *Forza* commission have already been mentioned, but the determinant reason was surely his recurrent urge to write a really successful grand opera.

The personal drama of Donna Leonora, Don Alvaro and Don Carlo is played out against an animated background of martial and monastic life across two countries. The vivandière Preziosilla and the voluble monk Melitone are prominent in a band of 'ordinary people' among whom the self-absorbed trio act out their tragedy. The chorus, very important, participates in every scene except the first. Verdi's invention is large, brilliant and generous. The St Petersburg audience was taken aback; a critic wrote, truly, that 'In place of a light opera in the ordinary Italian manner, the composer of *Rigoletto* has given us on this occasion a work more akin to the productions of Meyerbeer and Halévy'. Verdi complained later of an Italian performance in which the individual singers had been admirable and the solos and duets superbly well executed – but not 'the varied, ampler scenes that fill half the opera and really constitute the *dramma musicale*'. That was in 1869; in that year began the long series of letters to his Neapolitan friend Cesare De Sanctis in which he consciously formulated his belief, already noted, that in *La forza del destino, Don Carlos* and, later, *Aida* he had composed operas of a new kind, 'modern operas' made with ideas, not made up of numbers. Their production, he said, should be undertaken only by an ensemble company, directed by a single intelligence that had responsibility for every detail of the scenery, the staging and the musical execution. He had read Wagner's theoretical works and approved of many of the ideas expressed in them.

In *La forza*, destiny works overtime, bringing characters together in a most improbable fashion. Such coincidences Verdi had not ventured since *I lombardi*, and they even exceed those of that opera. The heroine and hero, parted in the first scene, do not meet again until the last, and Verdi confused a tangled tale still further by introducing a stretch of Schiller's *Wallensteins Lager*, which for a dozen years he had been wanting to set. A *Forza* in French was promised to Paris in 1866, but Verdi could not see how to tidy the piece, and the score was set aside. Many people made suggestions for its improvement; at length Antonio Ghislanzoni's, for an ending in a Manzoni-like spirit of Christian resignation, was adopted, and a somewhat reordered *Forza* had its first performance at La Scala in 1869. The new score began with an overture; the tenor lost his Act 3 cabaletta and no longer committed a spectacular suicide before the assembled monks.

But before the revised *Forza* there was a revision of *Macbeth* for the Théâtre-Lyrique, in 1865, and then *Don Carlos*, commissioned by the Opéra as its showpiece in the year of the 1867 Exhibition. From *Macbeth* Verdi removed two cabalettas, and to it he added Lady Macbeth's 'La luce langue', the infernal ballet and the duettino 'Ora di morte'. The opening and close of Act 4 were rewritten; so, among other things, was the apparitions scene. The revised *Macbeth* is, in Verdi's word, a 'mosaic', which until the mid-20th century did not achieve the popularity of its predecessor. The new music is noble, and the great things from 1847 remain: the dagger monologue, the Act 2 finale (in Verdi's early manner, but perhaps the finest, before the Act 3 finale in *Otello*, of all those slow 4/4–6/8 concerted movements) and the sleepwalking scene. But they no longer have their dominant positions; 'the skyline, so to speak, is altered' (Budden).

Schiller's *Don Carlos* as an Opéra subject was first suggested to Verdi in 1850, during the negotiations that led to *Les vêpres siciliennes*. It was submitted again, in the form of a scenario by Joseph Méry and Camille Du Locle, in 1865. Verdi accepted it (having rejected, among other subjects, *King Lear* as being insufficiently spectacular and difficult to cast), provided that a duet for Philip and Posa, another for Philip and the Grand Inquisitor, and more spectacle ('something like the skating scene or the church scene of *Le prophète*') were added. His requests were met; spectacle was supplied by the auto-da-fé of Act 3 and a final chorus of Inquisitors thundering denunciations. Verdi went to Paris to supervise the first drafting of the libretto and then, while composing the work at Sant'Agata, demanded from Du Locle the customary and extensive revisions. (Méry had died on 17 June 1866.)

Schiller's play proclaimed themes dear to the composer: love of individual and of national liberty, detestation of political and ecclesiastical tyranny. It was 'warmed' by five interesting and contrasting characters, enmeshed in a web of church and state where their decisions affect not only one another but also the fate of three nations. Public and personal destinies interact, and the hero is the common point of three emotional triangles: Elizabeth and Eboli both love Carlos; Philip and Carlos both love Elizabeth; and they both love Posa. But the heart of the opera, Verdi once said, is the public crisis of the auto-da-fé scene, and it was the only scene left unaltered when, 16 years later, he revised the work.

Don Carlos was composed on a very large scale. During rehearsals it proved so long that extensive passages, including some whole numbers, were cut before the first night. They remained unpublished and unknown until in 1970 they were found, crossed out, pinned, pasted or stitched up, in the parts used for the first performance. Verdi was dissatisfied by the Paris production, on which so much time and so many thousands of francs had been lavished; he contrasted it unfavourably with more spirited and fiery Italian performances achieved after only a few weeks' rehearsal. Even as published, the 1867 *Don Carlos* was a very long opera. The composer tried, but in vain, to insist on its being done uncut – for it was 'necessarily long', he said, and with it he had 'decided to transform our theatres'. Eventually, in 1882, he set about shortening it himself. But that revision, carried out in a 'anti-*grand opéra*' spirit, forms part of the last-period preparations for *Otello*.

The Suez Canal opened in November 1869, and a few days earlier Cairo's new Opera House had opened with *Rigoletto*. Verdi was asked to compose an opera for the following season, naming his own terms. He said 'no', and 'no' again, and then 'perhaps' when, in May 1870, there arrived a 23-page *Aida* synopsis that he found 'well made, splendid from a scenic point of view, and containing two or three situations that, while not exactly novel, are certainly very fine'. He said 'yes' when the terms were agreed. They were handsome indeed (150,000 francs for the Egyptian rights alone), but he was not a man to undertake a commission just for the money; it had to correspond to some inner need of his. At the time of the Cairo commission he was toying with quite a different idea, a piece for the Opéra-Comique on a subject that would be 'un po' di *comique*'. Several plays were considered, but no apt subject turned up. Instead, Verdi decided to tackle grand opera once again. Du Locle came to Sant'Agata, and he and Verdi worked up the scenario as a libretto in French prose. Antonio Ghislanzoni was engaged to turn it into Italian verse, and proceeded under close instruction.

The contract was signed in June 1870; early in November the composer said his score was almost ready for delivery. In fact he went on revising it for ten months more; Paris, where the décor was being prepared, was under siege, and the première was postponed to the end of 1871. Verdi did not attend it, but he supervised the first Italian performance, at La Scala, seven weeks later (February 1872), and in May another production in Parma. In 1873, as noted, he directed a production in Naples, and in 1880 an important production at the Opéra. By then the opera was established in the international repertory – where it has remained ever since.

Aida results from lessons practically learnt in those unwieldy, ambitious predecessors *La forza del destino* and *Don Carlos*. The situations, as Verdi remarked, are 'not exactly novel'. The characters are essentially stereotypes who had trod the operatic stage from the days of Metastasio, and there are only four principals. The plot is tight, and easy to follow. There is opportunity for stage spectacle on the Meyerbeerian scale; the 'production numbers' – the investiture in the temple, the decking of Amneris, the triumph scene – are conventional, but they directly concern the principals. Most of the movements are elaborated developments from the closed forms of traditional opera, handled on a large, sure scale. In dramatic scope and in psychological interest, *Aida* aims less high than its predecessors, but it is more securely achieved than they are, and is so strongly and beautifully written, for the voices and for the orchestra, that few have denied it greatness. *Aida*, at last, represents Verdi's personal transformation of grand opera.

In a sense, the Requiem can be considered a by-product of this period. Hans von Bülow's scornful reference to Verdi's 'latest opera in church vestments', often unthinkingly echoed, did not altogether miss the mark.

271

Musically, much of the score belongs with things like 'La Vergine degli angeli' in *La forza del destino*, the Act 3 finale of *Don Carlos* and the temple choruses of *Aida*. The 'Lacrimosa' is an enriched, extended and refined reworking of a duet for Carlos and Philip removed from *Don Carlos* before its first performance. Giuseppina Strepponi's well-known 'defence' of the style is not exactly a refutation of Bülow's charge:

> They talk a lot about the spirit, more or less religious, of Mozart, Cherubini, etc. I say that a man like Verdi must write like Verdi – that is, according to his own way of feeling and interpreting the text. . . . The religious spirit and the way in which it finds expression must bear the imprint of its time and the individuality of its author. I should, so to speak, have repudiated a mass by Verdi if it had been modelled on those of A, B or C.

Verdi's new command of large movements, of what is loosely termed 'symphonic development', and of a very full, very powerful choral and orchestral palette, could here be deployed without being tempered to theatrical and scenic requirements. In fact the Mass for the Dead provided him with one of the most dramatic texts and some of the most dramatic situations he had ever set, and he responded to them with high inspiration, rhythmic, sonic and structural. Several of the ideas, procedures, even motifs pay explicit tribute to Rossini by recalling the earlier composer's *Stabat mater*. The Requiem is at once a monument to Italian genius as Verdi perceived it in Rossini and Manzoni, an affirmation of his belief in an Italian music where the orchestra is very important but the sung word is paramount, and the climax of all those scenes, some tender, some terrifying, in which he sought to express his vision of suffering, suppliant humanity.

22. *Giuseppe Verdi: photograph*

CHAPTER TEN

Last works, last years

After the Requiem, a long silence. But in Milan in June 1879, when Verdi, Stolz and the mezzo Maria Waldmann all emerged from retirement for a charity performance of the Requiem, Giulio Ricordi astutely turned a dinner conversation to Shakespeare, Boito, and *Othello*, and caught a gleam of interest in the composer's eye. By November, Verdi had received Boito's *Otello* libretto. Although Giuseppina reported, disappointingly, that he had set it to rest beside Somma's for *King Lear*, letters of 1880 show that an opera was beginning to form in Verdi's mind. First, however, he and Boito tackled a revision of *Simon Boccanegra*. Perhaps he was unconsciously testing the possibility of a full-scale collaboration with the poet and also, in the magnificent new Council Scene and the new Iago-like recitatives of the villainous Paolo, testing his own ability to rise to the challenges of *Otello*. The revised *Boccanegra* was produced at La Scala in 1881, with Francesco Tamagno and Victor Maurel, the future Othello and Iago, as its tenor and baritone.

In 1882 Verdi set about revising and abridging *Don Carlos*, working now in French with Du Locle, his original librettist. (Because of a lawsuit over finance, Verdi was not on speaking, or even on writing, terms with his collaborator; the correspondence passed through an intermediary, Charles Nuitter, the Opéra archivist, who preserved things well.) A Vienna production of the opera had long been mooted; Vienna performances ended early, and if there had to be an amputation, Verdi said, he preferred to wield the knife himself. But it was not merely a question of abridgment. Verdi gave special attention to those passages where the dramatic motivation had been obscured or the musical shapes spoilt by the pre-performance cuts of 1867. He sought to bring the action closer to Schiller's. He removed Act 1, retaining only the tenor aria for insertion in the new opening scene. He reworked the important Philip–Posa duet, which had never quite satisfied him. (For the Naples production of 1872 there had already been an intermediate version of this crucial scene.) From the Carlos–Posa duet, he 'stripped everything that is purely musical, keeping just what is necessary for the action', and he did much the same when condensing the quartet of (the original) Act 4.

In a spoken tragedy . . . it does not matter if there is a word or phrase too many, to fill out the metre or provide a rhyme. Not so in music . . . there a word or phrase too many at dramatic moments kills things. . . . I believe that for an opera in modern music one should adopt unrhymed verse.

Verdi decided to scrap the 'stupid cantabile' in Act 4 in which Elizabeth had replied to Philip's reproaches

and have in its place something declamatory, something energetic. . . . The actress would have a chance of producing a strident outburst [*una strillacciata*] that would not be beautiful, either poetically or musically, but would be theatrical. And I need hardly tell you, my dear Nuitter, that when one writes for the theatre one must make *theatre*.

The final chorus was omitted. The insurrection at the end of the previous act was recomposed as a brief, most *Otello*-like passage, because 'those eternal massed forces weigh on my stomach'.

These new concerns – which are also old concerns, since before the *grands opéras* Verdi had counted brevity among the highest of theatrical virtues – point clearly towards *Otello*. The revised *Don Carlos* is something of a patchwork, being partly in the swift, taut-muscled, fine-tempered pre-*Otello* style, and partly in the lyrically expansive, long-breathed, ample manner of 1867, of which Posa's ballade in Act 2 and his death scene are notable examples. It was first performed, not in Vienna, but at La Scala, in 1884, in Italian translation. Tamagno took the title role. In 1886, with Verdi's permission, a composite score was made, containing Act 1 of 1867 and the other four acts as revised.

During these revisions of earlier pieces, *Otello* was not forgotten, and Verdi turned to it in earnest soon after the première of the revised *Don Carlos*. It was composed for the most part in three bouts: March 1884, December 1884 to April 1885, and September to early October 1885. The first interruption was caused by the misreporting of a speech by Boito to the effect (so Verdi read) that he wished he were composing the opera himself. Verdi at once offered to return the libretto, and it took all Boito's tact and skill to persuade him that 'you alone can set *Otello* to music'. The collaboration was resealed when Boito sent the composer a new version of Iago's Credo, no longer in regular verse but 'in broken metre, unsymmetrical', and Verdi replied with enthusiasm that it was 'most powerful and wholly Shakespearean'. The second interruption Verdi set down to a summer cure, the heat, and 'my unimaginable laziness'. The orchestration and some final revisions occupied another year, on and off, and *Otello* was first performed at La Scala in February 1887.

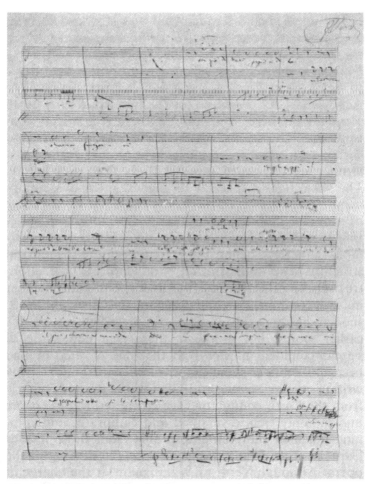

23. Autograph sketch for the Cassio–Iago–Othello trio from Act 3 of Verdi's 'Otello', first performed Milan, 5 February 1887

277

The opera includes much that was standard form in the operas of Verdi's youth: an *introduzione* in which the hero's solo entry is framed between choruses, a *brindisi*, a quartet of conflicting emotions, a duet finale to Act 2 (as in *Rigoletto*), a 4/4–12/8 ensemble finale to Act 3, a last-act *preghiera* for the heroine, a final death scene for the hero. Yet nothing about it is merely conventional. The score divides clearly into numbers, but within each number, free declamation and formal patterning are reconciled more skilfully than ever before. The vocal lines display at its highest pitch of development Verdi's genius for revealing character by the curve of a phrase. Subtle passing harmonies add their inflection to individual words while, on a larger scale, harmonic structures define and help to organize the musical structure. The orchestration is adventurous but unobtrusively so. Its delicacy, the unconventional chamber musical combinations, the poignant solo lines, the swift, sudden blazes – all these have precedent in Verdi's earlier scores, but in *Otello* there is a new sense of serene, confident mastery. At the time of *Aida* he had been unsure how some of his more unorthodox string writing would sound and anxiously awaited reports from the Cairo conductor. The string writing in *Otello*, uncommonly rich, diversified and elaborate, underpinning much of the dialogue, profits from those lessons learnt in *Aida*. Many things went to the making of the opera. Although Verdi grew indignant at the charge of 'Wagnerism', Desdemona's passage starting 'Poi mi guidavi ai fulgidi deserti', in the love-duet, closely reproduces the rhythms of Elsa's passage starting 'Fühl' ich von dir so süss mein Herz entbrennen', in the love-duet of *Lohengrin*. (Verdi owned a vocal score of

24. *Verdi with Arrigo Boito at Sant'Agata*

Lohengrin; and he went to Bologna in 1871 to hear the opera, and heard *Tannhäuser* in Vienna in 1875 – when, he confessed, 'I dozed, but so did the Germans'.) Verdi's ears were open to all that they encountered. In Rossini, Donizetti and Mercadante, in Meyerbeer, Berlioz and Wagner (inescapable as a general influence, however much the 'slowness and heaviness' might be deplored), he found things that could become his own. *Otello* results from Verdi's lifetime of learning by trial and effort, by striving, experimenting, discarding and refining, how best to give musical shape to the ideas about musical drama that had guided him from the start. It crowns his career as an operatic tragedian.

There was still *Falstaff* to come. Two years after *Otello*, early in July 1889, Boito sent Verdi a sketch of the *Falstaff* libretto, and his delighted response was immediate. He pleaded old age, and the possibility that he might not finish it, but Boito brushed such objections aside. Within days, Verdi had agreed to compose *Falstaff*, stipulating only that the fact he was doing so should be kept entirely secret until the work was ready. He composed it in rapid, intermittent bursts and in tearing high spirits. In February 1893 it had its first performance, at La Scala.

Verdi wanted very few libretto changes. Boito, skilfully and gracefully combining a condensed action from *The Merry Wives of Windsor* with elements from *Henry IV*, had provided a text that seemed 'to go straight into music'. The librettist wrote helpfully about his ideas. For example:

This love between Nannetta and Fenton must appear suddenly at very frequent intervals; in all the scenes in which they take part they will keep on kissing by stealth in corners, astutely, boldly, without letting themselves be discovered, with fresh little phrases and brief, very rapid little dialogues; it will be a most lively, merry love, always disturbed and interrupted and always ready to begin again.

To Camille Bellaigue, soon after the première, Boito wrote:

You say: this is the true modern and Latin lyric drama (or lyric comedy). But what you can't imagine is the immense intellectual joy that this Latin lyric comedy produces on the stage. It is a real outpouring of grace, of strength and gaiety. Shakespeare's sparkling farce is led back by the miracle of sound to its clear Tuscan source, to 'Ser Giovanni Fiorentino'.

To some extent, Boito was congratulating himself. His action derives from Shakespeare, but his diction, deliberately Boccaccian, contains many words that even to a 16th-century reader of the *Decameron* needed explanation. The lovers' refrain of 'Bocca baciata' is quoted directly from that book (where it appears in a very different context). Some Italian critics have regretted the determinedly 'literary' quality of Boito's poetry, in both *Otello* and *Falstaff*, but none has questioned his command of dramatic structure or his ability to inspire Verdi.

In this final opera, young love is triumphant but old age is triumphant too. Many of the great things about Verdi – his lifelong devotion to Shakespeare, his mistrust of the fickle public, his generous love for humanity, his tenderness towards young love, his respect for craftsmanship, his professionalism, his instinctive feeling for the theatre, and an acceptance, no longer bitter but now joyful, that new young men have risen to take the centre of the stage – all these and more seem to find their expression here. Musically, it is the comic counterpart to the new concise style of *Otello*.

281

25. 'L'illustrazione italiana': cover of the commemorative issue
'Verdi e il Falstaff' (1893)

There is not much in the earlier operas to adumbrate such gaiety (though there is something: ripe comedy in Melitone, zest in the ballet divertissements of the Paris scores, melodic and rhythmic sparkle in such pieces as Hélène's bolero in *Les vêpres siciliennes*). The new orchestral finesse bubbles over into such jokes as the cellos and piccolo, four octaves apart, that accompany the knight's 'Se Falstaff s'assottiglia', in the first scene. Only one solo number, Nannetta's fairy song in the last act, is in a set form – and it is by intention a 'song within the opera'. The situation is realistic: Nannetta, seconded by a chorus of Windsor girls, is pretending to be Queen of the Fairies. But the delicacy of Verdi's orchestration transfigures the episode, and for a while one seems to be transported to the supernatural world of *A Midsummer Night's Dream*. (That play, with its strands of poetic enchantment, robust comedy and lovers' tangles finally resolved, may underlie much of the last scene of *Falstaff*.) Fenton's sonnet, earlier in the scene, starts by proclaiming a regular rhythmic pattern but soon takes wing as freely as the 'canto estasiato' he sings of.

Falstaff is organized – the word is stiff for so quicksilver a composition, but the organization can be plotted – by supple, subtle patterns of rhythmic and melodic motifs, often developed by ostinatos that never outstay their welcome but are ever ready to scatter in bursts of orchestral and vocal laughter, and by recurrences of some pregnant themes. Beneath the freely declaimed monologues a secure structure can be observed. For example, the last vocal phrase of Ford's 'E sogno?', in Act 2, recalls his 'Due rami enormi crescon' at the start of the piece. As he reaches the final cadence, woodwind and strings pick up his 'E poi diranno', previously

283

unrepeated, from the centre of the monologue, while the brass hammer out the triplet figure of 'Dalle due alle tre' (the hour of Falstaff's assignation with Ford's wife) that has burnt in his ears since Falstaff first mentioned it. Often in *Falstaff* there is a sense that recitative – lyrical or declamatory – and aria have become one. The vocal line moves freely in response to the text, but there are glimpses along the way of the old, regular forms.

One of the glories of *Falstaff* is its melodic abundance. In 'arias' a few seconds long Verdi captured the essence of what another composer might take pages to express. Falstaff's eight bars in Act 1 starting 'So che se andiam, la notte' form a little *buffa* aria in themselves, and then the music goes on to something else (but, later, the first notes in diminution patter through the cellos and piccolo passage already mentioned). The sequence of melodies continues, episode after episode – a Falstaff monologue with brief interjections from Bardolph and Pistol – to the end of the scene, and it seems to be 'all one number'. Alice Ford's reading of Falstaff's letter, 'Come una stella', with the other women joining in, is at once a parody of a high romantic aria and a beautiful melody in itself. Alice is like one of Verdi's earlier grand heroines – an Elvira, Hélène, or Leonora – placed now in situations that call for only wit and laughter, not passion or despair. Her 'letter aria', like so much else in *Falstaff*, swiftly dissolves into a cascade of merriment. A second 'aria' for her, complete with 'cabaletta', is woven into the first scene of Act 3. At the end of the opera itself everything, everyone, falls into place in an exuberant fugue.

After *Falstaff*, Boito suggested to Verdi an *Antony and Cleopatra*, and did some work on a *King Lear*. But

26. Verdi at his desk in the Grand Hotel, Milan, 1900

the composer was 80 and, in Giuseppina's words, 'too old, too tired'. His last music for the theatre was a brief, striking ballet sequence for *Otello*, required for the Paris première in 1894. In 1880 he had composed two short sacred pieces, an *Ave Maria* and a *Pater noster*. In 1889, for his amusement he devised an *Ave Maria* based on an 'enigmatic scale' printed as a puzzle in the *Gazzetta musicale*. This was joined by *Laudi alla Vergine Maria*

285

(composed between *Otello* and *Falstaff*) and a *Stabat mater* and *Te deum* (1895–7), to form the group of *Quattro pezzi sacri* published in 1898. The *Ave Maria*, for four-part chorus unaccompanied, is slight, a curiosity, and Verdi did not wish to have it performed. The other three are noble. The *Laudi*, for two sopranos and two altos, unaccompanied, is a serene, tender composition. The *Stabat mater*, for mixed choir and orchestra, contains in small space the essence of a Passion (both in dramatic narrative and in meditations), a 'Dies irae', a 'Libera me' and an 'In paradisum'. The *Te Deum*, for double choir and orchestra, is harmonically adventurous and very dramatic. These pieces form no unworthy end to Verdi's career. He rated them highly, gave detailed instructions for their first performance (Paris, 1898), and wished to have the score of the *Te Deum* buried with him. But as his last and greatest work he regarded the Casa di Riposo per Musicisti, a home for aged musicians built in Milan at his expense, to designs by Boito's architect brother Camillo.

One by one his friends and former colleagues had died: Piave in 1876, Solera in 1878, Léon Escudier (his French publisher) in 1881, Maffei in 1885, Clarina Maffei the following year, Muzio in 1890. In 1894 he and Giuseppina paid their last visits to Paris, for the French premières of *Falstaff* at the Opéra-Comique and *Otello* at the Opéra. In November 1897 Giuseppina died, at Sant'Agata. Teresa Stolz, Boito and Giulio Ricordi and his wife came there at once to help sustain the composer. With the same company he spent Christmas 1900 in his usual suite in the Grand Hotel, Milan. On 21 January he suffered a stroke there, and he died six days later. His will specified a burial, without much ceremony, beside his wife, in the Casa di Riposo, but for that special authorization was required. At first Verdi was buried modestly in the city cemetery, but when his and Giuseppina's bodies were taken to the Casa di Riposo, on 28 February 1901, there was civic and national mourning on a very large scale.

CHAPTER ELEVEN

Posthumous reputation

When Alfred Noyes wrote in a poem that 'the music's only
Verdi' (it was a *Trovatore* tune he heard, ground out by
a barrel organ), that 'only' was a fair reflection of serious critical opinion early this century. Although
audiences the world over had taken *Rigoletto*, *Il trovatore*
and *La traviata* to their hearts, only *Otello* and *Falstaff*
and, to some extent, *Aida* and the Requiem were considered worthy of a serious musician's study. Giann-
andrea Mazzucato's article in the first edition of *Grove*
(1889) presents an opinion more sympathetic than most,
but, even in Italy, later musicians brought up under the
influence of Alfredo Casella did not rate Verdi very
high. The 'Verdi renaissance' and a willingness to consider him in a breath with Wagner began in Germany,
in the 1920s and 1930s, with writings by Werfel,
Bekker and Gerigk and performances of what were then
lesser-known operas. In England, in the early 1930s,
Bonavia and Toye published notable studies. Yet in
1933, when Beecham revived *Don Carlos* at Covent
Garden, Ernest Newman declared that most of the
music was bad, and that Verdi repeated the same
wretched formulae from one work to another and was
incapable of growth in the understanding of human
nature. After the war, all Verdi's operas were revived in
Britain and in Italy, while in New York, Rudolf Bing,
during his administration of the Metropolitan Opera
(1950–72), made Verdi the cornerstone of his

repertory. In previous decades *Luisa Miller, Simon Boccanegra, Un ballo in maschera* and *La forza del destino* were already done there more often than in most other non-Italian major houses; Bing revived them all in new productions, as well as *Ernani, Don Carlos, Otello* and *Falstaff,* and added to the repertory *Nabucco* and *Macbeth.* These performances brought scholarly reappraisal and also renewed popular enthusiasm. In the 1970s Verdi's operas dominated the international repertory more decisively than ever.

Biographical landmarks had been the publication of the *Copialettere* in 1913 and of several correspondences in the 1930s. Lives by Gatti (1931), Abbiati (1959) and Walker (1962) brought a good deal of material to light, but much remained unexamined. In 1959, the formation of the Istituto di Studi Verdiani, in Parma, provided a central archive where, printed or in photostat, the composer's voluminous correspondence and other documents, never systematically published or catalogued, could be assembled. The *Bollettini, Quaderni* and *Atti* of the institute and the exchange of ideas at its international congresses gave a new impetus and accuracy to studies biographical, bibliographical and critical. Budden's volume on the operas up to *Rigoletto* and Chusid's *Catalog* reflected the new approaches. In response to the growing enthusiasm for Verdi among both academics and general audiences, an American Institute for Verdi Studies was founded in 1976; its archive, in the Bobst Library of New York University, is even richer than the Parma Institute's. Verdi studies are still hampered by the lack of a complete edition of his music (some major operas are not generally available in score) and his correspondence (scattered among various volumes, with some important letters still unpublished), and by the unavailability of most of his sketches. However, in 1977 Ricordi and the University of Chicago Press announced plans for a complete critical edition of his works and the first volume, *Rigoletto*, appeared in 1983.

WORKS

(printed works published in Milan unless otherwise stated)

Numbers in the right-hand column denote references in the text.

Vocal scores were published by Ricordi of *Nabucco* (1842) and *Un giorno di regno* (c1845). All the other operas appeared in vocal score close to the time of their premières, and were first published by Ricordi, with the exceptions of *Attila*, *I masnadieri* and *Il corsare* (by Lucca), *Stiffelio* (by Blanchet, Paris, 1850; by Ricordi, 1852) and the operas for Paris (by the Bureau Central de la Musique/Escudier, Paris, and, almost simultaneously and in Italian translation, by Ricordi). Vocal scores of the Italian operas up to *La forza del destino* were also published in Paris (*Nabucco* by Schonenberger, *Il corsaro* by Chabal and the others by the Bureau Central de la Musique/Escudier or by Blanchet) often within a year or less of the Ricordi editions. In 1981 Ricordi published a vocal score of *Don Carlos* containing all versions of the opera.

Full scores circulated at first in manuscript copies. Ricordi printed (for hire only) *La traviata* (c1855), and (later in the century) all the operas except *Oberto*, *Un giorno di regno*, *Alzira*, *I masnadieri*, *Jérusalem*, *Il corsaro*, *Stiffelio* and the first versions of *Macbeth*, *Simon Boccanegra* and *Don Carlos*. The first published full score on public sale was Del Monaco's edition of *La traviata* (Naples, c1882). In 1913–14, Ricordi published 'study scores' of *Rigoletto*, *Il trovatore*, *La traviata*, *Un ballo in maschera*, *Aida*, *Otello* and *Falstaff*; in the 1950s, revised editions of these; and in 1951, a facsimile of the *Falstaff* autograph. Peters published a score of *La forza del destino* (1926) and a heavily edited version of *Don Carlos* (1954). All but three (*I lombardi*, *I due Foscari* and *Attila*) of the full scores printed by Ricordi have been reprinted and published by Kalmus (New York). A new complete, critical edition published by Ricordi and the University of Chicago Press was announced in 1977; the first volume, *Rigoletto* (ed. M. Chusid), appeared in 1983 and the Requiem (ed. D. Rosen) is in preparation.

In the list below, the genre and librettist (when not in square brackets) are as stated on the libretto of the first performance. Autographs are in the Ricordi archives, Milan, except where noted.

Title, Genre	Librettist, Source	First performance, Remarks	
Oberto, Conte di San Bonifacio (dramma, 2)	[T. Solera], ? from A. Piazza's lib(s) Rocester. Lord Hamilton	Milan Scala, 17 Nov 1839	199, 209, 219, 200, 246, 249
Un giorno di regno (Il finto Stanislao) (melodramma giocoso, 2)	[F. Romani, ? rev. Solera], from Romani's lib for Gyrowetz's Il finto Stanislao (1812), after A. V. Pineu-Duval: Le faux Stanislas (play, 1808)	Milan Scala, 5 Sept 1840; alternative title first used 1842	200, 209, 246, 248, 249
Nabucodonosor (Nabucco) (dramma lirico, 4 parts)	Solera, from A. Cortesi's ballet (1838), after Anicet-Bourgeois' and F. Cornue's play (1836)	Milan Scala, 9 March 1842	20, 113, 200ff, 203, 204, 205, 209, 214, 218, 228, 232, 243, 244, 245, 248, 249, 289
I lombardi alla prima crociata (dramma lirico, 4)	Solera, after T. Grossi's poem (1826)	Milan Scala, 11 Feb 1843	202, 203, 205, 209, 210, 232, 234, 248, 254, 263, 267
Ernani (dramma lirico, 4 parts)	F. M. Piave, after Hugo: Hernani (play, 1830)	Venice, Fenice, 9 March 1844	203, 205, 209, 213, 214, 220, 221, 227, 228, 238, 243, 245, 247, 248, 289
I due Foscari (tragedia lirica, 3)	Piave, after Byron: The Two Foscari (play, 1821)	Rome Argentina, 3 Nov 1844	205, 213, 218, 243, 265
Giovanna d'Arco (dramma lirico, 4)	Solera, in part after Schiller: Die Jungfrau von Orleans (play, 1801)	Milan Scala, 15 Feb 1845	205, 215, 249
Alzira (tragedia lirica, prol, 2)	S. Cammarano, after Voltaire: Alzire (play, 1736)	Naples, S Carlo, 12 Aug 1845	205, 217, 239, 246
Attila (dramma lirico, prol, 3)	Solera [and Piave], after Z. Werner's play (1808)	Venice, Fenice 17 March 1846; autograph CB-Lbm	203, 205, 232, 248

Title, Genre	Librettist, Source	First performance, Remarks	
Macbeth (4)	[Piave and A. Maffei], after Shakespeare	Florence, Pergola, 14 March 1847	204, 205, 212, 215, 228, 231, 236, 237, 238, 240, 242, 244, 245, 248, 254, 289
rev. version (opera, 4)	Piave, from 1847 lib; Fr. trans. by C. Nuitter and A. Beaumont	Paris, Théâtre-Lyrique, 21 April 1865; autograph F-Pn	239, 268
I masnadieri (tragic opera, 4 parts)	[Maffei], after Schiller: Die Räuber (play, 1781)	London, Her Majesty's, 22 July 1847	205, 212, 215, 234, 236, 242, 248
Jérusalem (opéra, 4)	A. Royer and G. Vaëz, from 1843 I lombardi lib	Paris, Opéra, 26 Nov 1847; autograph Pn	205, 242, 248, 249, 263
Il corsaro (3)	Piave, after Byron: The Corsair (poem, 1814)	Trieste, Grande, 25 Oct 1848	205, 239, 243, 244, 246
La battaglia di Legnano (tragedia lirica, 4)	Cammarano, after J. Méry: La bataille de Toulouse (play, 1828)	Rome, Argentina, 27 Jan 1849	203, 205, 207, 217, 243, 244
Luisa Miller (melodramma tragico, 3)	Cammarano, after Schiller: Kabale und Liebe (play, 1784)	Naples, S Carlo, 8 Dec 1849	31, 205, 207, 217, 221, 227, 230, 234, 242, 243, 244, 289
Stiffelio (3)	Piave, after E. Souvestre and E. Bourgeois: Le pasteur (play, 1849)	Trieste, Civico [Grande], 16 Nov 1850; autograph used for Aroldo (1857)	205, 217, 218, 219, 237, 246, 254, 264
Rigoletto (melodramma, 3)	Piave, after Hugo: Le roi s'amuse (play, 1832)	Venice, Fenice, 11 March 1851	113, 205, 217, 218, 227, 231, 232, 234, 236, 243, 254, 263, 267, 270, 278, 288, 289, 312
Il trovatore (dramma, 4 parts)	Cammarano [and L. E. Bardare], after A. García Gutiérrez: El trovador (play, 1836)	Rome, Apollo, 19 Jan 1853	205, 216, 217, 219, 222, 226, 228, 229, 235, 236, 237, 238, 244, 263, 266, 288, 312
La traviata (3)	Piave, after A. Dumas fils: La dame aux camélias (play, 1852)	Venice, Fenice, 6 March 1853	205, 207, 217, 229, 234, 235, 237, 242, 243, 244, 246, 263, 288, 312
Les vêpres siciliennes (opéra, 5)	E. Scribe and C. Duveyrier, from lib for Donizetti's inc. Le duc d'Albe (1839)	Paris, Opéra, 13 June 1855; autograph Pn	106, 205, 207, 223, 227, 237, 241, 242, 253, 254, 264, 265, 268, 283
Simon Boccanegra (prol, 3)	Piave [and G. Montanelli], after Gutiérrez: Simón Bocanegra (play, 1843)	Venice, Fenice, 12 March 1857	205, 207, 208, 228, 233, 239, 241, 253, 264, 265, 289
rev. version (melodramma, prol, 3)	Piave [rev. A. Boito], from 1857 lib	Milan, Scala, 24 March 1881	274
Aroldo (4)	Piave, from 1850 Stiffelio lib	Rimini, Nuovo, 16 Aug 1857	205, 253, 264
Un ballo in maschera (melodramma, 3)	A. Somma, from Scribe's lib for Auber's Gustave III (1833)	Rome, Apollo, 17 Feb 1859	205, 218, 221, 228, 239, 253, 254, 257, 265, 266, 289

La forza del destino (opera, 4)	Piave, after A. P. de Saavedra, Duke of Rivas: Don Alvaro, o La fuerza del sino (play, 1835) with scenes from Schiller: Wallensteins Lager (play, 1799)	St Petersburg, Imperial Theatre, 10 Nov 1862	171, 207, 213, 221, 234, 236, 249, 256, 257, 259, 266, 267, 271, 272, 289
rev. version (opera, 4)	Piave [rev. A. Ghislanzoni]. from 1862 lib	Milan, Scala, 27 Feb 1869	268
Don Carlos (opéra, 5)	Méry and C. Du Locle, after Schiller's play (1787); W. H. Prescott: History of Philip II (1856) and E. Cormon: Philippe II, roi d'Espagne (play, 1849)	Paris, Opéra, 11 March 1867; autograph Pn	207, 208, 214, 220, 223, 224, 225, 226, 228, 233, 237, 239, 244, 253, 256, 259, 266, 267, 268, 269f, 271, 272, 283, 288, 289
rev. version (opera, 4)	Méry and Du Locle [rev. Du Locle], from 1867 lib and Schiller's play; It. trans. by A. de Lauzières and A. Zanardini	Milan, Scala, 10 Jan 1884	274ff
Aida (opera, 4)	Ghislanzoni, from A. Mariette's scenario amplified as Fr. prose lib by Du Locle	Cairo, Opera, 24 Dec 1871	18, 207, 208, 214, 218, 220, 223, 233, 236, 237, 238, 239, 240, 256, 257, 258, 259, 261, 265, 267, 270, 271, 272, 278, 288, 312
Otello (dramma lirico, 4)	Boito, after Shakespeare: Othello	Milan, Scala, 5 Feb 1887	207, 208, 230f, 237, 239, 243, 265, 270, 274, 276ff, 277, 280, 281, 285, 288, 289
Falstaff (commedia lirica, 3)	Boito, after Shakespeare: The Merry Wives of Windsor, King Henry IV	Milan, Scala, 9 Feb 1893	207, 208, 229, 231, 233, 237, 265, 280ff, 282, 283, 289, 323

For alternative or additional numbers in the operas *Oberto, Nabucco, I lombardi, Ernani, I due Foscari, Giovanna d'Arco* and *Attila*, see D. Lawton and D. Rosen: 'Verdi's Non-definitive Revisions: the Early Operas', *3 congresso internazionale di studi verdiani: Milano 1972*. 189–237. Four alternative arias are in *Inediti per tenore* (Milan, 1978).

CHORAL

Inno popolare (Suona la tromba) (G. Mameli), TTB, pf, 1848 (1848)

Inno delle nazioni (A. Boito), solo v, mixed vv, orch, 1862, London, Her Majesty's, 24 May 1862, vocal score (1862)   256

Libera me, S, mixed vv, orch, 1868–9 [from collab. Requiem for Rossini; incorporated in Messa da Requiem, 1874]   258

Messa da Requiem, S, A, T, B, mixed vv, orch, 1874, Milan, S Marco, 22 May 1874, vocal score (1874); with new setting of Liber scriptus, 1875, London, Albert Hall, May 1875, vocal score (1875), full score pr. (c1877), pubd (1913), autograph [with both settings of Liber scriptus] I-Ms, facs. (1941)   239, 244, 256, 261, 262, 271, 272, 274, 288

Pater noster (attrib. Dante), SSATB, 1880 (1880), Mr   285

Quattro pezzi sacri, pubd together in vocal score (1898), full score   285f
(London, 1971):
    Ave Maria (Scala enigmatica armonizzata a quattro voci miste), SATB, orig. version, 1889, Parma, 1895, 8 bars in Gazzetta musicale di Milano, I (1895), 454; rev. version (1898)
    Laudi alla Vergine Maria (Dante: Paradiso, xxxiii), S, S, A, A, c1890, Paris, 7 April 1898 (1898)
    Te Deum, SA-B, SATB orch, 1895–6, Paris, 7 April 1898, full score pr. (1898), pubd (Leipzig, c1935)
    Stabat mater, SATB, orch, 1896–7, Paris, 7 April 1898, full score pr. (1898), pubd (Leipzig, c1935)

SONGS AND VOCAL TRIO
(for 1v, pf unless otherwise stated)
Edition: *G. Verdi: Composizioni da camera per canto e pianoforte* (Milan, 1935) [CC]

Brindisi (Maffei), 1st version, ?1835 (1935), CC, *Mr*

6 romanze (1838), CC, *Mr*: Non t'accostare all'urna (J. Vittorelli),   199
More, Elisa, lo stanco poeta (T. Bianchi), In solitaria stanza (Vittorelli), Nell'orror di notte oscura (C. Angiolini), Perduta ho la pace (Goethe, trans. L. Balestra), Deh, pietoso, oh Addolorata (Goethe, trans. Balestra)

Notturno (Guarda che bianca luna) (Vittorelli), S, T, B, fl obbl, pf (1839), *Ms*

L'esule (Solera) (1839), CC, *Mr*

La seduzione (Balestra) (1839), CC, *Mr*

Chi i bei di m'adduce ancora (Goethe, trans. ?Balestra), 1842, ed. in *MR*, ix (1948), 13

Il tramonto (Maffei), 1st version, 1845, *US-NYpm*

6 romanze (1845), CC, *I-Mr*: Il tramonto (Maffei) [2nd version], La zingara (S. M. Maggioni), Ad una stella (Maffei), Lo spazzacamino (F. Romani), Il mistero (Romani), Brindisi (Maffei) [2nd version]

Il poveretto (Maggioni) (1847), CC

L'abandonnée (M. L. E[?scudier]) (1849)

Barcarola (Piave), 1850, facs. in G. Stefani: *Verdi e Trieste* (Trieste, 1951)

La preghiera del poeta (N. Sole), ?1858, ed. in *RMI*, xiv (1941), 230

Il brigidino (F. dall'Ongaro), 1863, facs. in *Scenario*, x/2 (1941)

Stornello (anon.) (1869), CC

Cupo è il sepolcro mutolo, 1873, *Ms*

Pietà, Signor (Boito) (1894)

OTHER VOCAL

Io la vidi (from C. Bassi: Il solitario ed Elosa), aria, T, [T], orch, ?1832–5, *US-NYpm*, facs. 3 pp. [of 24] in *Verdiana*, vi (1951), 14ff, in Abbiati: *Verdi*, i (1959), facing p.160, and in M. Chusid: *A Catalog of Verdi's Operas* (Hackensack, 1974), 19, ed. in *Inediti per tenore* (Milan, 1978)   *196, 197*

Tantum ergo, T, orch, c1836, *Ms*, ed. in *Inediti per tenore* (Milan, 1978)   199

Ave Maria (Dante), S, str, 1880, arrs. incl. for v, pf (1880), *Mr*   285

INSTRUMENTAL

Romanza senza parole, pf (1865)

Waltz, pf, facs. in *Discoteca*, iv/30 (1963), 19

String Quartet, e. 1873 (1876), *Nc*   258

Bibliography

BIBLIOGRAPHY

BIBLIOGRAPHICAL

L. Torri: 'Saggio di bibliografia verdiana', *RMI*, viii (1901), 379

C. Vanbianchi: *Nel I° centenario di Giuseppe Verdi, 1813–1913: saggio di bibliografia verdiana* (Milan, 1913)

C. Hopkinson: 'Bibliographical Problems concerned with Verdi and his Publishers', *1° congresso internazionale di studi verdiani: Venezia 1966*, 431

D. Lawton: 'Per una bibliografia ragionata verdiana', *1° congresso internazionale di studi verdiani: Venezia 1966*, 437

M. Pavarani: 'Per una bibliografia e documentazione verdiana', *1° congresso internazionale di studi verdiani: Venezia 1966*, 446

O. Strunk: 'Verdiana alla Biblioteca del Congresso', *1° congresso internazionale di studi verdiani: Venezia 1966*, 452; Eng. orig. in *Essays on Music in the Western World* (New York, 1974), 192

G. Tintori: 'Bibliografia verdiana in Russia', *1° congresso internazionale di studi verdiani: Venezia 1966*, 458

D. Kämpfer: 'Das deutsche Verdi-Schriften: Hauptlinien der Interpretation', *AnMc*, no.11 (1972), 185

M. Mila: *La giovinezza di Verdi* (Turin, 1974), 501ff

Newsletter of the American Institute for Verdi Studies (1976–); from no.3 (1977) as *Verdi Newsletter* [incl. detailed lists of publications, 1975–]

E. Surian: 'Lo stato attuale degli studi verdiani: appunti e bibliografia ragionata', *RIM*, xii (1977), 305

CATALOGUES

D. Lawton and D. Rosen: 'Verdi's Non-definitive Revisions: the Early Operas', *3° congresso internazionale di studi verdiani: Milano 1972*, 189–237

C. Hopkinson: *A Bibliography of the Works of Giuseppe Verdi, 1813–1901*, i (New York, 1973) [vocal and inst works excluding operas]; ii (New York, 1978) [operas]

M. Chusid: *A Catalog of Verdi's Operas* (Hackensack, 1974)

ICONOGRAPHICAL

G. Monaldi: *Saggio d'iconografia verdiana* (Bergamo, n.d.)

G. Bocca: 'Verdi e la caricatura', *RMI*, viii (1901), 326–59

H. Schultz: *Giuseppe Verdi 1813–1901: sein Leben in Bildern* (Leipzig, 1938)

C. Gatti: *Verdi nelle immagini* (Milan, 1941) [incl. sketches, pp.64f, 184, 186f]

F. Walker: 'Vincenzo Gemito and his Bust of Verdi', *ML*, xxx (1949), 44

H. Kuehner: *Giuseppe Verdi in Selbstzeugnissen und Bilddokumenten* (Reinbek bei Hamburg, 1961)

R. Petzoldt: *Giuseppe Verdi 1813–1901: sein Leben in Bildern* (Leipzig, 1961)

M. T. Muraro: 'Le scenografie delle cinque "prime assolute" di Verdi alla Fenice di Venezia', *1° congresso di studi verdiani: Venezia 1966*, 328

M. Chusid and others: 'The Verdi Archive at New York University', *Verdi Newsletter*, no.7 (1979)

LETTERS AND DOCUMENTS

I. Pizzi: *Ricordi verdiani inediti* (Turin, 1901)

A. Pascolato: *Re Lear e Ballo in maschera: lettere di Giuseppe Verdi* (Città di Castello, 1902)

T. Costantini: *Sei lettere di Verdi a Giovanni Bottesini* (Trieste, 1908)

G. Cesari and A. Luzio: *I copialettere di Giuseppe Verdi* (Milan, 1913/*R*1973; Eng. trans., abridged, 1971, as *Letters of Giuseppe Verdi*, ed. C. Osborne)

J. G. Prod'homme: 'Unpublished Letters from Verdi to Camille du Locle', *MQ*, vii (1921), 73–103; Fr. orig., *ReM*, x (1928–9), no.5, p.97; no.7, p.25

——: 'Verdi's Letters to Léon Escudier', *ML*, iv (1923), 62, 184, 375; Fr. trans., *Bulletin de la société Union musicologique*, v (1925), 7; It. orig., *RMI*, xxxv (1928), 1, 171, 519–52

A. Damerini: 'Sei lettere inedite di Verdi a G. C. Ferrarini', *Il pianoforte* (1926), Aug–Sept

A. Della Corte: 'Lettere a Maria Waldmann', *Il pianoforte* (1926), Feb

F. Werfel and P. Stefan: *Das Bildnis Giuseppe Verdis* (Vienna, 1926; Eng. trans., enlarged, 1942, as *Verdi: the Man in his Letters*)

A. Luzio: 'Il carteggio di Giuseppe Verdi con la contessa Maffei', *Profili biografici e bozzetti storici*, ii (Milan, 1927), 505–62

G. Morazzoni: *Verdi: lettere inedite* (Milan, 1929)

A. Alberti: *Verdi intimo: carteggio di Giuseppe Verdi con il conte Opprandino Arrivabene (1861–1886)* (Verona, 1931)

L. A. Garibaldi: *Giuseppe Verdi nelle lettere di Emanuele Muzio ad Antonio Barezzi* (Milan, 1931)

R. De Rensis: *Franco Faccio e Verdi: carteggio e documenti inediti* (Milan, 1934)

A. Luzio: *Carteggi verdiani*, i–ii (Rome, 1935), iii–iv (Rome, 1947)

C. Bongiovanni: *Dal carteggio inedito Verdi-Vigna* (Rome, 1941)

A. Oberdorfer: *Giuseppe Verdi: autobiografia dalle lettere* (Verona, 1941 [under pseud. C. Graziani and censored]; complete, Milan, 2/1951; rev., enlarged M. Conati, 3/1981)

Bibliography

F. Walker: 'Verdi and Francesco Florimo: some Unpublished Letters',
ML, xxvi (1945), 201

——: 'Four Unpublished Verdi Letters', *ML*, xxix (1948), 44
'Cinque lettere verdiane', *RaM*, xxi (1951), 256

F. Schlitzer: 'Inediti verdiani nella collezione dell'Accademia musicale
chigiana', *Giuseppe Verdi*, Chigiana, viii (1951), 30; pubd
separately, enlarged as *Inediti verdiani nell'archivio dell'Accademia
chigiana* (Siena, 1953)

F. Walker: 'Verdi and Vienna: with Some Unpublished Letters', *MT*,
xcii (1951), 403, 451

——: 'Verdian Forgeries', *MR*, xix (1958), 273; xx (1959), 28; It.
trans., *RaM*, xxx (1960), 338

J. W. Klein: 'Verdian Forgeries: a Summing-up', *MR*, xx (1959), 244

T. Jauner: *Fünf Jahre Wiener Operntheater, 1875–1880: Franz Jauner
und seine Zeit* (Vienna, 1963)

E. Zanetti: 'La corrispondenza di Verdi conservata a S Cecilia', *Verdi:
Bollettino dell'Istituto di studi verdiani*, iii (1969–73), 1131

U. Günther: 'Documents inconnus concernant les relations de Verdi
avec l'Opéra de Paris', *3° congresso internazionale di studi verdiani:
Milano 1972*, 564

M. Conati: 'Saggio di critiche e cronache verdiane dalla *Allgemeine
musikalische Zeitung* di Lipsia (1840–48)', *Il melodramma italiano
dell'ottocento: studi e ricerche per Massimo Mila* (Turin, 1977), 13–
43

W. Weaver: *Verdi: a Documentary Study* (London, 1977)

M. Medici and M. Conati, eds.: *Carteggio Verdi–Boito* (Parma, 1978)

G. Marchesi: *Verdi, merli e cucù: cronache bussetane fra il 1819 e il
1839* (Busseto, 1979)

M. Conati: *Interviste e incontroviste con Verdi* (Milan, 1980)

PUBLICATIONS OF THE ISTITUTO DI STUDI VERDIANI, PARMA

Verdi: Bollettino dell'Istituto di studi verdiani, i (1960) [mainly on *Un
ballo in maschera*]

Verdi: Bollettino dell'Istituto di studi verdiani, ii (1961–6) [mainly on
La forza del destino]

Verdi: Bollettino dell'Istituto di studi verdiani, iii (1969–73) [mainly on
Rigoletto]

[*Atti del*] *1° congresso internazionale di studi verdiani: Venezia 1966*
(1969)

[*Atti del*] *2° congresso internazionale di studi verdiani: Verona 1969*
(1971)

[*Atti del*] *3° congresso internazionale di studi verdiani: Milano 1972*
(1974)

[*Atti del*] *4° congresso internazionale di studi verdiani: Chicago 1974* (in preparation) ·
Quaderni dell'Istituto di studi verdiani, i: *Il Corsaro* (1963), ii: *Gerusalemme* (1963), iii: *Stiffelio* (1968), iv: *Genesi dell'Aida* (1971)

SPECIAL PERIODICAL NUMBERS

(*article titles listed in M. Mila: *La giovinezza di Verdi* (Turin, 1974), 514f)
* *Gazzetta musicale di Milano*, lvi (1901), March
Natura ed arte (1901)
**RMI*, viii/2 (1901)
Die Musik, xiii (1913–14) [incl. articles by A. Weissmann, E. Istel, R. Specht]
**Nuova antologia*, clxvii (16 Oct 1913)
**Aurea Parma*, xxv (1941), Jan–Feb
Illustrazione italiana (26 Jan 1941)
**La regione Emilia-Romagna* (1950), nos.9–12
**ZfM*, Jg.112 (1951), Jan
**Das Musikleben*, iv (1951), Feb
**Il diapason* (1951), Feb
**Melos*, xviii (1951), Feb
**Opera*, ii/2 (1951)
**La fièra letteraria* (22 April 1951)
**RaM*, xxi (1951), July
Verdiana: bollettino di notizie (1950–51) [12 issues]
HMYB, vii (1952), 494
High Fidelity, xiii (1963), Oct [incl. articles by A. Moravia, W. Weaver, and on early New York productions]
19th Century Music, ii/2 (1978–9)

BIOGRAPHY, LIFE AND WORKS

G. Demaldè: *Cenni biografici* (MS, archives of Monte di Pietà, Busseto, c1853); pubd in *Newsletter of the American Institute for Verdi Studies*, nos.1–2 (1976), *Verdi Newsletter*, no.3 (1977)
H. Cavalli: *José Verdi* (Madrid, 1867)
M. Lessona: 'Parma: Giuseppe Verdi', *Volere è potere* (Milan, 1869), 287
G. Monaldi: *Verdi e le sue opere* (Florence, 1878)
A. Pougin: *Giuseppe Verdi: vita aneddotica* (Milan, 1881 [trans. and annotated by Folchetto (pseud. of J. Caponi) from biographical articles in *Le ménestrel*, 1878]; Fr. orig., incorporating Caponi's additions, 1886; Eng. trans., 1887)
G. Monaldi: *Verdi* (Turin, 1899, 4/1951)

Bibliography

F. Werfel: *Verdi: Roman der Oper* (Berlin, 1925/*R*1972, rev. 2/1930;
   Eng. trans., 1947) [novel]
F. Bonavia: *Verdi* (London, 1930)
C. Gatti: *Verdi* (Milan, 1931, 2/1951; Eng. trans., 1955, as *Verdi: the
   Man and his Music*)
F. Toye: *Giuseppe Verdi: his Life and Works* (London, 1931)
H. Gerigk: *Giuseppe Verdi* (Potsdam, 1932)
D. Hussey: *Verdi* (London, 1940, 5/1973)
G. Cenzato: *Itinerari verdiani* (Parma, 1949, 2/1955)
M. Mila: *Giuseppe Verdi* (Bari, 1958)
F. Abbiati: *Giuseppe Verdi* (Milan, 1959)
F. Walker: *The Man Verdi* (London, 1962)
G. Martin: *Verdi* (New York, 1963, rev. 2/1964)
M. J. Matz: 'The Verdi Family of Sant'Agata and Roncole: Legend and
   Truth', *1° congresso internazionale di studi verdiani: Venezia 1966*,
   216
   ——: 'Verdi: the Roots of the Tree', *Verdi: Bollettino dell'Istituto di
   studi verdiani*, iii (1969–73), 333–64
W. Weaver: 'Verdi the Playgoer', *Musical Newsletter*, vi/1 (1976), 3
P. Southwell-Sander: *Verdi, his Life and Times* (Tunbridge Wells,
   1978)
G. Marchesi: *Verdi* (Milan, 1979)
W. Weaver and M. Chusid, eds.: *The Verdi Companion* (New York,
   1979)
D. Kimbell: *Verdi in the Age of Italian Romanticism* (Cambridge,
   1981)
M. De Angelis: *Le carte dell'impresario: melodramma e costume
   teatrale nell'ottocento* (Florence, 1982)

LOCATIVE STUDIES

F. Resasco: *Verdi a Genova* (Genoa, 1901)
G. M. Ciampelli: *Le opere verdiane al Teatro alla Scala* (*1839–1929*)
   (Milan, 1929)
Verdi e Roma (Rome, 1951)
La passione verdiana di Trieste (Trieste, 1951)
G. Steffani: *Verdi e Trieste* (Trieste, 1951)
Verdi e la Fenice (Venice, 1951)
Verdi e Firenze (Florence, 1951)
P. P. Várnai: 'Verdi in Hungary', *Verdi: Bollettino dell'Istituto di studi
   verdiani*, ii (1961–6), 949–1029, 1429–1503; iii (1969–73), 246–
   332, 718–89, 1038–1130, 1409–84
M. Labroca: 'Verdi e Venezia', *1° congresso internazionale di studi
   verdiani: Venezia 1966*, 367
R. Massarani: 'Giuseppe Verdi a Rio de Janeiro', *1° congresso inter-*

nazionale di studi verdiani: Venezia 1966, 383
G. Gualerzi and C. M. Roscioni: 'Il Verdi "minore" dal 1945 al 1971',
    La Fenice programme book (Venice, 1970–71), 335 [list of perfs. in
    Italy]
M. Chusid: 'Casts for the Verdi Premières in the U.S. (1847–1976)',
    Newsletter of the American Institute for Verdi Studies, no.2 (1976);
    Verdi Newsletter, no.3 (1977)
——: 'Casts for the Verdi Premières in London (1845–1977)', *Verdi
    Newsletter*, no.5 (1978); no.6 (1979)
D. L. Hixon: *Verdi in San Francisco, 1851–1899* ([Irvine, Calif.], 1981)

MUSICAL STUDIES

A. Basevi: *Studio sulle opere di Giuseppe Verdi* (Florence, 1859)
H. F. Chorley: *Thirty Years' Musical Recollections* (London, 1862,
    2/1926), 182ff
E. Hanslick: *Die moderne Oper*, i (Berlin, 1875/R1971), 217–55
F. Filippi: *Musica e musicisti: critiche, biografie ed escursioni* (Milan,
    1876)
G. B. Shaw: 'A Word More about Verdi', *Anglo-Saxon Review* (1901),
    March; repr. in *London Music in 1888–89* (London, 1937, 2/1950),
    405
A. Soffredini: *Le opere di Verdi: studio critico analitico* (Milan, 1901)
L. Torchi: 'L'opera di Giuseppe Verdi e i suoi caratteri principali', *RMI*,
    viii (1901), 279–335
D. Alaleona: 'L'evoluzione della partitura verdiana', *Nuova antologia*,
    clxvii (1913), 521
G. Roncaglia: *Giuseppe Verdi: l'ascensione dell'arte sua* (Naples, 1914)
M. Mila: *Il melodramma di Verdi* (Bari, 1933/R1960)
P. Bekker: *Wandlungen der Oper* (Leipzig, 1934; Eng. trans., 1935),
    192
J. Loschelder: *Das Todesproblem in Verdis Opernschaffen* (Cologne and
    Stuttgart, 1938)
G. Roncaglia: *L'ascensione creatrice di Giuseppe Verdi* (Florence,
    1940)
Verdi: studi e memorie (Rome, 1941)
G. Roncaglia: 'Il "tema-cardine" nell'opera di Giuseppe Verdi', *RMI*,
    xlvii (1943), 220
A. Della Corte: *Le sei più belle opere di Giuseppe Verdi: Rigoletto, Il
    trovatore, La traviata, Aida, Otello, Falstaff* (Milan, 1946; pubd
    separately, 1923–43)
M. Mila: 'Verdi e Hanslick', *RaM*, xxi (1951), 212
I. Pizzetti: 'Contrappunto ed armonia nell'opera di Verdi', *RaM*, xxi
    (1951), 189
U. Rolandi: *Il libretto per musica attraverso i tempi* (Rome, 1951), 126

Bibliography

R. Vlad: 'Anticipazioni nel linguaggio armonico verdiano', *RaM*, xxi (1951), 237

G. Roncaglia: 'Il cammino e l'insegnamento di Giuseppe Verdi', *RMI*, liv (1952), 114

A. Porter: 'Verdi and Schiller', *Opera Annual*, no.3, ed. H. Rosenthal (London, 1956), 52

F. I. Travis: *Verdi's Orchestration* (Zurich, 1956)

G. Roncaglia: *Galleria verdiana: studi e figure* (Milan, 1959)

W. A. Herrmann jr: *Religion in the Operas of Giuseppe Verdi* (diss., Columbia U., 1963)

L. Dallapiccola: 'Parole e musica nel melodramma', *Quaderni della Rassegna musicale*, ii (1965), 117; Eng. trans. as 'Words and Music in Italian XIX Century Opera', *Quaderni dell'Istituto italiano di cultura* (Dublin, 1964), no.3; repr. in *PNM*, v/1 (1966), 121

M. Chusid: 'The Organization of Scenes with Arias: Verdi's Cavatinas and Romanzas', *I° congresso internazionale di studi verdiani: Venezia 1966*, 59

F. Lippmann: 'Verdi e Bellini', *I° congresso internazionale di studi verdiani: Venezia 1966*, 184; Ger. version in *Beiträge zur Geschichte der Oper*, ed. H. Becker (Regensburg, 1969), 77

J. Kovács: 'Zum Spätstil Verdis', *I° congresso internazionale di studi verdiani: Venezia 1966*, 132

P. P. Várnai: 'Contributo per uno studio della tipizzazione negativa nelle opere verdiane: personaggi e stiuazioni', *I° congresso internazionale di studi verdiani: Venezia 1966*, 268

P. Pinagli: *Romanticismo di Verdi* (Florence, 1967)

L. K. Gerhartz: *Die Auseinandersetzungen des jungen Giuseppe Verdi mit dem literarischen Drama: ein Beitrag zur szenischen Strukturbestimmung der Oper*, Berliner Studien zur Musikwissenschaft, xv (Berlin, 1968)

S. Hughes: *Famous Verdi Operas* (London, 1968)

J. Kerman: 'Verdi's Use of Recurring Themes', *Studies in Music History: Essays for Oliver Strunk* (Princeton, 1968), 495

M. Mila: 'L'unità stilistica nell'opera di Verdi', *NRMI*, ii (1968), 62

A. A. Abert: 'Über Textentwürfe Verdis', *Beiträge zur Geschichte der Oper*, ed. H. Becker (Regensburg, 1969), 131

Colloquium Verdi–Wagner: Rom 1969 [AnMc, no.11 (1972)]

C. Osborne: *The Complete Operas of Verdi* (London, 1969)

G. Baldini: *Abitare la battaglia: la storia di Giuseppe Verdi* (Milan, 1970; Eng. trans., 1980, as *The Story of Giuseppe Verdi: 'Oberto' to 'Un ballo in maschera'*)

P. Petrobelli: 'Osservazioni sul processo compositivo in Verdi', *AcM*, xliii (1971), 125 [incl. sketches]

A. A. Abert: 'Leidenschaftsausbrüche zwischen Recitativ und Arie', *3°*

congresso internazionale di studi verdiani: Milano 1972, 56

C. Casini: 'L'analogo sintattico: sul recitativo del primo Verdi', *Spettatore musicale*, vii/4 (1972), 38

W. Dean: 'Some Echoes of Donizetti in Verdi's Operas', *3° congresso internazionale di studi verdiani: Milano 1972*, 122

F. Noske: 'Verdi and the Musical Figure of Death', *3° congresso internazionale di studi verdiani: Milano 1972*, 349–86

J. Budden: *The Operas of Verdi*, i: *From Oberto to Rigoletto* (London, 1973); ii: *From Il trovatore to La forza del destino* (London, 1978); iii: *From Don Carlos to Falstaff* (London, 1981)

D. Lawton: *Tonality and Drama in Verdi's Early Operas* (diss., U. of California, Berkeley, 1973)

F. Noske: 'Ritual Scenes in Verdi's Operas', *ML*, liv (1973), 415

F. Lippmann: 'Der italienische Vers und der musikalische Rhythmus: zum Verhältnis von Vers und Musik in der italienischen Oper des 19. Jahrhunderts, mit einem Rückblick auf die 2. Hälfte des 18. Jahrhunderts', *AnMc*, no.12 (1973), 253–369; no.14 (1974), 324–410; no.15 (1975), 298–333

W. Dean: 'Donizetti's Serious Operas', *PRMA*, c (1973–4), 123

M. Mila: *La giovinezza di Verdi* (Turin, 1974)

F. Lippmann: 'Verdi und Donizetti', *Opernstudien: Anna Amalie Abert zum 65. Geburtstag* (Tutzing, 1975), 153

V. Godefroy: *The Dramatic Genius of Verdi: Studies of Selected Operas*, i: *'Nabucco' to 'La traviata'* (London, 1975); ii: *'I vespri siciliani' to 'Falstaff'* (London, 1977)

F. Noske: *The Signifier and the Signified: Studies in the Operas of Mozart and Verdi* (The Hague, 1977)

G. Tomlinson: 'Verdi after Budden', *19th Century Music*, v (1981–2), 170

P. Weiss: 'Verdi and the Fusion of Genres', *JAMS*, xxxv (1982), 138

TEXTUAL STUDIES

D. Vaughan: 'Discordanze tra gli autografi verdiani e la loro stampa', *La Scala* (1958), no.104, pp.11, 71

G. Gavazzeni: 'Problemi di tradizione dinamico-fraseologica e critica testuale, in Verdi e in Puccini', *RaM*, xxix (1959), 27, 106; repr. with Eng. trans. (Milan, 1961) [see also D. Vaughan and G. Gavazzeni, *RaM*, xxx (1960), 60; *Musica d'oggi*, iv (1961), 65 168]

D. Vaughan: 'Meeting Verdi on his Own Ground', *Verdi: Bollettino dell'Istituto di studi verdiani*, i (1960), p.lvii

———: 'The Inner Language of Verdi's Manuscripts', *Musicology*, v (1979), 67–153; abridged, 'Markings and Meanings in Verdi', *World of Opera*, i/1 (1978–9), 43

Bibliography

INDIVIDUAL WORKS

Oberto

C. Sartori: '*Rocester*, la prima opera di Verdi', *RMI*, xliii (1939), 97

M. Conati: 'L'*Oberto, conte di San Bonifacio* in due recensioni straniere poco note e in una lettra inedita di Verdi', *1° congresso internazionale di studi verdiani: Venezia 1966*, 67

D. R. B. Kimbell: 'Poi . . . diventò l'*Oberto*', *ML*, lii (1971), 1

Nabucco

P. Petrobelli: 'Nabucco', *Conferenze 1966–67: Associazione Amici della Scala*, 17–47

D. Lawton: 'Analytical Observations on the *Nabucco* Revisions', *3° congresso internazionale di studi verdiani: Milano 1972*, 208

I lombardi

'Gerusalemme', *Quaderni dell'Istituto di studi verdiani*, ii (1963)

Ernani

L. K. Gerhartz: *Die Auseinandersetzungen des jungen Giuseppe Verdi mit dem literarischen Drama: ein Beitrag zur szenischen Strukturbestimmung der Oper*, Berliner Studien zur Musikwissenschaft, xv (Berlin, 1968), 30–82, 453ff

J. Kerman: 'Notes on an Early Verdi Opera', *Soundings*, iii (1973), 56

I due Foscari

C. Simone: 'Lettere al tenore Mario de Candia sulla cabaletta de *I due Foscari*', *Nuova antologia*, lxix (1934), 327

Alzira

M. Mila: 'Lettura dell'*Alzira*', *RIM*, i (1966), 246

Attila

M. Noiray and R. Parker: 'La composition d'*Attila*: étude de quelques variantes', *RdM*, lxii (1976), 104

Macbeth

G. C. Varesi: 'L'interpretazione del *Macbeth*', *Nuova antologia*, cclxxxi (1932), 433

L. K. Gerhartz: *Die Auseinandersetzungen des jungen Giuseppe Verdi mit dem literarischen Drama: ein Beitrag zur szenischen Strukturbestimmung der Oper*, Berliner Studien zur Musikwissenschaft, xv (Berlin, 1968), 82–193, 465ff

W. Osthoff: 'Die beiden Fassungen von Verdis *Macbeth*', *AMw*, xxix (1972), 17

D. Kimbell: 'The Young Verdi and Shakespeare', *PRMA*, ci (1974–5), 59

G. Badacsonyi: 'Verdi's Two *Macbeths*', *Opera*, xxvii (1976), 108

F. Noske: 'Schiller e la genesi del Macbeth verdiano', *NRMI*, x (1976), 196

F. Degrada: 'Lettura del *Macbeth* di Verdi', *Studi musicali*, vi (1977), 207–67

D. Goldin: 'Il *Macbeth* verdiano: genesi e linguaggio di un libretto', *AnMc*, no.19 (1979), 336–72

M. Rinaldi: 'Il "Macbeth" di Verdi: un'opera "più difficile delle altre" ', *Studi musicali*, x (1982), 293–331

D. Rosen and A. Porter, eds.: *Verdi's 'Macbeth': a Sourcebook* (New York, 1983)

see also 'Shakespeare operas'

Jérusalem

'Gerusalemme', *Quaderni dell'Istituto di studi verdiani*, ii (1963)

D. Kimbell: 'Verdi's First Rifacimento: *I lombardi* and *Jérusalem*', *ML*, lx (1979), 1

Il corsaro

'Il corsaro', *Quaderni dell'Istituto di studi verdiani*, i (1963)

G. Barblan: 'La lunga quarantena de Il Corsaro', La Fenice programme book (Venice, 1970–71), 291

R. Celletti: '*Il Corsaro* e la vocalità di Verdi dall'*Oberto* ai *Vespri*', La Fenice programme book (Venice, 1971–2), 321

La battaglia di Legnano

J. Budden: '*La battaglia di Legnano*: its Unique Character, with Special Reference to the Finale of Act I', *3° congresso internazionale di studi verdiani: Milano 1972*, 71

F. Noske: 'Verdi und die Belagerung von Haarlem', *Convivium musicorum: Festschrift Wolfgang Boetticher* (Berlin, 1974), 236

Luisa Miller

L. K. Gerhartz: *Die Auseinandersetzungen des jungen Giuseppe Verdi mit dem literarischen Drama: ein Beitrag zur szenischen Strukturbestimmung der Oper*, Berliner Studien zur Musikwissenschaft, xv (Berlin, 1968), 193–270, 475ff

Stiffelio

V. Levi: '*Stiffelio* e il suo rifacimento (*Aroldo*)', *1° congresso internazionale di studi verdiani: Venezia 1966*, 172

'Stiffelio', *Quaderni dell'Istituto di studi verdiani*, iii (1968)

Rigoletto

C. Gatti: Introduction to *L'abbozzo del Rigoletto di Giuseppe Verdi* (Milan, 1941) [sketches]

G. Roncaglia: 'L'abbozzo del *Rigoletto* di Verdi', *RMI*, xlviii (1946), 112; repr. in G. Roncaglia: *Galleria verdiana* (Milan, 1959)

P. Petrobelli: 'Verdi e il *Don Giovanni*: osservazioni sulla scena iniziale del *Rigoletto*', *1° congresso internazionale di studi verdiani: Venezia 1966*, 232

Bibliography

Verdi: Bollettino dell'Istituto di studi verdiani, iii (1969–73)

M. Chusid: 'Rigoletto and Monterone: a Study in Musical Dramaturgy', *IMSCR*, xi *Copenhagen 1972*, 325

N. John, ed.: *Rigoletto*, [English National] Opera Guide, no.15 (London, 1982)

Il trovatore

P. Petrobelli: 'Per un'esegesi della struttura drammatica del *Trovatore*', *3° congresso internazionale di studi verdiani: Milano 1972*, 387

D. Rosen: '*Le trouvère*: Comparing Verdi's French Version with his Original', *Opera News*, xli/22 (1977), 16

La traviata

F. Merkling, ed.: *The Opera News Book of 'Traviata'* (New York, c1967)

M. Chusid: 'Drama and the Key of F major in *La traviata*', *3° congresso internazionale di studi verdiani: Milano 1972*, 89

C. and M. J. Matz: 'Verdi's Revenge', *High Fidelity* (1972), March, 62

J. Budden: 'The Two *Traviatas*', *PRMA*, xcix (1972–3), 43

D. Rosen: 'Virtue Restored', *Opera News*, xlii/9 (1977–8), 36; repr. in *About the House*, vi (1981), 40

N. John, ed.: *La traviata*, English National Opera Guide, no.5 (London, 1981)

Les vêpres siciliennes

P. Bonnefon: 'Les métamorphoses d'un opéra', *Revue des deux mondes*, xli (1917), 877

J. Budden: 'Varianti nei *Vespri siciliani*', *NRMI*, vi (1972), 155

M. Mila, R. Celletti and G. Gualerzi: *Opera: collana di guide musicali*, 1st ser., i (Turin, 1973) [essays with Fr./It. lib]

A. Porter: '*Les vêpres siciliennes*: New Letters from Verdi to Scribe', *19th Century Music*, ii (1978–9), 95

Simon Boccanegra

F. Walker: 'Verdi, Giuseppe Montanelli and the libretto of *Simon Boccanegra*', *Verdi: Bollettino dell'Istituto di studi verdiani*, i (1960), 1373

W. Osthoff: 'Die beiden *Boccanegra*-Fassungen und der Beginn von Verdis Spätwerk', *AnMc*, no.1 (1963), 70

4° congresso internazionale di studi verdiani: Chicago 1974

Aroldo

V. Levi: '*Stiffelio* e il suo rifacimento (*Aroldo*)', *1° congresso internazionale di studi verdiani: Venezia 1966*, 172

Un ballo in maschera

A. Pascolato: *Rè Lear e Ballo in maschera: lettere di Giuseppe Verdi* (Città di Castello, 1902)

Verdi: Bollettino dell'Istituto di studi verdiani, i (1960)
G. Salvetti and R. Celletti: *Opera: collana di guide musicali*, 1st ser., ii (Turin, 1973) [essays with lib]

La forza del destino
Verdi: Bollettino dell'Istituto di studi verdiani, ii (1961–6)

Don Carlos
E. Fabrini: *Il Don Carlos del Maestro Verdi* (Florence, 1869)
2° congresso internazionale di studi verdiani: Verona 1969
A. Porter: 'A Sketch for *Don Carlos*', *MT*, cxi (1970), 882
———: 'The Making of *Don Carlos*', *PRMA*, xcviii (1971–2), 73
U. Günther: 'La genèse de *Don Carlos*', *RdM*, lviii (1972), 16–64; lx (1974), 87–158
———: 'Zur Entstehung der zweiten französischen Fassung von Verdis *Don Carlos*', *IMSCR*, xi *Copenhagen 1972*, 396
A. Porter: 'A Note on Princess Eboli', *MT*, cxiii (1972), 750
U. Günther: preface to vocal score (Milan, 1974, 2/1981)
U. Günther and G. Carrara Verdi: 'Der Briefwechsel Verdi–Nuitter–Du Locle zur Revision des *Don Carlos*', *AnMc*, no.14 (1974), 1–31; no.15 (1975), 334
A. Porter: 'Preamble to a New *Don Carlos*', *Opera*, xxv (1974), 665
M. Clémeur: 'Eine neuentdeckte Quelle für das Libretto von Verdi's *Don Carlos*', *Melos/NZM*, iii (1977), 496
A. Porter: 'Observations on *Don Carlos*', *World of Opera*, i/3 (1978–9), 1

Aida
E. Prime-Stevenson: 'Verdi and the Theme-structure of *Aida*', *Long-haired Iopas* (Florence, 1928)
A. Luzio: 'Come fu composta l'*Aida*', *Carteggi verdiani*, iv (Rome, 1947), 5
E. Lendvai: 'Verdis Formgeheimnisse', *1° congresso internazionale di studi verdiani: Venezia 1966*, 157
'Genesi di Aida', *Quaderni dell'Istituto di studi verdiani*, iv (1971)
A. Geck: '*Aida*', *Die Oper: Schriftenreihe über musikalische Bühnenwerke* (Berlin, 1973)
U. Günther: 'Zur Entstehung von Verdis *Aida*', *Studi musicali*, ii (1973), 15–71
G. Marchesi: '"Aida" come fiaba', *Quadrivium*, xiv (1973), 283
P. Gossett: 'Verdi, Ghislanzoni, and *Aida*: the Uses of Convention', *Critical Inquiry*, i (1974), 291–334
J. Humbert: 'A propos de l'égyptomanie dans l'oeuvre de Verdi: attribution à Auguste Mariette d'un scénario anonyme de l'opéra *Aïda*', *RdM*, lxii (1976), 229
L. Alberti: 'I progressi attuali [1872] del dramma musicale: note sulla

Bibliography

Disposizione scenica per l'opera 'Aida'', *Il melodramma italiano dell'ottocento: studi e ricerche per Massimo Mila* (Turin, 1977), 125–55

H. Busch: *Verdi's Aida: the History of an Opera in Letters and Documents* (Minneapolis, 1978)

N. John, ed.: *Aida*, English National Opera Guide, no.2 (London, 1980)

Otello

'L'Otello di Verdi', *Corriere della sera* (1887), Feb, suppl.

F. Busoni: 'Verdi's *Otello*: eine kritische Studie', *NZM*, liv (1887), 125

J. Kerman: 'Verdi's *Otello*, or Shakespeare Explained', *Hudson Review*, vi (1953–4), 266; rev. in J. Kerman: *Opera as Drama* (New York, 1956), 129–67

H. Schueller: '*Othello* Transformed: Verdi's Interpretation of Shakespeare', *Studies in Honor of John Wilcox* (Detroit, 1958), 129

W. Dean: 'Verdi's *Otello*: a Shakespearian Masterpiece', *Shakespeare Survey*, xxi (1968), 87

D. Lawton: 'On the "bacio" theme in *Otello*', *19th Century Music*, i (1977–8), 211

N. John, ed.: *Otello*, English National Opera Guide, no.7 (London, 1981)

see also 'Shakespeare operas'

Falstaff

H. Gál: 'A Deleted Episode in Verdi's *Falstaff*', *MR*, ii (1941), 266

E. T. Cone: 'The Stature of *Falstaff*: Technique and Content in Verdi's Last Opera', *Center*, i (1954), 17

G. Barblan: *Un prezioso spartito del 'Falstaff'* (Milan, 1957)

——: 'Spunti rivelatori nella genesi del *Falstaff*', *I° congresso internazionale di studi verdiani: Venezia 1966*, 16

D. Sabbeth: 'Dramatic and Musical Organization in *Falstaff*', *3° congresso internazionale di studi verdiani: Milano 1972*, 415

W. Osthoff: 'Il Sonetto nel *Falstaff* di Verdi', *Il melodramma dell'ottocento: studi e ricerche per Massimo Mila* (Turin, 1977), 157

see also 'Shakespeare operas'

Il re Lear

A. Pascolato: *Rè Lear e Ballo in maschera: lettere di Giuseppe Verdi* (Città di Castello, 1902)

M. Medici: 'Lettere su Re Lear', *Verdi: Bollettino dell'Istituto di studi verdiani*, i (1960)

L. K. Gerhartz: 'Il *Re Lear* di Antonio Somma ed il modello melodrammatico dell'opera verdiana: principi per una definizione del libretto

307

verdiano', *1° congresso internazionale di studi verdiani: Venezia 1966*, 110

——: *Die Auseinandersetzungen des jungen Giuseppe Verdi mit dem literarischen Drama: ein Beitrag zur szenischen Strukturbestimmung der Oper*, Berliner Studien zur Musikwissenschaft, xv (Berlin, 1968), 277ff, 497ff

G. Martin: 'Verdi, *King Lear* and Maria Piccolomini', *Columbia Library Columns*, xxi (1971), 12

see also 'Shakespeare operas'

Shakespeare operas

P. Nardi: *Vita di Arrigo Boito* (Milan, 1942), 458–516, 587ff

E. T. Cone: 'Verdis letzte Opern: die Spielzeuge eines alten Mannes: die Spätwerk Verdis im Lichte der modernen Kritik', *Perspektiven*, vi (1953), 127; Eng. orig., 'The Old Man's Toys', *Perspectives USA*, vi (1954), 114

W. Dean: 'Shakespeare and Opera', *Shakespeare in Music*, ed. P. Hartnoll (London, 1964), 89–175

——: 'Shakespeare in the Opera House', *Shakespeare Survey*, xviii (1965), 75

A. Porter: 'Translating Shakespeare', *Opera*, xxxi (1980), 527, 753

see also 'Macbeth', 'Otello', 'Falstaff', 'Il re Lear'

Requiem

I. Pizzetti: 'La religiosità di Verdi: introduzione alla Messa da Requiem', *Nuova antologia*, i (1941)

D. Rosen: 'Verdi's "Liber scriptus" Rewritten', *MQ*, lv (1969), 151

——: 'La *Messa* a Rossini e il *Requiem* per Manzoni', *RIM*, iv (1969), 127; v (1970), 216

——: *The Genesis of Verdi's Requiem* (diss., U. of California, Berkeley, 1976)

Quattro pezzi sacri, etc

M. C. Caputo: 'La Scala-Rebus e le *Ave Maria* di G. Verdi', *Gazzetta musicale di Milano*, l (1895), 453

H. Scherchen: 'I quattro pezzi sacri', *Il diapason* (1951), Feb

F. Walker: 'Verdi's *Four Sacred Pieces*', *Ricordiana*, vi/2 (1961), 1

D. Stivender: 'The Composer of *Gesù mori*', *Newsletter of the American Institute for Verdi Studies*, no.2 (1976), 6

M. Conati: 'Le *Ave Maria* su scala enigmatica di Verdi dalla prima alla seconda stesura (1889–1897)', *RIM*, xiii (1978), 280–311

GIACOMO PUCCINI

Mosco Carner

CHAPTER ONE

Life

I Education and early compositions

Giacomo Puccini was born in the Tuscan city of Lucca on 23 December 1858 and baptized as Giacomo Antonio Domenico Michele Secondo Maria Puccini. He was the most eminent member of a family that had long been prominent in the musical life of the city. His great-great-grandfather, also Giacomo (1712–81) and his great-grandfather Antonio (1747–1832) were both organists at the church of S Martino and composed a large number of works, mainly sacred. Antonio's son Domenico (1772–1815, Puccini's grandfather) enjoyed much esteem as a composer: his works, in particular his operas (he was a pupil of Paisiello), reveal an outstanding theatrical sense. Puccini's father Michele (1813–64), a pupil of Donizetti and Mercadante, was an important teacher, but he died when Giacomo was a little over five. As the latter was expected to follow the family tradition as organist and choirmaster at S Martino, the city fathers in 1864 issued a decree that his uncle Fortunato Magi hold the post until Giacomo should be old enough to take it over. Magi was his first teacher but had little success with the boy, and at the instigation of his energetic mother, Puccini continued his studies with the director of the Istituto Musicale Pacini, Carlo Angeloni, who, like Magi, had been a pupil of Michele Puccini. At the age of ten Puccini joined the choirs at S Martino and S Michele and four years later started his career as organist at these and other churches in the vicinity of Lucca, including those of Mutigliano, Celle and Pascaglia.

When he was 17 he began composing in earnest, writing organ pieces that were largely the result of improvisations into which he worked, much to the surprise of the congregation, snatches from Tuscan folksongs and from operas such as *Rigoletto*, *Il trovatore* and *La traviata*, to which he had been introduced by Angeloni. A performance of *Aida* at Pisa in 1876 made such an impact on him that he decided to break with the family tradition and follow his instinct for operatic composition. He later said that this Pisa performance opened a musical window to him. Lucca, however, was not the place to acquire the operatic craft, and it became Puccini's most ardent wish to go to Milan, which with its Teatro alla Scala and conservatory was the mecca for all aspiring composers.

Four years were to pass before his wish could be realized. From those early Lucca days date two symphonic preludes (1876), a cantata, *I figli d'Italia bella*, written for a competition (1877), and a motet and Credo (1878) which Puccini later used in the Mass in A♭ composed as his final exercise at the Istituto Musicale Pacini (1880). With the help of a scholarship instituted by Queen Margherita for talented sons of poor families and financial support from a great-uncle, Dr Nicolao Cerù, Puccini entered the Milan Conservatory in the autumn of 1880 and remained there three years. His chief teachers were Antonio Bazzini and Ponchielli. His experiences in those three years had much in common with those of the poor young artists so vividly depicted in *La bohème*. In July 1883 he ended his studies with an instrumental piece, the *Capriccio sinfonico*, which was performed by the

312

student orchestra under Franco Faccio, revealing for the first time his talent for melodic invention and colourful orchestration.

II 1884–1904

In the preceding April of 1883 the music publishing firm of Edoardo Sonzogno in Milan had announced in its house journal, *Il teatro illustrato*, a competition for a one-act opera (Mascagni's *Cavalleria rusticana* was to be discovered in this way in 1889), and Puccini, then still a pupil at the conservatory, had decided with Ponchielli's encouragement to enter it. Through Ponchielli's intervention he won as librettist Ferdinando Fontana, who suggested to him a subject with fantastic, supernatural features, *Le villi*. Based on a legend first related by Heine, it was used by Adolphe Adam in his ballet *Giselle, ou Les willis* (Paris, 1841) and by Edward Loder in his opera *The Night Dancers* (London, 1846). Such subjects were then in vogue in Italian opera in the wake of the German Romantic operas of Weber, Marschner and early Wagner. (Catalani's *Loreley* of 1880 is another example of this influence.) When the result of the competition was announced early in 1884, *Le villi* was not even mentioned: the jury seems not to have taken the trouble to examine the score as, written in haste, it was all but illegible. Soon after, at a party in the house of the wealthy Milan music lover Marco Sala, at which a number of influential people including Arrigo Boito were present, Puccini played and sang his opera at the piano to such general acclaim that it was decided to stage it at the Teatro del Verme. Performed there on 31 May 1884 with resounding success, it was acquired by

*27. Giacomo
Puccini (centre)
with his wife
Elvira and son
Antonio at Torre
del Lago*

314

Ricordi, on whose advice Puccini extended it to two acts
(Turin, 1884). Moreover, the publisher commissioned
another opera, again with Fontana as librettist. This was
the beginning of Puccini's lifelong association with the
house of Ricordi, in whose director he was to find a
fatherly mentor and friend. The new opera was the four-
act *Edgar*, based on Alfred de Musset's involved and
turgid book-drama *La coupe et les lèvres*, apparently
chosen by Fontana because of a superficial resemblance
of its plot to that of *Carmen*. For Puccini's particular
dramatic talent it was a most unsuitable libretto, on
which he worked four years. *Edgar* was first given at La
Scala on 21 April 1889 and was coolly received, and
although the composer subsequently compressed it into
three acts (Ferrara, 1892) and further revised it in 1901
and 1905, it has not survived. In Puccini's own words it
was 'una cantonata' – 'a blunder'. Into the time of
Edgar falls the beginning of Puccini's association with
Elvira Gemignani, the wife of a wholesale merchant at
Lucca, who in 1886 bore him a son, Antonio. It was not
until after the death of Elvira's husband in 1904 that her
union with Puccini could be legalized.

Manon Lescaut was the first of Puccini's operas for
which he selected the subject himself. The international
success of Massenet's *Manon* (1884) attracted his
attention to Abbé Prévost's famous novel, whose
narrative, characters and atmosphere he felt to be
eminently suited to his particular genius. The libretto
was fashioned by five different authors – first
Leoncavallo, then Marco Praga and Domenico Oliva,
and finally Luigi Illica and Giuseppe Giacosa, with
Ricordi lending a helping hand and Puccini controlling
the whole operation. Because of the multiple paternity

of its libretto, *Manon Lescaut*, so called to distinguish it from Massenet's opera, was published without the names of the librettists. At its first production (Turin, 1 February 1893) it achieved a success such as Puccini was never to repeat, and it made his name known outside Italy. Its London production in 1894 prompted Bernard Shaw, then a music critic, to the prophetic words: 'Puccini looks to me more like the heir of Verdi than any of his rivals'. In 1891, while at work on the opera, the composer acquired a house at Torre del Lago on the lake of Massaciuccoli, where he lived until 1921 and wrote all his later operas except *Turandot*. After Puccini's death his son transformed the house into a mausoleum-cum-museum in which the composer and his wife, who died in 1930, were interred.

La bohème was the first of the three operas in which Puccini enjoyed the exclusive collaboration of Illica and Giacosa, an association to which Ricordi jokingly referred as the 'Holy Trinity'. It was perhaps the best team of poets Puccini had in his entire career. There was a clear division of labour: Illica elaborated the scenario and invented picturesque incidents, Giacosa saw to the poetic side and the versification, with Puccini taking a highly active part in the shaping of the libretto. This inevitably led to frequent quarrels among the three, with Giacosa, an eminent writer and poet in his own right, threatening to resign a number of times. In the end, however, it was Puccini who won, because of his extraordinary sense of the theatre. For example, he developed, from a mere hint in Prévost's novel, the unique Embarkation act of *Manon Lescaut*, added a manhunt in the final act of *La fanciulla del West* and invented the character of Liù and her suicide in *Turandot*. The new opera, based on Henry Murger's autobiographical *Scènes de la vie de Bohème*, was first produced at Turin on 1 February 1896 under Toscanini, but did not have an immediate success, since the critics had come expecting to hear an opera in the romantically tragic vein of *Manon Lescaut*. *La bohème*, in its mixture of lighthearted and sentimental scenes and its largely conversational style, was reminiscent of operetta and, in addition, displayed impressionist features in its harmony and orchestration. The progression of parallel 5ths at the opening of Act 3 was particularly castigated. Today the work is considered by some writers to be Puccini's masterpiece.

The plan to set Victorien Sardou's *Tosca* dates from 1889, shortly after the première of *Edgar*. For some time Puccini seriously doubted whether this blood-and-thunder melodrama suited him at all. It was his first excursion into the sphere of *verismo*. The first night was staged in Rome (Teatro Costanzi, 14 January 1900) in an atmosphere charged with high tension and with wild rumours that a bomb would be thrown. However, nothing happened, and *Tosca* achieved an outstanding success with the Roman public. The critics, on the other hand, attacked it for the sadistic cruelty and brutality of the action, which they thought seriously interfered with the composer's inborn lyricism. Yet they admitted his immense skill in the musical characterization of the atmosphere and the *dramatis personae* and in the ideal adjustment of the music to the swift changes of mood on stage. In the modern view it is the lyricism that Puccini was able to extract from the 'strong' scenes of the libretto that is so admirable.

In the summer of 1900 Puccini saw in London David Belasco's one-act play, *Madam Butterfly*, derived from a magazine story by John Luther Long based on a real incident. Although he knew scarcely any English, he was deeply impressed by the character and fate of the little geisha, and the exotic ambience fascinated him. Following the play, Puccini first thought of a one-act opera with a prologue (the present Act 1), but then decided on two acts, with the second in two parts separated from each other by Butterfly's night vigil which was accompanied by an orchestral intermezzo. Since he considered this opera the best and technically most advanced that he had written, he looked forward with great expectation to its première at La Scala on 17 February 1904. Yet the evening proved a fiasco rare in the annals of opera, with the public whistling, shouting and making ironic remarks about the heroine. It appears that this pandemonium was engineered by his jealous rivals, who, as in the case of the *Tosca* première, wanted to ruin the performance. Puccini withdrew the opera after a single showing, revised it by judicious cuts in both text and music and recast it into three acts, with the orchestral intermezzo leading into Act 3. In this version it was given with great acclaim at Brescia the following May. There are two more versions (London, 1905, and Paris, 1906), the last version being the definitive one.

III Middle and late years

Six years elapsed before Puccini's next opera. One of the chief reasons for his slow work was a domestic tragedy which in January 1909 culminated in the suicide of Doria Manfredi, a servant girl of the Puccinis whom the abnormally jealous Elvira had accused of an intimate relationship with her husband. The affair led to a court case which, basing itself on the evidence of the autopsy, established the girl's innocence and found against

Elvira. The case provoked an enormous sensation in Italy, and the publicity associated with it affected the hypersensitive and extremely vulnerable composer to such an extent that for some time afterwards his creative energy and desire to work were impaired. Moreover, he had arrived at a point of his career when he wanted to turn away from the *tragédie larmoyante* of his previous operas and attempt something of a harder, more masculine fibre, such as he had first tried in *Tosca*. He found a subject of this nature in Belasco's *The Girl of the Golden West*, which he happened to see in New York in 1907, where he was attending a Puccini festival at the Metropolitan Opera. What seemed to appeal to him most strongly was the mixture of stark realism and sentimental romanticism of this Wild West melodrama, which takes place among miners at the time of the first California gold rush. Carlo Zangarini and Guelfo Civinini were the librettists, since Illica, after Giacosa's death in 1906, no longer satisfied Puccini as sole collaborator. The fact that *La fanciulla del West* was an 'American' opera prompted Gatti-Casazza, then director of the Metropolitan, to secure the world première for his theatre, where it was given on 10 December 1910 with Toscanini conducting and with Caruso as Johnson and Emmy Destinn as Minnie (see fig.28, p.320). With such a cast the opera could not have failed to be a success with the public; the reaction of the critics, however, was guarded. In all technical respects, notably in its Debussian harmony and Straussian orchestration, the opera is a masterpiece and was Puccini's reply to the criticism that he repeated himself in every new opera. What it lacks is the incandescent lyrical phrase, which was largely intentional as it seemed to conform to the composer's change of his melodic style.

28. Final scene in the first production of 'La fanciulla del West' (New York, Metropolitan, 1910), with Emmy Destinn (Minnie), Enrico Caruso (Johnson) and Pasquale Amato (Rance)

In the meantime, a new generation of Italian composers was growing up (Pizzetti, Casella, Malipiero) which condemned the native *melodramma* of the 19th century and vocalism in general (it is worth observing, however, that in later years this group of erstwhile firebrands wrote operas themselves). What this anti-operatic movement advocated was a rejuvenating return to the spirit and character of the ancient masters of Italian instrumental music (Frescobaldi, Corelli, Legrenzi, Vivaldi). The chief attack was directed at Puccini, who was accused of bourgeois mentality, lack of ideals and pure commercialism; the intellectual mouthpiece of this movement was the musicologist Fausto Torrefranca, who in 1912 published a book with the significant title *Giacomo Puccini e l'opera internazionale*. As far as is known, Puccini never replied to these attacks in public.

Serious differences with Giulio Ricordi's son Tito, who became head of the firm after his father's death in 1912, were the main reason why in 1913 Puccini accepted a lucrative offer by Eibenschütz and Berté, directors of the Vienna Karltheater, to write an operetta. He was to compose eight or ten numbers only, the rest to be spoken dialogue. He rejected the first libretto submitted by the Viennese, the next he entrusted to the young writer Giuseppe Adami, who after much rewriting produced an acceptable 'book' with the title *La rondine*. Although it was warmly received at its first production at Monte Carlo on 27 March 1917, it has proved the weakest of Puccini's works, uneasily hovering between opera and operetta and devoid of striking lyrical melody. But it is written with consummate technical skill and possesses a certain allure, notably in the waltz music. *La rondine* is Puccini's only work published by

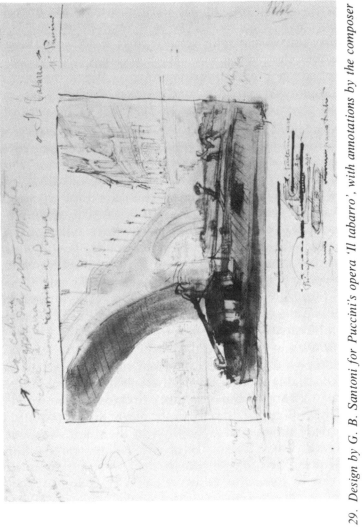

29. *Design by G. B. Santoni for Puccini's opera 'Il tabarro', with annotations by the composer*

Ricordi's rival Sonzogno. Because of this work Puccini was accused of lack of patriotism by Léon Daudet and his nationalist paper *L'action française* after Italy had entered the war on the side of the Allies.

While still at work on the operetta Puccini began the composition of *Il tabarro*, after the French play *La houppelande* by Didier Gold, which he had seen in Paris in 1913. This was the first of the three one-act operas, known under the collective title *Il trittico*, in which Puccini followed the scheme of the Parisian Grand Guignol – a horrific episode, a sentimental tragedy and a comedy or farce. Adami was the librettist of *Il tabarro*, and the texts of *Suor Angelica* and *Gianni Schicchi* are by Giovacchino Forzano, who derived the comedy from a few lines in canto xxx of Dante's *Inferno*. Since the war was still on, with the majority of Italian artists serving in the armed forces, Puccini in early 1918 willingly accepted the offer by the Metropolitan to stage the first production, which took place on 14 December. The first European performance was given in Rome on 11 January 1919. On both these occasions the comedy achieved the widest acclaim, while the reception of the first two episodes was lukewarm. *Gianni Schicchi*, which displays an unexpected *vis comica* in Puccini (a striking parallel to Verdi and his *Falstaff*), was in the following years, much to the composer's dislike, given without the other two, usually in a double bill. But more recently *Il tabarro*, outstanding for its painting of a sombre atmosphere and its dramatic concentration, has come into its own, and occasional productions of the entire triptych have proved the theatrical viability of Puccini's conception.

323

By his early 60s Puccini had arrived at an important turning-point: he was determined to 'tentar vie non battute' ('strike out on new paths') and was looking for a subject with a fantastic, fairy-tale atmosphere, but characters of flesh and blood. He eventually decided on Gozzi's *Turandotte*, which was suggested to him by Renato Simoni, an authority on Gozzi and the author of a play on him; Simoni and Adami were to collaborate with the composer. For Puccini this five-act play was the most human of Gozzi's dramatic *fiabe*, and Gozzi himself had felt the same way when writing it. With *Turandot* Puccini felt that he was moving on to a loftier plane, that an 'original and perhaps unique work is in the making', compared with which all his previous music seemed to him 'a farce'. But no other opera cost him so much labour and toil, notably the great love duet in Act 3, and no other opera filled him with such strong doubts about his creative powers. His letters to the two poets expressed a feverish urgency and anguish, and he constantly implored them to get on with the work on the libretto; it was as if he had a premonition that he would not live to complete the opera. In a moment of abject despair he wrote a letter to Adami in which he clearly recognized the limitations of his genius:

I touch the keyboard of my piano and my hands get dirty with dust! My writing desk is a sea of letters – and not a trace of music! Music? It is useless. I have the great weakness of being able to compose only when my puppet executioners [*carnefici burattini*] move on the stage. If I could be a pure symphonic composer, I would then cheat time and my public. But I am not! I was born many years ago – so many, far too many, almost a century . . . and the Almighty touched me with his little finger and said: 'Write for the theatre–mind, only for the theatre!' And I have obeyed the supreme command. Had he intended me for some other profession . . . well, I should perhaps not now find myself without the essential material. Oh you who say you're working . . . you ought to think of a man who has the earth under his feet, yet feels the ground receding under him with every hour and every day, as if a precipice would swallow him up!

In the midst of his work on *Turandot* Puccini decided to move from his beloved Torre del Lago, where the erection of a peat factory had made life impossible for him, and settle in Viareggio (December 1921). Towards the end of 1923 he began to complain of pains in his throat. In the autumn of 1924 three specialists diagnosed cancer. Accompanied by his son, he went to Brussels, where he entered the clinic La Couronne and was treated with X-rays. Though the treatment seemed successful, his heart could not stand the strain and he died on 29 November. The body was brought to Milan and temporarily buried in Toscanini's family tomb. The whole of Italy went into mourning, and Mussolini gave the funeral oration. Two years later his remains were interred at Torre del Lago.

Puccini left a bundle of sketches for the final two scenes of *Turandot,* in all 23 leaves which are fragmentary and incomplete (see fig.31, p.337). They were used, though not in their entirety, by Franco Alfano for the completion of the opera. The first production was given at La Scala on 25 April 1926, when Toscanini ended the performance with the death of Liù, the last scene Puccini was able to finish. Two evenings later (27 April) the opera was performed with a revised and much cut version of Alfano's ending.

CHAPTER TWO

Puccini and opera

1 Concept of opera

Puccini had a firm concept of opera, representing a consistent and original view in musico-dramatic thinking. To be sure, it was a narrow concept – though he tried to enlarge it with *Gianni Schicchi* and *Turandot* – and one tarnished by neurotic features. Compared with the greatest musical dramatists, Puccini worked in an operatic world constricted in subject matter, in variety and range of characters and musical depth. It is significant for the ethos of his operas that of the 12 he wrote, seven are named after their heroines, who, with the exception of Minnie and Turandot, are essentially all of the same type. Puccini does not engage us on as many different levels as do Mozart, Wagner, Verdi and Strauss, but on his own, most characteristic level, the level where erotic passion, sensuality, tenderness, pathos and despair meet and fuse, he was an unrivalled master.

Like every born musical dramatist, he considered work on the libretto a creative act and as important as its musical setting. As he put it: 'The basis of an opera is the subject and its dramatic treatment'. Whatever criticism might be brought against the limitations of the subject matter and his dramatic and psychological handling of it, the fact remains that his librettos are eminently stage-worthy and offered him precisely the opportunities he needed for the full exercise of his imagination. Puccini did not aim at music-drama in the

Wagnerian sense, but at musical drama; yet in his own way he thought in terms of a *Gesamtkunstwerk* in which the whole stage apparatus – singing, acting, declamation, facial expression, gesture and movement, costumes, scenery and lighting – should be engaged to create the maximum effect. He thus insisted that the lighting, in following closely the dramatic changes, be regulated 'with an attentive ear', and he was obsessed (as was Berg in *Wozzeck*) with the precise moment at which the curtain should be raised or dropped – 'a curtain dropped too soon or too late often means the failure of an opera'. From *Tosca* onwards his stage directions were far more elaborate than Verdi's, and his operas require singer–actors more flexible in their acting technique than do the majority of the older composer's works.

II Dramaturgy

Puccini's dramaturgy has much in common with that of the short story writer. The plot always develops clearly and logically, showing a definite point of departure, a middle and an end. The story line was for Puccini the chief means of directing and holding the spectator's attention, and he always wanted it to be straightforward and simple so that the action and its motivation remained, as far as possible, self-explanatory. He insisted on what he called 'l'evidenza della situazione', which would enable the spectator to follow the drama even without understanding the actual words. This was one of his supreme criteria when, in his constant searches for a suitable subject, he saw productions of plays in foreign languages, like *Madam Butterfly* and *Tosca*. He wanted dramatic material of the utmost economy and so, except in *La bohème*, sub-plots in the original play or novel were eliminated and historical and local details excised unless they served the evocation of a particular atmosphere. This concern for compression and concentration resulted in a swift unfolding of the drama and a steadily mounting tension. Once the action gets under way in a Puccini opera, there is little lingering or dispersal of interest; suspense and surprise are produced by well-timed incidents and the catastrophe is approached in rapid strokes. Yet in his concern to achieve maximum concentration, he at times overshot the mark. He over-compressed and/or suppressed narrative and psychological details necessary for a fully convincing motivation of the characters. He was not alone in this: over-compression was also the blind spot in the dramaturgy of early and middle Verdi.

Five of Puccini's operas observe the classical unities of action, time and place – an imponderable but important factor contributing subliminally to the concentrated effect on the spectator. In *Tosca* and *Turandot* the action takes place within 24 hours, in *Il trittico* the one-act form of the episodes inevitably compelled the composer to adhere strictly to the classical unities. Each episode takes less than an hour to perform, yet each is so well constructed that it represents a foreshortened version of a full-length, three-act opera with exposition, development and dénouement.

Puccini's gifts as a man of the theatre include one that many playwrights might envy and that only a few opera composers have possessed. This is what the French call 'l'optique du théâtre', an eye for the purely visual effect of a scene. 'Be sparing with words and try to make the incidents clear and brilliant to the eye rather than the

30. Giacomo Puccini

ear', Puccini wrote to Adami about *Turandot*. Every Puccini opera contains at least one scene striking as a stage spectacle, such as the Embarkation act of *Manon Lescaut* or Liù's funeral cortège in Act 3 of *Turandot*. These scenes, in consequence, fired the composer's imagination particularly strongly. From this sense of the purely visual as a dramatic means sprang Puccini's predilection for dumb-shows; in these he relied almost exclusively on the stage action for the intended effect, accompanying it with, as it were, only incidental music. This is superbly illustrated by the silent scene that follows Tosca's murder of Scarpia and by the arrival and departure of the aunt in *Suor Angelica*. Mention must also be made of the composer's masterly use of the dramatic pause, especially at the point of highest tension, where it achieves an effect far greater than any that words or music could. Puccini called this 'musica sottintesa' – 'implied music'. In this he echoed Verdi's remark that 'there are moments in the theatre where poets and composers must have the talent to write neither poetry nor music'.

For Puccini the theatre had its fixed, immutable laws: it must, he said, interest, surprise, touch or move to laughter. Part of the secret of his success lay in the fact that he fully met these demands in virtually all his operas. Moreover, he was acutely aware that an opera, however dramatic, is not all action, movement and conflict, but must have its moments of stasis and repose, moments to be filled with music of a poetic lyricism. Puccini ranks far above Mascagni, Leoncavallo, Giordano, Cilea and his other Italian contemporaries because of his superior power of melodic invention, his insight into the imponderables of the musical and dramatic structure and his highly developed sense of the relationship between words and music. Even his *verismo* operas, *Tosca*, *Butterfly*, *La fanciulla* and *Il tabarro*, have a dimension that raises them above the constricted canon of pure realism. Hence his constant demands to his librettists to allow him scope for spreading his colours more lyrically, for an 'affectionate little phrase', for 'episodes delicate, tender, luminous and exquisite' and with a 'touch of gay, fresh laughter'. He possessed most sensitive antennae for 'le cose piccole', the little things in the lives of little, unimportant people and for 'grande dolore in piccole anime'. But this represented only one side of his genius. He was equally strongly drawn to the full-blooded, as is shown by *Tosca*, *La fanciulla* and *Turandot*.

III The Puccini heroine

'Chi ha vissuto per amore, per amore si mori' sings the street vendor in *Il tabarro*. It might be a description of the fate suffered by his protagonists, notably his heroines, for the most part frail creatures who live and die for love. This equation of Eros with Thanatos, or the concept of love as tragic guilt to be atoned for by death, is of course a perennial theme in drama and opera and has nowhere been shown in such grandeur and elaborated to such psychological and metaphysical depths as in Wagner's *Tristan*. With Puccini this concept carried no such implications, but was essentially the expression of an erotic nihilism that stands in marked contrast to the hedonism of his private life. What is striking, however, is the peculiar dramatic pattern in which he presented this theme. In the Puccinian opera the heroine, who is the pivot around which the action

331

revolves, is shown as a woman of true and unbounded love. This, in the composer's view, constitutes a guilt for which she must be punished by physical and mental suffering and gradually ground down until she perishes. It is in this grinding-down process, in which refined cruelty is matched by deep compassion, that Puccini established an individual dramatic pattern. The male characters perform, with one or two exceptions, the role of catalyst (the tenor lovers) or of persecutor (baritone). In *Suor Angelica* and *Turandot* the part of the persecutor is assigned to a female character –the aunt in the former and the Chinese princess in the latter. The fact that Puccini adhered to this dramatic pattern almost from his first to his last opera suggests that it sprang from an image deeply anchored in his unconscious, assuming therefore the force of a compulsion.

IV Depiction of atmosphere

Another fingerprint of Puccini's dramatic style is his technique for the projection of atmosphere. Three kinds are apparent in his work. One is 'documentary' atmosphere, like that of the bell music in Act 3 of *Tosca*, for which Puccini made a special journey to Rome to obtain a first-hand impression of the matin bells from the churches around the Castel Sant'Angelo. This is reminiscent of Zola's descending into the coal mines of northern France for his novel *Germinal*. And Flaubert's preparatory archaeological studies for his *Salammbô* are paralleled by Puccini's study of books on the ethnography and music of Japan and China for *Butterfly* and *Turandot*. The musical exoticism of these operas and of *La fanciulla* was, however, not only intended to suggest an authentic atmosphere but also sprang from the composer's desire to evoke a poetic ambience. The Japanese, Chinese and North American tunes employed in these works are not merely quotations but are organically worked into the fabric of Puccini's own music to saturate it with local colour. Puccini absorbed their melodic, rhythmic and instrumental inflections so completely into his own style that there is no dichotomy between his 'western' and 'exotic' manners. *Butterfly*, *La fanciulla* and *Turandot* are stylistically completely homogeneous. The fertilizing effect of this exotic material on his work can be compared with that of native folksong on the music of Bartók, Falla and Vaughan Williams.

In addition to the documentary and poetic atmospheres there is the psychological atmosphere, which is the nerve centre of each Puccini opera and determines its particular emotional character. Although the dramatic world is small, each opera has its peculiar emotional tone which sets it apart from its sister works. Only a composer possessed of so highly developed a sense of psychological atmosphere could have conceived *Il trittico*, in which three episodes immensely contrasted in their emotional ambience are juxtaposed. Part of the measure of Puccini's stature as a musical dramatist is this ability to bend his inventive power so completely to the psychological character of a libretto. Moreover, virtually every one of his 12 operas opens with a theme, called by him 'motivo di prima intenzione', which catapults the spectator into its ambience. Significant in this context are his words to Adami: 'The difficulty is how to begin an opera, that is, how to find its musical atmosphere. Once the opening is fixed and composed, there is no more to fear'.

v **Melody and aria types**

Puccini once wrote that 'without melody, fresh and poignant, there can be no music'. With this he put his finger on what many consider to be his greatest gift as an opera composer. It is indeed questionable whether his stage works, in spite of his extraordinary theatrical instinct and the attention he paid to the story line, would have achieved such universal and lasting acclaim, had he not possessed remarkable powers as a melodist. In this he showed his deep roots in the tradition of Italian opera and proved himself the true successor of Verdi, although his fund of melody was not as rich and varied as that of the older master. His melodic style can best be studied in his arias, which arise naturally from the action and represent the culmination of a character's lyrical expression. Puccini was too fine a dramatist to subscribe to Giordano's half-joking prescription: 'Find a good song and then write an opera around it!' In later years he even thought that Tosca's 'Vissi d'arte' tended to hold up the drama and wanted to scrap it. Nevertheless, it is the aria that displays his cantilena at its most perfect. Marked by great sensous warmth and melting radiance, its singability is considerably heightened by the predominantly diatonic movement of the vocal line. His arias most often start in a slow, hesitant manner, with the theme first played by the orchestra, while the voice glides in, chantlike, on softly reiterated notes, as in Massenet and Debussy. Tender, graceful and infinitely supple, Puccini's cantilena in its languor proclaims an affinity with Massenet's typical *phrase décadente* transplanted to Italian soil. Like all born musical dramatists, Puccini concentrated into a single phrase all there was to express at a given point of the drama, thus achieving a close union of words, sentiment and situation – hence the irresistible impact the Puccinian cantilena has on the listener.

There are various types of aria in Puccini, but the most characteristic is to be found in his 'farewell' and 'death' arias, more particularly in those 'povera faccia' themes reflecting, as it were, the habitual expression of melancholy on his face   so often remarked upon by those who knew him. These themes show certain constant features – a minor key, a slow, dragging pace, a dropping of the melodic line mostly in 4ths and 5ths and an effort to counteract this by a forced screwing up of the phrase. There is about these limping, spineless themes an air of utter weariness and despair (a characteristic example is already to be found in *Le villi*). In marked contrast to this are Puccini's *ballabile* tunes, those dance-like, pirouetting strains in 2/4 and/or 6/8 which are always associated with lighthearted emotions, youthful gaiety (*Bohème* and *Butterfly*), playfulness and insouciance (love duet in *Tosca*, Act 1) and grotesque comedy (the sacristan in *Tosca*, the three masks in *Turandot* and innumerable passages in *Gianni Schicchi*).

VI Harmony and leitmotif

Puccini's harmonic idiom, too, is part of his superiority over his Italian contemporaries. Fragrant, delicate, brilliant, bittersweet and pungent, it displays not only richness and variety but a remarkable flux, reflecting the turns of the drama and, on a more personal level, the rise and fall of the composer's inner tension. It was Puccini's maxim to keep abreast of the innovations of his time, and this is nowhere better seen than in his

harmonic vocabulary. He began with chromatic alterations of the triad and chromatic side-slipping of secondary 7ths and 9ths in *Le villi* and *Edgar*. He turned to
Tristan harmonies in *Manon Lescaut*, in which he also
used parallel 5ths before Debussy. Under the influence
of French impressionism he cultivated faburden-like
progressions, chords of the added 6th, augmented triads
and unresolved dissonances (*Bohème*). From about
1900 he began to make pointed use of the whole-tone
scale (*Tosca, Butterfly* and *La fanciulla*) and subsequently experimented with bitonality, chords of the
4th and exposed, naked discords (*Il trittico, Turandot*).
Even the atonality of Schoenberg's *Pierrot lunaire*,
which Puccini heard in Florence in April 1924, seems
to have left its mark on the Chorus of Spectres in Act 1
of *Turandot*. It is significant that the majority of
Puccini's most striking harmonic devices occur in situations charged with 'negative' emotions: fear, terror, despair, mental pain and death. Moreover, it is in such
situations that the composer resorted, in the orchestra,
to ominous, sinister ostinatos, like that accompanying
the preparations for the execution of Cavaradossi in Act
3 of *Tosca*. Puccini obviously derived this device from
Verdi, who used it to establish a dramatic mood and
impress it on the spectator. The younger composer
turned it into a means of creating mounting suspense.

No post-Wagnerian composer could afford to
dispense with the leitmotif and Puccini was no exception. His leading motifs are clearcut and sharply defined
(the theme of the Bohemians, the 'Scarpia' and 'Turandot' motifs) but his application of this device is not
strict, and the same figure may symbolize several things
– a character, a situation, an atmosphere, an object

31. First page of Puccini's autograph sketches for the finale of 'Turandot', completed by Alfano in 1926

(notably in *Tosca*), or it may be used merely to add interest to the texture without any perceptible relevance to the stage action. Puccini's leitmotifs are employed in the manner of the old 'reminiscence'; they keep their melodic shape and change only in tempo and harmony. Real metamorphosis in the Wagnerian sense is almost entirely confined to the themes of the aunt in *Suor Angelica* and the Chinese princess in *Turandot*.

VII Orchestral mosaic

The orchestra provides a continuous background, but displays only a semblance of symphonic technique. This should not be held against a composer for whom the musical weight of an opera rested on the singers. Orchestral continuity is achieved not so much by the interweaving of different themes as by the juxtaposition of tiny motifs. It is the technique of the mosaic, in which diminutive melodic 'squares' are repeated and treated sequentially, after which the process is repeated with the next square. However, Puccini handled this technique with such consummate skill that it gives the impression of almost organic growth.

In Puccini's orchestral style two basic and strongly contrasted elements can be discerned. There is, on the one hand, the Puccini who, like Strauss, loved rich, saturated colours and, on the other, the Puccini with an ear for the most refined sensory stimuli, who, like Debussy, seemed to relish sound for itself and used his palette with an aristocratic restraint. A characteristic feature of his luxuriant style is the instrumental doubling, trebling and even quadrupling of the vocal melody – a device known as *sviolinata*. Puccini was severely criticized for it, yet it had been used by Rossini, Bellini and Donizetti and, indeed, by the 18th-century Neapolitan school (Rousseau, in his *Lettre sur la musique française* of 1753, mentioned this device specifically). What lay behind these doublings and treblings was the urge to impart to the vocal lines a maximum of sensuousness and vibrancy. However, the impact of a special effect stands in inverse ratio to the frequency of its use, and Puccini's too-frequent use of the *sviolinata* tended to become self-defeating.

Orchestra and chorus

Puccini always wrote for a large orchestra, one considerably augmented in his 'grand' operas *Tosca, La fanciulla* and *Turandot*. As with all the Italian opera composers of the 19th century, the central element of the orchestra is the warm and expressive string section. Often the first half of a Puccini aria or duet is accompanied by strings alone, or supported only slightly by the woodwind. The woodwind dominates in lighthearted scenes, whereas the brass is used mostly to add tension and to underline the dramatic climax. In his three 'exotic' operas Puccini combined brass, woodwind and percussion (including a number of unpitched instruments) to create local colour. Each of his operas has its special orchestral 'tone' or character, and there can hardly be a greater contrast than that between the liquescent and diaphanous timbres of *Butterfly* and the explosive *fauve* sound of *La fanciulla* and *Turandot*.

VIII The chorus

Like Verdi, Puccini was a master in the handling of large choral scenes. His treatment of the chorus was not as a mere adjunct to the action nor as a scenic prop, but as a collective character with an active part in the drama, as for instance in *Manon Lescaut* (Embarkation Act), *La fanciulla* (Manhunt, Act 3) and *Turandot* (Act 1). Even when the chorus represents only a decorative element Puccini enlivened its effect by seemingly effortless musical exchanges between soloists and crowd, as in the opening acts of *Manon, Butterfly* and *La fanciulla* and the splendid Latin Quarter Act in *Bohème*. And what could be more evocative than the humming chorus at the start of Butterfly's night vigil?

IX **Assessment**

Puccini was a perfectionist. Even in the hapless *La rondine*, he paid almost obsessive attention to the minutest details. He may well have owed this high level of professionalism to his position as the scion of four generations of most respectable craftsmen, whose history may be said to be the musical history of Lucca. Puccini exemplified Henry James's memorable phrase: 'An artist is fortunate when his theories and limitations exactly correspond'. He was fully aware of his limitations and only once or twice made the mistake of venturing beyond them, since within them he was able to achieve all that he wished to. Yet this does not make him a *petit maître* any more than it makes a Chopin, a Wolf, a Ravel or, in literature, a Maupassant and a Chekhov minor masters. They were all artists with an acute awareness of the extent of their creative range and were stylists in the true sense of the word, in that they knew how to adapt their imagination and technique completely to the exigencies of their particular medium; this explains Puccini's constant and unremitting search for a subject that would exactly suit his talent. Puccini the man had by no means a fully integrated personality, as had Verdi – there were too many seemingly irreconcilable contradictions in his psychological make-up. But the artist in him succeeded in creating a style that was wholly original, homogeneous and compelling. A lesser genius than Verdi, he represents Verdi's only true successor, and his greatest masterpiece and swansong, *Turandot*, must belong among the last 20th-century stage works that have remained in the regular repertory of the world's opera houses.

WORKS

(published in Milan unless otherwise indicated; detailed bibliographical information in Hopkinson)

OPERAS

Numbers in the right-hand column denote references in the text.

Title	Text	First performance	Sources and remarks	
Le villi	1, F. Fontana	Milan, Verme, 31 May 1884	autograph I-Mr, unpubd	313
2nd version	2	Turin, Regio, 26 Dec 1884	vocal score (1885)	315, 335, 336
Edgar	4, Fontana, after de Musset: La coupe et les lèvres	Milan, La Scala, 21 April 1889	autograph Acts 1, 3, Mr, vocal score (1890)	315, 317
2nd version	3	Ferrara, 28 Feb 1892	copy of 1st version with autograph changes, Mr, vocal score (1892)	315
final version		Buenos Aires, 8 July 1905	vocal score (1905)	315, 336
Manon Lescaut	4, Leoncavallo, M. Praga, D. Oliva, L. Illica, G. Giacosa, after Abbé Prévost	Turin, Regio, 1 Feb 1893	autograph Mr (1891), vocal score (1893)	315f, 317, 330, 336, 339
La bohème	3, Illica, Giacosa, after Murger	Turin, Regio, 1 Feb 1896	autograph Mr (1896), vocal score (1896)	316, 317, 328, 335, 336, 339
Tosca	3, Illica, Giacosa, after Sardou	Rome, Costanzi, 14 Jan 1900	autograph Mr (1899), vocal score (1899)	317, 318, 319, 328, 331, 332, 334, 335, 336, 337, 339
Madama Butterfly	2, Illica, Giacosa, after D. Belasco's stage version of a magazine story by J. L. Long	Milan, La Scala, 17 Feb 1904	autograph Mr, vocal score (1904)	318
2nd version	2	Brescia, Grande, 28 May 1904	changes in autograph Mr, vocal score (1904)	318
3rd version	2	London, Covent Garden, 10 July 1905	vocal score (1905)	318
4th version	3	Paris, Opéra Comique, 28 Dec 1906	full score (1906), (1907) with changes to text	318, 331, 332, 333, 335, 336, 339
La fanciulla del West	3, G. Civinini, C. Zangarini, after Belasco	New York, Metropolitan, 10 Dec 1910	autograph Mr (1910), vocal score (1910)	319, 320, 331, 332, 333, 336, 339
La rondine	3, G. Adami	Monte Carlo, 27 March 1917	autograph lost (1917), vocal score (1917)	321, 340
Il tabarro	1, Adami, after D. Gold: La houppelande	New York, Metropolitan, 14 Dec 1918	autograph Mr (1918), vocal score (1918)	323, 328, 333, 336
Suor Angelica	1, G. Forzano			322, 323, 331
Gianni Schicchi	1, Forzano, developed from a few lines in Dante's Inferno xxx			323, 330, 332, 337 323, 326, 335
Turandot	3, Adami, R. Simoni, after Gozzi	Milan, La Scala, 25 April 1926	autograph Mr, vocal score (1926); inc., finished by F. Alfano	316, 324f, 326, 328, 330, 331, 332, 333, 335, 336, 337, 339, 340

341

Sacred: Motet, Credo, in honour of S Paolino, 1878, unpubd; Mass, T, 312 Bar, B, vv, orch, 1880, autograph *I-TLP*, vocal score (New York, 1951)[incorporating Motet, Credo]; Salve del ciel regina, S, harmonium, before 1880, autograph *Li*, unpubd; Requiem, S, T, B, org/harmonium, before 1905, autograph frag. *Ms*

Choral: I figli d'Italia bella, cantata, solo vv, orch, 1877; Cantata a 312 Giove (1897)

Songs: Melancolia (A. Ghislanzoni), 1881, unpubd; Allor ch'io sarò morto (Ghislanzoni), 1881, unpubd; Spirto gentil (Ghislanzoni), 1882, unpubd; Noi leggeremo (Ghislanzoni), 1882, unpubd; Storiella d'amore (Ghislanzoni), 1883, in *Musica popolare* (4 Oct 1883); Menti all'avviso (Romani), romanza, 1883: Sole e amore (Puccini), mattinata, 1888, in *Paganini* (1888): Avanti, Urania! (R. Fucini) (Florence and Rome, 1899); E l'uccellino (Fucini) (1899); Inno a Diana (C. Abeniacar [F. Salvatori]) (Florence and Rome, 1899); Terra e mare (E. Panzacchi) in *Novissima* (1902); Morire? (Adami), in *Per la Croce rossa italiana* (c1917–18); Inno di Roma (Salvatori) (Florence and Rome, 1923)

Pedagogical: Solfeggi, 1888, unpubd

Orch: Preludio sinfonico, A, 1876, autograph *Li*, unpubd; Preludio 312 sinfonico, e, 1876, autograph, private collection of Natale Gallini, Milan, unpubd; Adagietto, 1883, autograph sketch *Li*, unpubd; Capriccio sinfonico, perf. Milan, 14 July 1883, autograph *M-c*, arr. pf 4 hands (1884), full score (1978); Preludio, A, for production of Edgar in Madrid, 1892 (1978); Scossa elettrica, march, 1896, unpubd

Chamber: Scherzo, str qt, c1880–83, autograph *Li*, unpubd; Str Qt, D, c1880–83, autograph parts *Li*, unpubd; Crisantemi, str qt (1890): 3 minuets, str qt (1892), nos.1, 3 rev. (Paris, 1898); La sconsolata, vn, pf, 1883, unpubd

Kbd: several unpubd org pieces, before 1880; Foglio d'album, pf, ?1907 (New York, 1942); Piccolo tango, pf, ?1907 (New York, 1942)

Bibliography

BIBLIOGRAPHY

SOURCE MATERIAL

G. Adami: *Giacomo Puccini: epistolario* (Milan, 1928; Eng. trans., 1931, rev. 2/1974)

G. M. Gatti: *Puccini in un gruppo di lettere inedite a un amico* (Milan, 1944)

E. Gara: *Carteggi pucciniani* (Milan, 1958)

C. A. Hopkinson: *Bibliography of the Works of Giacomo Puccini 1858–1924* (New York, 1968)

A. Marchetti: *Puccini: com'era* (Milan, 1973)

G. Pintorno: *Puccini: 276 lettere inedite* (Montecatini, 1974)

P. Ross and D. Schwendimann Berra: 'Setta lettere di Puccini a Giulio Ricordi', *NRMI*, xiii (1979), 851

S. Puccini: *Giacomo Puccini: lettere a Riccardo Schnabl* (Milan, 1982)

BIOGRAPHY AND CRITICISM

F. Fontana: 'Giacomo Puccini', *Gazzetta musicale di Milano*, xxxix (1884), 381; repr. as 'Puccini visto dal suo primo librettista', *Musica d'oggi*, xv (1933), 148

F. Torrefranca: *Giacomo Puccini e l'opera internazionale* (Turin, 1912)

I. Pizzetti: 'Giacomo Puccini', *Musicisti contemporanei: saggi critici* (Milan, 1914)

A. Coppotelli: *Per la musica d'Italia: Puccini nella critica del Torrefranca* (Orvieto, 1919)

A. Weissmann: *Giacomo Puccini* (Munich, 1922)

A. Coeuroy: *La Tosca de Puccini: étude historique et critique* (Paris, 1923)

G. Monaldi: *Giacomo Puccini e la sua opera* (Rome, 1924)

A. Fraccaroli: *La vita di Giacomo Puccini* (Milan, 1925)

A. Neisser: *Giacomo Puccini: sein Leben und sein Werk* (Leipzig, 1928)

R. Specht: *Giacomo Puccini: das Leben – der Mensch – das Werk* (Berlin, 1931; Eng. trans., 1933)

A. Bonaccorsi: 'Le musiche sacre dei Puccini', *Bollettino storico lucchese*, vi (1934), 29

W. Maisch: *Puccinis musikalische Formgebung, untersucht an der Oper 'La Bohème'* (Neustadt an der Aisch, 1934)

G. Adami: *Puccini* (Milan, 1935)

K. G. Fellerer: *Giacomo Puccini* (Potsdam, 1937)

H. Gerigk: *Puccini* (Potsdam, 1937)

V. Seligman: *Puccini among Friends* (London, 1938)

P. Panichelli: *Il 'Pretino' di Giacomo Puccini racconta* (Pisa, 1940, 3/1949)

G. Adami: *Il romanzo della vita di Giacomo Puccini* (Milan, 1944)

343

M. Carner: *Of Man and Music: Collected Essays and Articles* (London, 1944, 3/1945) [incl. 'In Defence of Puccini', 'The First Version of *Madama Butterfly*', 'The Two *Manons*', 'Puccini's Early Operas', 'Puccini's Chief Symphonic Venture: the *Capriccio sinfonico*', 'A Puccini Operetta: *La Rondine*', 'The Exotic Element in Puccini']

F. Thiess: *Puccini: Versuch einer Psychologie seiner Musik* (Vienna, 1947)

L. Marchetti: *Puccini nelle immagini* (Milan, 1949)

G. Marotti: *Giacomo Puccini* (Florence, 1949)

A. Bonaccorsi: *Giacomo Puccini e i suoi antenati musicali* (Milan, 1950)

W. Dean: 'Giacomo Puccini', *The Heritage of Music*, ed. H. Foss, iii (London, 1951), 153

G. R. Marek: *Puccini: a Biography* (New York, 1951)

D. Del Fiorentino: *Immortal Bohemian: an Intimate Memoir of Giacomo Puccini* (London, 1952)

L. Ricci: *Puccini interprete di se stesso* (Milan, 1954)

M. Carner: *Puccini: a Critical Biography* (London, 1958, rev. 2/1974)

E. Greenfield: *Puccini: Keeper of the Seal* (London, 1958)

C. Sartori: *Puccini* (Milan, 1958)

P. C. Hughes: *Famous Puccini Operas* (London, 1959)

C. Sartori, ed.: *Puccini* (Milan, 1959) [collection of essays by various authors]

W. Ashbrook: *The Operas of Puccini* (London, 1968)

N. A. Galli: *Puccini e la sua terra* (Lucca, 1974)

G. Magri: *Puccini e le sue rime* (Milan, 1974)

L. Pinzauti: *Puccini: una vita* (Florence, 1974)

A. Marchetti: 'Tutta la verità sull'"Inno a Roma" di Puccini', *NRMI*, ix (1975), 396

J. Meyerowitz: 'Puccini: musica a doppio fordo', *NRMI*, x (1976), 3

E. Siciliano: *Puccini* (Milan, 1976)

C. Casini: 'Introduzione a Puccini', *Il melodramma italiano dell'ottocento: studi e ricerche per Massimo Mila* (Turin, 1977)

L. Gherardi: 'Appunti per una lettura delle varianti nelle opere di Giacomo Puccini', *Studi musicali*, vi (1977), 269–321

S. Martinotti: 'I travagliati Avant-Propos di Puccini', *Il melodramma italiano dell'ottocento: studi e ricerche per Massimo Mila* (Turin, 1977)

C. Sartori: 'I sospetti di Puccini', *NRMI*, xi (1977), 233

C. Casini: *Giacomo Puccini* (Turin, 1978)

H. Greenfield: *Puccini* (London, 1981)

C. Osborne: *The Complete Operas of Puccini* (London, 1981)

M. Carner: *Tosca* (in preparation)

Index

345

Index

Index

Index

Index

353